The Festival of Indra

SUNY series in Hindu Studies

Wendy Doniger, editor

The Festival of Indra

Innovation, Archaism, and Revival in a South Asian Performance

MICHAEL C. BALTUTIS

SUNY
PRESS

Cover image: Indra sits on a low table in the center of Nasal Chowk. Photo by author.

Published by State University of New York Press, Albany

Printed in the United States of America

For information, contact State University of New York Press, Albany, NY
www.sunypress.edu

Library of Congress Cataloging-in-Publication Data

Name: Baltutis, Michael C., author.
Title: The festival of Indra : innovation, archaism, and revival in a South Asian performance / Michael C. Baltutis.
Description: Albany : State University of New York Press, [2023] | Series: SUNY series in Hindu Studies | Includes bibliographical references and index.
Identifiers: ISBN 9781438493336 (hardcover : alk. paper) | ISBN 9781438493343 (ebook) | ISBN 9781438493329 (pbk. : alk. paper)
Further information is available at the Library of Congress.

10 9 8 7 6 5 4 3 2 1

Contents

Illustrations

Acknowledgments

This book has taken much longer to see the light of day than I thought it would. An easy option would have been to edit my 2008 dissertation, publish it right away, and move on to other projects. I cannot express how glad I am that I did not do this. By sitting on this project for more than a decade and working on other odds and ends, I was able to wait out the vagaries of history, especially the many ways that life in Nepal has adapted and adjusted to the downfall of the 240-year-long Shah monarchy in 2006, portions of which process I describe at relevant points in this book. One of the most significant adjustments in this period has been how local communities have filled the cultural vacuum of power from the absence of the Hindu king. During my first visit to Nepal, many people told me that within a few years the Indra festival (and other festivals and elements of Nepal's rich culture) would no longer be celebrated because the younger generation was no longer interested. For complex reasons that are worthy of their own study—including the end of the Shah dynasty in 2006, the pair of devastating earthquakes that struck Nepal in 2015 and killed some ten thousand people and destroyed many heritage sites, and the COVID-19 pandemic that prevented the Indra festival from being celebrated for the first time in centuries—young people have never been more interested in their heritage. At the center of this interest and participation in Kathmandu's heritage, and especially in its entertaining and accessible festival culture, is the Indra festival that has maintained its place as the core festival of Kathmandu.

And what a festival it is! In culturally and linguistically diverse Nepal, a festival is celebrated nearly every day of the year somewhere: pan–South Asian Hindu festivals such as Holi, Durga Puja, and Diwali;

Buddha Jayanti, Mani Rimdu, and Losar celebrated by Nepal's Newar, Tibetan, Sherpa, and other Buddhist communities; and processions of local gods and goddesses that are nearly unknown outside of their immediate neighborhoods. In the larger and multicultural context of Nepal, these festivals take on a bit of the identity that residents of Kathmandu's northeastern Handigaon neighborhood ascribe to the Satya Narayan festival they celebrate there: "There is no jātrā like the one in Handigaon!" (Nep. *kahī na bhaeko jātrā Hāḍigauṃ mā*!). Taking nothing away from this local one-day festival in the neighborhood where I lived for a year while conducting research for this project, there is also certainly nothing like the autumnal and city-wide festival of the Indrajatra, the subject of this book.

I am indebted to the people of the Kathmandu Valley who have welcomed, conversed with, assisted, and challenged me during my visits there, especially during the festival seasons of 2003, 2005, 2014, and 2018. Their guidance and friendship has helped me appreciate the festival itself—from its earliest appearance in the Sanskrit *Mahābhārata* up to the present day—and the city it celebrates and the larger nation of which it is a part. The Indra festival is intense, complex, and exhausting, as dedicated spectators rush from one neighborhood to another following tight schedules drawn up by court officials, organizational heads, and local performers. The end of each year's festival is bittersweet. After following Indra's pole to the riverbank, its final destination on the festival's final day, I thought of the old man at the end of Linda Hess's essay on the thirty-day Rāmlīlā festival of Ramnagar, held across the Ganges River from Varanasi: appearing to some as drunk, though actually "absorbed in God," the man was distraught at the final and inevitable conclusion of the festival that had taken over his life for the past month (2007: 136). Although not devotionally absorbed as he was, I feel a palpable absence in the city upon the festival's conclusion, with all of its visual and performative cues packed away for another year.

Having observed the festival on four separate occasions across approximately fifteen years, I have seen many of the specific rites several times, others only once or twice, and yet others I have been made aware of only through conversations and interviews. In the following chapters, I draw heavily on my own experiences watching its constituent rites, my conversations with local performers, leaders, and observers, and occasionally my active participation in it. In most cases, I provide a largely synchronic account of the festival without naming which particular year I am referring to; in other cases I might combine festivals from different years into the same narrative where the details have not appreciably changed; and in most cases, I have recourse to the body of Sanskrit literature that informs the contemporary tradition.

My dissertation, which still serves as something of the core of this book, was conceived and composed in the friendly confines of Iowa City: the temporarily vacated offices of Fred Smith and Janine Sawada in the Department of Religious Studies at the University of Iowa, Ken Kuntz's generously donated third-floor library carrel, and Joe's Place on a Tuesday night or two. With the financial support of the University of Iowa I was able to visit South Asia those first few times: the Stanley-University of Iowa (UI) Foundation Support Organization supported language and research trips to Pune, Mussoorie, and ultimately Kathmandu. A UI Summer Fellowship in 2006 and a Ballard and Seashore Dissertation Year Fellowship in the academic year 2007–2008 followed my Fulbright Institute of International Education grant for the academic year 2005–2006, a term only slightly abbreviated by the April 2006 collapse of Nepal's government. The inaugural Workshop on Transforming a Dissertation into a Book in 2009, sponsored by the American Institute of Indian Studies and hosted at the Annual South Asia Conference in Madison, was immensely helpful for navigating the writing process and putting together a book that is both insightful and, I hope, engaging. The University of Wisconsin, Oshkosh, supported the final stages of this book with assistance from its wonderful research librarians and financially with a Faculty Development Grant in 2017 and a fall 2018 sabbatical, both of which allowed for additional travel back to Kathmandu, where portions of this book were written.

In addition to the financial support required for a study like this, an immense amount of local assistance was necessary and greatly appreciated. For much of the day-to-day research assistance in Kathmandu, I am indebted to Sailesh Rajbhandari, Anil Maharjan, Jujuman Maharjan, and Manoj Srestha, whose willingness to ask difficult (and easy) questions and whose ability to jump in with both feet (sometimes very literally) opened many otherwise unopened and unseen doors.

For graciously engaging my requests for interviews and conversations regarding local rites and stories, I am in varying degrees of debt to Triratna Manandhar, Mina Srestha, Baburatna Maharjan, Jit Bahadur Manandhar, Uden Nhusayami, Ratna Maharjan, Binod Srestha, Sambhu Maharjan, Mohan Krishna Dangol, Gautam Shakya, Tulsi Narayan Maharjan, Laxman Ranjitkar, Jeevan Kumar Maharjan, and Rajendra Man Vajracharya.

For assistance with language, obtaining research materials, and checking facts and narratives on the ground in Kathmandu, my thanks go to Geeta Manandhar, Kashinath Tamot, Krishna Pradhan, Nutendhar Sharma, Monalisa Maharjan, Alok Tuladhar, Diwakar Acarya, Sudarshan Raj Tiwari, and Mahesh Raj Pant. Much appreciation to the anonymous readers that SUNY brought on to make this manuscript so much more clear and concise. Thanks to those kind folks I have worked with at conferences and elsewhere who have engaged me in insightful conversations over the years, including Jessica Vantine Birkenholtz, Megan Adamson Sijapati, Anne Mocko, Marko Geslani, Ellen Gough, Gudrun Bühnemann, Richard Davis, Simon Brodbeck, Niels Gutschow, Axel Michaels, Nadine Plachta, Christoph Vieth, Jeremy Saul, Luke Whitmore, Tim Lubin, Gérard Toffin, Brian Pennington, Amy Allocco, Gaurav Shrestha, and Louis Breton.

I am forever indebted to Fred Smith and Philip Lutgendorf, whose scholarship, lectures, conversations, and interventions have been integral to this entire work. I thank the wonderful people at SUNY Press who navigated a global pandemic to ensure that this book saw the light of day. And I thank Kelly Matthews and Gloria and Robert Baltutis for their support throughout all phases of this work.

Earlier versions of several chapters of this book have been revised from previous publications. I cite these sources here once rather than throughout the body of the book:

Chapter 1 original appeared as "Innovating the Ancient, Instantiating the Urban: the South Asian Indra Festival," in *Ritual Innovation: Strategic Interventions in South Asian Religion*, edited by Amy Allocco and Brian Pennington (Albany: SUNY Press, 2018), 53–70. Parts of this chapter's section on the *Mahābhārata* were published in "Reinventing Orthopraxy and Practicing Worldly Dharma: Vasu and Aśoka in Book Fourteen of the *Mahābhārata*," *International Journal of Hindu Studies* 15, no. 1 (2011): 55–100.

Chapter 2 includes material from "Speaking Obscenely and Carrying a Big Stick: The Limits of Textuality in Kathmandu's Indrajatra

Festival," *Journal of Ritual Studies* 28, no. 1 (2014): 1–13, and "The Indrajatra festival of Kathmandu, Nepal," in *Contemporary Hinduism*, edited by P. Pratap Kumar (Durham, UK: Acumen, 2013), 83–96.

Portions of Chapter 3 appeared in "Entering the South Asian City: *Praveśa* in Literature and Religion," in *Modern Hinduism in Text and Context*, edited by Lavanya Vemsani (London: Bloomsbury, 2018), 23–40.

Much of Chapter 6 comes from "Sacrificing (to) Bhairav: The Death, Resurrection, and Apotheosis of a Local Himalayan King." *Journal of Hindu Studies* 9, no. 2 (2016): 205–25 with some insight from "Renovating Bhairav: Fierce Gods, Divine Agency, and Local Power in Kathmandu," *International Journal of Hindu Studies* 13, no. 1 (2009): 25–49.

Introduction

The Archetypal Indra Festival

On the third day of Kathmandu's Indra festival in 2005, I pressed in with the crowd gathering underneath the overhanging balcony of Gaddi Baithak on the west side of the royal palace. Standing in stark contrast to the brick pagoda-style temples throughout the palace area, its neoclassical architecture recalls the intertwined history of Nepal and Europe and the British empire. Surrounded by a community of diplomats, ambassadors, and officials from across the globe at this most festive moment of the eight-day festival, and anticipating the first and most significant chariot procession of the living goddess Kumari, King Gyanendra distributed to the crowd the symbolic largesse of one-rupee coins. No one could have predicted that this would be the final time in Nepal's history that this particular scene would play out.

On February 1, 2005, Gyanendra dismissed the government and suspended the seven major political parties. With the intention of bringing to an end the decade-long civil war with Maoist rebels, Gyanendra only succeeded in alienating local and international allies as well as the general public. Political strikes turned into five days of nationwide protests. Gyanendra's government responded with a "shoot to kill" curfew that brought the whole country to a near standstill for three weeks, completely disrupting life. Nearly fourteen months later, in April 2006, and under pressure from all quarters, Gyanendra reinstated the government and stepped down from the throne, essentially ending Nepal's monarchy.

Over the next two years, Gyanendra was gradually stripped of all of his real and symbolic power. As the most public expression of his status as the king of Nepal—then referred to as the "the only Hindu kingdom in the world"—the Indra festival charted his fall from power. For the 2006 festival, his official domestic and international circles abandoned him, and by 2007 he was replaced by the prime minister, Girija Prasad Koirala. This symbolic act is one of many that would make up the "New Nepal" that will, it is hoped, further the country's path toward democracy and integration into a global economy.[1]

The role of Kathmandu's Indra festival in this fourteen-month period from February 2005 to April 2006 is instructive for understanding the history of the festival, as far back as its earliest appearance in the Sanskrit text of the *Mahābhārata*. A festival whose textual origins lie in the fuzzy boundaries between late Vedic and early medieval periods, the autumnal Indra festival celebrates Hindu kingship in all of its urban glory. Its narrative of origin variously is told in the *Mahābhārata, Brihat Saṃhitā,* and *Nāṭyaśāstra,* and the story of its demise is found in the *Bhāgavatā Purāṇa*. The Indra festival continues to be celebrated in Kathmandu according to the Sanskrit textual tradition. This book covers the Indra festival from its narrative inception in these texts up to the present, noting the consistent ways it innovates. Like the 2007 festival in Kathmandu that communicated a shift in the political situation in Nepal, the Indra festival has consistently stood as a cipher for innovation, signaling shifts in religious practices, royal dynasties, and architectural styles.

The performance of the festival can be summarized rather easily. It begins when a small coterie of local officials charged by the king travels to a nearby forest, where they cut down a tree. The tree is pulled to the city where it is twice celebrated as a king: in its majestic entrance down the royal road and again in its grand installation in the center of the city. The festival concludes after a number of days when the tree is taken down and pulled to a nearby body of water. The names of the festival are only slightly more complicated. In the Sanskrit of classical India, it is the Indradhvajotsava, Indramaha, or Śakramahotsava; in Nepali, the Indrajātrā or the slightly more Sanskritized Indrayātrā; and in the Newar language of the Kathmandu Valley, the *yeṃ yāḥ* (*punhi*). All of these terms translate to "the festival of Indra" except the first one, Indradhvajotsava, which adds a reference to Indra's *dhvaja*—the forty-foot-tall wooden pole raised in the city's royal square—and the last one, the Newar *yeṃ yāḥ* (*punhi*), which refers to the chronological and geographical setting of its celebration as "the (full moon) festival of Kathmandu," eliding any direct reference to Indra or his ritual pole.[2] First mentioned in the epic *Mahābhārata* some two thousand years ago, the South Asian festival of Indra has been celebrated within a variety of overlapping settings throughout India and Nepal: urban and rural; royal and agricultural; and Hindu, Jain, and Newar.[3]

Despite Indra's precipitous post-Vedic decline, scholars writing on early medieval India or contemporary Kathmandu have occasionally attended to the central role of the Indra festival. Art historian Mary Shepherd Slusser asserts that Indra is "still an important and honored deity [in Nepal, whose] name is familiar to every tongue, his images abound, and he is the center of an annual festival whose duration is exceeded only by that of the premier goddess, Durga" (1982: 1:267). Slusser might be overstating her case here. Even in Nepal, Indra has no temple, no priests, and no regular devotees, and once his festival ends, he and his images go into mothballs for the remainder of the year, with a periodicity that replicates the temporariness of his worship from the Vedic period (Kuiper 1975: 111, 1977: 42).[4]

Discussing the continuity of the epics with the Vedas, John Brockington points to the possibility of the festival's significance. "The epic evidence suggests in fact what other evidence also points to: that Indra maintained a degree of supremacy in more popular belief longer than most Vedic deities. In the early to middle layers of both epics he is prominent and frequently mentioned, both as the ruler of the gods and as the performer of various heroic deeds" (2001: 67). Despite the epics' continued references to the supremacy of the king of the gods—whose decline in prestige Brockington immediately acknowledges—contemporary scholars have allowed Indra's festival to remain squarely on the periphery. Thus, whereas such Hindu festivals as the Rāmlīlā, Durgā Pūjā, Ganesh Chaturthī, and Kumbha Mela have all come to be part of the general academic consciousness (studies of which have greatly assisted my own research into how Hindu festivals operate), very little secondary literature exists on Indra's festival. I am still mildly shocked, this many years on, when I encounter any reference to this festival in scholarship on South Asia. Of the references that I have come across, many have been little more than brief asides that acknowledge the festival's potential past glory but do not provide any larger cultural context for its performance and certainly do not acknowledge its survival into any contemporary South Asian performative tradition. In translating the Jain *Triśaṣṭiśalākapuruṣacaritra,* Helen Johnson footnotes the text's single reference to the festival: "The Indrotsava is described in the Natyasastra I. 55 ff. It apparently does not survive in any extant festival" (Hemacandra 1962: 343, n386). In his translation of chapter 150 of the *Kauśika Sūtra* of the Atharva Veda, Jan Gonda cautiously asserts: "The worship of the sal tree as the Indradhvaja is still prevalent in the western parts of Bengal. . . . According to H. A. Oldfield['s 1880 study of Nepal] . . . the Nepalese Gurkhas had, at least 80 years ago, likewise retained this custom" (1967: 413, n4). Brockington speaks to the inclusion in both Sanskrit epics of similes featuring Indra's banner, although he acknowledges that such references become increasingly rare in their later sections (2001: 70).

This book argues that the Indra festival had long been a significant part of the religious history of early medieval India, especially for the religion commonly referred to as Hinduism. The majority of the places where the festival has been celebrated have been Hindu kingdoms with the intellectual resources to produce the texts that used the Indra festival as a significant component of the reproduction of their rule. Thus, whatever the language used to name it, these celebrations focus on the performing king, who is identified with Indra, presides over the festival and its raising of the pole, and receives its ultimate benefits and blessings.

Such consistency can only occur because powerful agents responsible for producing ritual texts and actions (to borrow language from theories of practice) reconstructed the festival with "interested action" (Marshall Sahlins) that referred back and contributed to structuring dispositions (Pierre Bourdieu), provided strategic and practical orientations for acting (Bell 1992: 85), and applied features of asymmetry, inequality, and domination to this archetypal annual festival (Ortner 1989: 11–12). Although such flexible applications initially represent "subjective risks" for the performing culture, the process results in creative and meaningful cultural and symbolic change, Sahlins's "functional revaluation of the categories" (1985: ix). Produced rather than passively recorded by classical and contemporary agents drawing on culturally meaningful actions, narratives, and materials, the Indra festival has consistently been used to support an intimate relationship to these basic themes, its own *habitus* that is "constituted in practice and is always oriented towards practical functions" (Bourdieu 1990: 52).

Questions over the identity of the festival extend from the Sanskrit record into its new Nepalese home, where authors have wrestled with its flexibility and multiplicity. Henry Oldfield, surgeon for the British resident in Kathmandu whose work Gonda briefly referred to, provides an interpretation of how this festival, by the time of his writing in 1880, incorporated elements from several different festivals: the Newar festival said to be initiated by Guṇakāmadeva in the tenth century and the Hindu Nepali one maintained by Pratap Singh in the eighteenth century. Amid a brief description of the daily performances that local Newar people celebrate nightly—dances, displays of images of deities, and processions within and outside of Kathmandu—Oldfield asserts: "The Indrajatra, though commonly regarded as one festival, is in reality two distinct festivals: one, the Indrajatra proper, in honour of Indra; the other, the Ruthjatra [chariot festival], in honour of Devi Kumari (one of the eight goddess mothers). They have properly *no connection with each other* beyond the fact of their occurring at the same time" (1974 [1881]: 313–14, emphasis added). The dichotomy that Oldfield proposes here is remarkably insightful, though overly simplistic, because it results in two unrelated festivals that just happen to be celebrated at the same time and at the same place. D. R. Regmi, considering the same ritual material—the concurrent rites devoted to Indra, Kumari, and Bhairav—similarly concludes "Although the cult is ancient, the worship of Indra . . . is again so mixed up with the *jātrās* of Kumari and Bhairav that even though the festival is celebrated in the name of Indra, the latter has to share the devotion offered while others tend to dominate" (1966: 615).

Much of the scholarship on the Nepalese Indrajatra has concerned itself with this very issue: the extent to which the festival's diverse constituent rites are "mixed up" and thus the degree to which they might constitute a single archetypal festival. Rajendra Pradhan argues that the festival's thematically separate rites and themes are "relatively independent of each other," yet are "different aspects of the same basic idea which is the victory of order over chaos" (1986: 378–79). A. W. van den Hoek similarly asserts a classical Indic foundation for the festival: its "context shows features of a sacrificial arena" (2004: 14) whose "combined features . . . all point to one direction, that of a sacrificial concourse" (15) that has "the unifying notion of sacrificial death" (60) and that is a sacrificial prelude to the ensuing goddess-oriented Dasain festival (52, 61).

Using such structural language as "innovations, inventions and additions," "accretion" (37, 48, 50), and "embedded" (60), van den Hoek applies the related language of syncretism from his description of the simultaneous appearances of Hindu and Buddhist imagery during the Dasain festival (67) to his analysis of the large golden-colored mask of Seto Bhairav that dispenses beer to Kathmandu's youth during the Indra festival.[5] This mask is located immediately underneath a smaller replica of the temple to the goddess Taleju, the tutelary goddess of the erstwhile Malla dynasty whose original and larger temple was built nearly two centuries earlier and remains at the core of the old Newar palace approximately one hundred meters to the northeast.[6] Installed by Rana Bahadur Shah in 1795 several decades after the defeat of the Mallas and prominently displayed only during the Indra festival, Bhairav's mask represents part of the "cult of Svet Bhairav at Hanumāndhokā" whose image, "installed by the present Shāhī rulers but with a completely Newar cast and script, is thus a beautiful example of how the new rulers were integrated in the old ritual" (van den Hoek 2004: 46).[7]

Finally, in the writings of Gérard Toffin, a prolific anthropologist who has written on the urban Newar communities of Nepal for several decades, we can see the real difficulties in discerning the festival's unity. Though Toffin has shown an increasing flexibility toward the historical development of Kathmandu's Indra festival, his approach, like those of Oldfield and Regmi, has treated the festival in a similar piecemeal fashion that has presumed a gradual accumulation over time. In a 1992 article, he highlights the place of prominence that the festival gives to the living goddess Kumari and the transgressive deity Bhairav, writing that the "Indra Jatra is made up of three different series of rituals: Kumārī Jātrā, Indra Jātrā and Bhairava Jātrā, each one concentrated on a specific god. Though [they] are more or less related to each other, these three complex ceremonial components have their own myths and can be analysed quite independently. An hypothesis worth considering is that they originated separately and were brought together in a latter stage" (1992: 74). In a 2006 article, he increases the number of constituent elements from three to five, although he considers the organization and development of the festival to be based on a somewhat haphazard method of interpolation that is rooted in a central festival core, in much the same way that an earlier generation of scholars of the Sanskrit epics had considered their literary development. "The Indrajatra is composed of five parts: Indra, Kumari, Bhairav, funerary rites, masked dances. These five had probably developed independently and then had been progressively combined" (2006: 54). Finally, Toffin reverts to his original tripartite structuring and questions his approach to these three components:

> The Nepalese refer to the Kumārī Jātrā, the Bhairava Jātrā and the Indra Jātrā as they consider them three distinct entities. Should one consider these associated rites as one single festival or as three celebrations incorrectly grouped together under one name? The more one would like to interpret this delicate matter according to the facts, and especially to all the facts, the more difficult a goal this is to achieve. We are inclined, however, towards a thesis of structural unity, even if the structured system lacks a completely closed loop. (2010: 16; translation mine)

These citations—especially those that describe the arc of Toffin's scholarship—help us understand the complexity of the Indra festival: the multiple historical, thematic, and performative threads woven together throughout it and the multiple meanings attached to it. We might place the positions of these scholars into three loose categories, considering the degree of unity they attribute to the festival. Oldfield and Regmi assert the festival's absence of unity, saying that it contains such diverse and "mixed-up" components that we must see the festival as "two distinct festivals . . . [that] have properly no connection with each other."[8] Pradhan and Toffin offer a moderated unity, arguing that the festival has an underlying basic idea or structural unity, though the relative independence of its rites prevents it from achieving a "completely closed loop."

Only van den Hoek provides a reading whereby the festival attains an absolute unity, whose "combined features . . . all point to one direction, that of a sacrificial concourse." In reducing the Indra festival to "the unifying notion of sacrificial death," however, he overstates the relationship between a classical pan-Indian Hinduism and the system of Newar religious performance that effectively blends Hindu,

Vajrayana Buddhist, and local traditions. Although violent conflict is integral to the Indra festival tradition, it operates fairly independently of the robust textual corpus on classical Vedic and Hindu sacrifice that "has to be agonistic" (Heesterman 1993: 42). Moreover, van den Hoek frequently hedges on the sacrificial unity that he proposes, qualifying his general assertions by acknowledging specific rites that seem not to fit, stretching other examples to fit, or simply asserting it so frequently and in so reductive a manner that it starts to no longer ring true.[9]

The festival's survival in contemporary Kathmandu indicates its ability to survive in multiple environments, adapting as it shifts historical eras and geographical areas. The Indra festival is consistently connected to a common fund of related ideas: urban power, kingship and rivalry, and innovation and archaism. These related themes define the festival across time and space, as it is periodically regenerated, renewed, and revived. This thematic continuity allows the festival, despite its adaptability, to remain archetypal. Borrowing Humphrey and Laidlaw's definition that describes rituals as "perceived as discrete, named entities, with their own characters and histories," the Indra festival possesses and has retained its own "facticity and independent existence" (1994: 89, 100). By treating the Indra festival as "comprehensive" or "archetypal," I mean that I consider the festival as a singular entity, treating all of its parts together: thematically, systematically, and comprehensively without ahistorically essentializing the festival or the people who celebrate it.

In handing the festival in this holistic way, I seek to neutralize the power of the Sanskrit text, allowing for local performances of the Indra festival tradition to be considered as both independent performances that drive local, regional, and pan–South Asian interpretations and part of the larger Indra festival tradition whose roots are partially in the classical Sanskritic tradition. The festival's powerful authors and ritualists can then be seen as "contributing to the creative processes of making, remaking, and disseminating *proposed* meanings, some of which are more successful [than] others and some of which lead, in turn, to changes in the way the rite is performed" (Humphreys and Laidlaw 1994: 196).[10] Treating the textual tradition as just one part of the holistic Indra festival tradition, I am drawing on literature on Himalayan performances of the epic *Mahābhārata*, with which this book will conclude. William Sax writes of the epic as not being contained within the printed and published Sanskrit text but serving for the local community as "a kind of ancestral history that is remembered by the wise and periodically enacted" (2002: 56). Rather than separating "local" from "classical" festival performances (as if the Sanskrit record were not also local), and certainly rather than using the "authoritative" text to explain local performances, I hope to use these local performances to fill in the historical and narrative gaps that clearly exist in the textual record. In doing so, I intend to treat these texts more in the way that Leela Prasad treats the shastras as an "imagined text [in which] the normative manifests as emergent, situated in the local and the larger-than-local, the historical, and the interpersonal" (2007: 119).

Jātrā: Politics, Violence, and Power

The Nepali word *jātrā*, one component of the festival's most commonly known name Indrajātrā, is ultimately derived from the Sanskrit verbal root √*yā* (to go). This emphasis on motion refers to much more than the respectful movement of people, goods, and gods through the streets and neighborhoods of Kathmandu's old city. The term *jatra*, which simply means festival, implies a certain degree of energy or "effervescence" that is related to its Sanskrit synonym *utsava*. Such an event, Jan Gonda writes, is intended "to set in motion, to impel, to rouse, etc." (1947: 148), the goal of which is the strengthening of the deity through the celebratory actions of human beings. Considering the energy that permeates the Indra festival, it may not be coincidental that the only two hymns in which the word *utsava* occurs in the ancient Hindu text of the *Rig Veda* are directed to and celebrate Indra (1.100.8 and 1.102.1). More than any other, Nepal's Indra festival embodies Gonda's definition in all of its parts.

The public nature of the Indra festival is a major contributor to the frenetic energy it generates. Although the festival does include private family rites, as do nearly all major festivals, these domestic components are eclipsed by the concentration of vibrant and intense rites performed in some of Kathmandu's most public areas. Between its formal and scheduled rites and the very public manner in which people might observe and participate in them, the festival includes elements of mild to moderate violence, sometimes by design and sometimes as a result of its public and inclusive nature. Typically perpetrated by and against the thousands of young men who come from the city and its surrounding villages, the festival is used as a setting to assert their social positions. Late at night the young men fight to obtain a taste of the alcoholic *prasād* blessing from the six-foot-tall golden mask of Seto Bhairav, they fight one other as they try to settle scores accumulated throughout the year, and they are sometimes beaten bloody by the bamboo sticks of police who claim to be keeping order. Having seen multiple festivals in cities and towns throughout the Kathmandu Valley, I am quite sure that the unique and concentrated violence I have repeatedly witnessed—along with the regular sacrifice of multiple animals offered to various forms of Bhairav—is a necessary part of Kathmandu's Indra festival.

Gonda's definition of the Sanskrit *utsava* contains another conception that is relevant here: "the generating, stimulating, producing (viz. of power)" (1947: 151). Used throughout the classical texts as a weapon to destroy one's enemies, Indra's pole is a symbol of military power. This theme of political violence is inherent in the festival and relates to the construction of modern Nepal, the pole's installation marking the moment of the 1768 victory of the Hindu Shah dynasty over the Newar Mallas.[11] In the mid-eighteenth century, the Shah family reigning in the central hill town of Gorkha began a series of military incursions into the Kathmandu Valley, and by 1769 it had conquered the valley's four largest cities of Kirtipur, Kathmandu, Patan, and Bhaktapur. Defeating each city's king in turn, the Shah king made Kathmandu the capital of a single empire whose geographic extent came to be represented by the nation's current borders. The primary goal of the early Shah kings was the establishment of Nepal, unified as an *asal Hindustān* (a true Hindu kingdom) that served as a political and cultural bulwark against the Mughal and British imperial threat to the immediate south in India. Just as royal dynasties have done periodically throughout South Asian history, the Shah dynasty in the late eighteenth and early nineteenth century used the obscure festival of the Vedic god Indra as a strategic means for asserting its power throughout the expanding and increasingly unified Nepal.

More than simply using, performing, or celebrating the festival, and rather than seeing the Kathmandu Valley only as "a particularly conservative place which has preserved old Indian traditions elsewhere vanished," as Toffin suggests (1992: 82), I argue that the Shah kings conscientiously and strategically brought the Indra festival back into existence—they revived, reconstructed, and innovated around it after several centuries of general disuse. This revival took performative and textual forms and developed into what is sometimes referred to as the *mūl jātrā* (root festival) of Kathmandu.[12] This revival of an ancient and moribund festival celebrating Indra signaled their assertion of a festival that was explicitly Hindu in form and that represented a cultural victory over the Buddhist Newars. Though ancient and moribund, the Indra festival still represented a part of the cultural memory of Hindu South Asia, which this book will attempt to unpack. Despite the official processes that transformed Nepal's monarchy—"the only Hindu kingdom in the world"—into the secular Federal Democratic Republic of Nepal in the 2010s, the festival has survived and continues to be celebrated, maybe now especially celebrated, in the absence of the Hindu king.

This notion of political power is directly related to the particularly tantric aspect of many facets of religion in Nepal. Nascently present in the Sanskrit textual tradition, powerful tantric goddesses are omnipresent in Kathmandu's festival because they historically supported Nepal's Hindu king. Most notable is the figure of the Kumari, the living goddess who resides in a special house adjacent to the old royal palace. During the festival, accompanied by her brothers Bhairav and Ganesh, she goes on three chariot processions and dispenses blessings to the city's residents. Independently of Kumari, masks, wooden posts, and human representations of Bhairav are visible and audible during the festival. Narratives of Bhairav recall and celebrate the ancestors, beings who trouble the notion of the festival as a top-down, state-sponsored, and Indra-directed festival. Rather, its situatedness in Kathmandu allows for an oscillation between universal kingship and local kinship, often in the same ritual performance, location, and character.[13]

We can observe in this larger context how the South Asian religious festival represents a genre of strategic action that serves as an appropriate and successful strategy for the complementarity of innovation and archaism. The Ramlīlā of Rāmnagar at Benares requires the presence of the reigning Mahārājā (Lutgendorf 1991: 259); the Bengali Durgā Pūjā reflects the changing socioeconomic interpretations of the goddess and the demonic Mahiṣa (Rodriguez 2003: 289–90); the Ganesh festival in Maharashtra includes tableaux of the elephant-headed god placed amid the images of Indian political figures (Courtright 1985: 194); and the Kumbha Melā is attended by itinerant groups of *sadhus* whose simultaneous occupation as traders required them to acquire the warrior skills required to protect their goods" (Maclean 2008: 12).

More than just political interpretations and applications of religious materials, persons, and performances, however, the origins of these festivals, ancient though they might seem and ancient though some of their roots might be, "inescapably and unmistakably" reflect the politics of the era in which they were strengthened, retooled, fortified, popularized, and in some cases revived (Pennington and Allocco 2018: 9). All of these renovating actions were strategically performed in the context of a relationship with a powerful and contiguous Other, if not in the face of the threat of colonial occupation. Likewise, Hindu agents constructed, fortified, innovated, and revived the Indra festival several times at moments of political upheaval.

The examples throughout this book show how the somewhat contradictory functions of the Indra festival, both conservatively political and flexibly innovative, connect to the process that has come to be known as Sanskritization or even what we might more specifically call Hinduization.[14] The authors of these Indra festival texts have used a highly Sanskritic concept—the ancient Hindu and, more particularly, Vedic deity Indra—as the festival's focus of divine attention. Despite Slusser's assertion of Indra's place in the religious life of post-Vedic South Asia—"whereas in India Indra's cult seems to have survived only to the tenth century, it is exactly from then that images of Indra begin to be abundant in Nepal" (1982: 1:267)—Indra is an ancient and moribund deity who has no temple or priestly infrastructure. But it is precisely his quality of being ancient that makes him a prime candidate for a festival that reinforces a self-consciously Hindu tradition and identity. There is no way Indra can be confused for or conflated with a divine being from any other religious tradition. Indra's long-standing identity as a king and victorious combatant over primeval enemies—beginning with his victory over the primordial serpent Vṛtra in *Rig Veda* 1.32—helps define the specifically royal and hegemonic uses to which his festival has been put.

Though the use of the Indra festival as a literary and performative technique was applied infrequently, it attained a degree of consistency that has shown the power that it continued to exert on court poets and their royal patrons, periodically across approximately one and a half millennia. More than simply a celebration of a particular deity or a moment in the agricultural calendar, performances of the Indra festival show that it is an explicitly Hindu response to potential incursions from religious others. In his study of the Shah dynasty, which revived the Indra festival in early nineteenth-century Nepal in the Buddhist Newar society of the Kathmandu Valley, Subho Basu refers to the ultimate Shah goal of "state-sponsored Hinduism," asserting, "The quasi-feudal monarchical regime used religion to establish its hegemonic ideological presence in the political landscape" (Basu 2010: 111, 112). This "hegemonic ideological presence" refers to the (largely successful) attempts at national unification that the Shah family effected through techniques we now recognize as standard: the establishment of a single form of government (a monarchy), one language (Nepali), and one religion (Hinduism).[15]

This holy trinity of national unification has long been part and parcel of state formation in South Asia (and elsewhere), and the Indra festival has been at the vanguard of these Hindu-centered movements. During opportune times, ritualists, authors, poets, and priests have highlighted if not revived the festival, which publicly displays culturally resonant concepts, practices, and materials, transforming recognizable religious gestures into transhistorical acts of political power. Moreover, the explicit use of Hindu forms in performances of the Indra festival has regularly worked against Buddhist Others.[16] The production of the epic *Mahābhārata* in the post-Aśokan period (Fitzgerald 2004), of the *Vishnudharmottara Purāṇa* among north Indian courts of the seventh century (Inden 1978), and of the *Indradhvajotsava Kathanam* from the Nepali Shah dynasty in the early nineteenth century are all examples of this conservative use of the Indra festival against Buddhist regimes, indicating to its audience the specifically Hindu-based hegemony these dynasties sought to produce.[17] By viewing Nepal's festival as a revival and as the endpoint of a particular performative lineage with multiple cultural points of origin—local Newar festivals, regional Himalayan *Mahābhārata* performances, and pan–South Asian Hindu forms—we can more easily see how the contemporary festival represents a concerted effort to continue this comprehensive performative tradition, despite local rites and readings that might seem to point elsewhere.[18] If we view these texts as part of a comprehensive Indra festival tradition and their authors as dependent on the ties between political patronage and Hindu sectarian affiliation, we should not be surprised when overt notions of imperialistic agendas and political hegemony interrupt an otherwise imaginative, mythological, or religious narrative.

The Chronology of the Indra Festival and an Introduction to the Chapters

The Indra festival has a fluid chronology that reflects its larger flexibility over time and helps us understand the main themes of this book. In Nepal, the most popular way of conceiving of the festival duration is to assert that it is an eight-day festival that begins when the pole goes up and ends when it is dropped, pulled away, and disposed of on the final day.[19] By accounting for and troubling this seemingly simple fact, we can see more clearly how acts of revival and archaism have structured the festival throughout its history. Always bracketed by rites dedicated to the pole, the festival's fluid chronology helps us see how all of the festival's rites, even those that precede the pole's installation, are part of the comprehensive and archetypal Indra festival that celebrates both kingship and kinship.

The classical Sanskrit texts fit the festival into the fifteen days of the second, bright half of the autumnal month of Bhādrapad. The *Viṣṇudharottara Purāṇa* states that the royal coterie should proceed to the forest "on the first day of the bright half of Prauṣṭhapāda [Bhādrapad]" (2.155.4a). Lying on display on the outskirts of the city, the pole makes its ritual entrance into the core of city on Bhādra 8 and is installed on Bhādra 12, prominently remaining on display in the center of the city for another four days until the full-moon day at the end of the month (*pūrṇimā*, Bhādra 15).[20] Up to this point the classical and contemporary festival calendars are identical. With the classical texts unceremoniously lowering and disposing of the pole on the following day (Āśvin/Asoj 1), the festival thus occupies the entire bright half of Bhādra, from *pratipad* to *pūrṇimā*, neatly bounded by the dark halves of Bhādra and Asoj/Āśvin, inauspicious times typically devoted to rites to the ancestors.[21]

The contemporary Nepalese festival begins on Bhādra 2 and spills over into the first four days of the dark half of Asoj, thus celebrated over eighteen days. This difference is mainly due to the pole remaining upright in the center of the city for another four days (eight days total), with the festival concluding on the somewhat anomalous day of Asoj kṛṣṇa 4, a chronological shift that is quite evident in the Nepalese performance.[22] Whereas the festival's first half (Bhādra śukla 12–15, the final four days of the month ending with the full moon) is full of activities, the festival's second half (Asoj kṛṣṇa 1–4, the first four days of the next month) is nearly devoid of any unique ritual activities. In fact, the only major activity that occurs in these final four days—aside from the pole's lowering (*pātana*) and disposal (*visarjan*), which must occur on the festival's final day—is the third and final chariot procession of Kumari that also occurs on the final day and is also seen locally as a later addition. There is no easy answer as to why the Nepalese festival continues into the month of Asoj. It is possible that the royal astrologers had wanted to accommodate the festival in a chronological scheme that maintains an eight-day duration with the pole's installation on Bhādra 12, although no documentation exists to support such a claim.[23]

We do know that this new chronology was established in the early nineteenth-century Shah court of Kathmandu. Court astrologers in 1843 introduced the specific language of the five *sāit*, the festival's five core events that name and schedule the rites surrounding the pole (Pant 1995: 37, 39).[24] These times are now provided by the office of Śākhā Kāryālaya Kāṭhmaḍauṃ (Branch Office of Kathmandu) of Gūṭhī Saṃsthān, the Nepali government office that funds local *guthi* organizations upholding facets of local and national heritage. For 2017 (V.S. 2074), the office provided the following *sāit* list, which I transcribe as follows. The first line of each *sāit* copies the official document as accurately as possible—with the name of the event, *gate* date of the Nepali secular calendar, day of the week, and time of day—while the second line provides a translation of the event name, *tithi* Hindu lunar festival date, and date from the Western calendar.

1. Ban Yātrā. Wednesday, Bhadra 7, 11:15 a.m.
    - Journey to the Forest. Bhādra śukla 2 (August 23)
2. Vṛkṣa-kartana. Wednesday, Bhadra 7, 7:33 p.m.
    - Cutting the tree. Bhādra śukla 2 (August 23)

3. Nagara-praveśa. Tuesday, Bhadra 13, 9:32 a.m.
    - Entrance into the city. Bhādra śukla 8 (August 29)
4. Indra-dhvajotthāna. Sunday, Bhadra 18, 8:15 a.m.
    - Raising the pole. Bhādra śukla 12 (September 3)

    Indrajātrā (talloṭol jātrā). Tuesday, Bhadra 20
    - Kumari's lower-city chariot procession (September 5)[25]

    Māthilo ṭol jātrā. Wednesday, Bhadra 21
    - Kumari's upper-city chariot procession (September 6)

    Nānichā Yātrā. Sunday, Bhadra 25, nighttime of this day
    - Kumari's central-city chariot procession (September 10)
5. Indradhvajapatana. Sunday, Bhadra 25, 10:25 p.m.
    - Lowering of the pole, Asoj kṛṣṇa 4 (September 10)[26]

In coining this language, the Hindu court astrologers made these events tally with the content of the Sanskrit textual tradition, helping establish the continuity of the revived Nepalese Indrajatra with its classical textual and performative forebears, thus bolstering the *asal Hindustān* and imperial successes of the Shah dynasty. As I read the classical Sanskrit textual record and the contemporary Nepalese performative tradition together as part of the same festival tradition, with each able to interpret the gaps and ambiguities in the other, this *sāit* structure, rather than being anachronistic, will be helpful for establishing, sequencing, and understanding the corresponding rites in both modes of the festival tradition. Each chapter will detail how ritual actors and agents in classical India and contemporary Nepal innovated around the archaic nature of the Indra festival and its central pole, adapting it to their sociocultural needs.

Chapter 1 details five Sanskrit texts, beginning with the rustic and archaic origin story at the start of the *Mahābhārata*, that use the Indra festival as a framing device for an aspect of social or cultural innovation in medieval India. Steeped in the classical textual tradition, this first chapter will observe changes effected by the classical festival in dharma, drama, royal power, architecture, and devotion, concluding with a few observations on how the contemporary Nepalese festival similarly draws on these classical themes to highlight the capital city. This urban focus sets up much of the remainder of this book, as the city provides the locus for activities devoted to all of the festival's human and divine players.

Chapter 2 details the festival's first two *sāit*, the rural and royal rites of the Ban Yātrā (the Forest Journey) and the Vṛkṣa-karttana (the Cutting of the Tree) that connect the capital city with the jungles outside of the city. Chapter 3 covers the festival's three urban *sāit*, the rites of the Nagara-praveśa (the Entrance into the City), the Indra-dhvajotthāna (the Raising of Indra's Pole), and the festival's concluding Visarjan (the Disposal) that reify and celebrate the city. These movements of the pole celebrate the urban kingship for which the festival was classically known, while incorporating the parallel internal processions of the goddess Kumari throughout the many neighborhoods of Kathmandu's upper and lower halves.

Chapters 4 and 5 focus squarely on the early nineteenth century and the Shah revival of the Indra festival, each chapter handling one text produced in that period. Chapter 4 handles the text commonly known as the *Wright Vamsavali*, recently retranslated and republished in a multivolume critical edition. This chapter follows recent scholarship that considers the genre of the *vaṁśvalī* (chronicle) as more literary than historical and will investigate the twin applications in this particular text of the Indra festival and Kumari toward the origins of the Shah dynasty. Chapter 5 considers Śaktivallabh Arjyāl's *Indradhvajotsava Kathanam*, a text whose compilation of and commentary on classical Sanskrit texts, several of which appeared in chapter 1, supported the military incursions of the Shah dynasty and their intentions of constructing a single Nepali nation.

The Shah revival hardly resulted in a single uncontested meaning for the festival, however. The final two chapters attend to the many occasions when Kathmandu's festival diverts from or even challenges its classical focus on the urban king. Local Newar processions for the ancestors and celebrations of the power of the goddess frequently work together to highlight the ways the Indra festival draws on a common Himalayan fund of rhetoric, imagery, and performances connected to the *Mahābhārata*. Chapter 6 focuses on the local story of Bhairav and his victimhood at the hands of Krishna at the epic war in Kurukshetra as a way of thinking about political hierarchies in modern Nepal.

Chapter 7 concludes by considering the role of the ancestors led by Indra's powerful mother against a number of disparate epic elements brought together in Kathmandu's festival that simultaneously celebrates kingship and kinship. Rather than disrupting the festival and despite their absence from the *sāit* schedule, these events trace the multiple boundaries of the city and highlight Kathmandu's multiple royal histories, honoring the local powerful beings whose continued power sustains city and citizen alike. A brief conclusion analyzes the continued significance of the Indra festival in an ever-changing Nepal.

A Note on Language

In describing the contemporary Indra festival in Kathmandu, I use the term *Newar* to refer to those cultural elements specific to the Newar people of the Kathmandu Valley. I use the Nepali-language term *Nepali* to refer to non-Newar Parbatiya people whose Hindu religious culture, promoted by the Shah dynasty after their successful military invasions of the valley in the 1760s, is found throughout Nepal. I use the English-language term *Nepalese* to refer more generally to historical eras, places, and practices that are such a part of the modern nation that it is not possible or relevant to distinguish among ethnic or culture groups. Those readers for whom such a distinction is irrelevant are welcome to ignore it. Despite the difficulties in shifting—culturally, historically, and linguistically—between classical Sanskrit, contemporary Nepali, and Newar, I have attempted to maintain some consistency as I try to weave together these disparate but related cultures while adhering to standard spelling, transliteration, and diacritics, but some idiosyncrasies will doubtless remain.

Chapter One

The Early Medieval Indra Festival

The Vedic identity regularly attributed to the Indra festival and its central ritual pole is commonly based on a number of passages from the *Rig Veda*: in 3.8, where the poets sing a hymn of praise to the Vedic *yūpa* (sacrificial post); in 10.173, where the king stands up firmly like Indra; and in *Rig Veda* 1.10, where Brāhmaṇs raise Indra like a *vaṃśa* pole.[1] In several studies of Vedic narrative and performance, F. B. J. Kuiper repeatedly asserts the festival's basis in the foundational cycle of stories of the Vedic Indra, stating that the festival, celebrated at the end of the year, re-creates the battle between good and evil—between Indra and the asura demons—in an only temporarily resolved conflict that remains latent for the rest of the year (1975: 115). In this reading, the festival's central victory banner ultimately and definitively depends on the Vedic myth of Indra propping up the sky such that he is "identical with the tree . . . [and] with the pillar at the moment of creation, when he himself literally *was* the world axis. . . . This inference is confirmed by data about the Indra festival of much later times" (110–11). In a later publication, Kuiper states this point about the festival more strongly: "The character of the banner, mostly a bamboo pole . . . then admits of no other interpretation than that the erection of the pole was a ritual re-enactment of Indra's 'propping up' the sky by means of the cosmic pillar. . . . The banner festival was, consequently, a reiteration of the creation and must as such have inaugurated the new year, that is, a new life in a renovated world" (1977: 129–30).

Despite the presence of Indra and his proximity to poles and posts in the *Rig Veda*, I will argue throughout this book that the complete absence of the festival in the Vedic textual record suggests that we should reject the notion of an ancient Vedic Indra festival.[2] This does not preclude us from considering how medieval Sanskrit authors applied Vedic rhetoric to "the Indra festival of much later times," as courtly literature and royal performances certainly drew on local folk festivals that operated independently of but coterminous with the Vedic tradition. Alf Hiltebeitel's argument about the applications of Vedic rhetoric to epic narratives can be readily applied to our consideration of the rhetorical history of the Indra festival: detailing ritual performances and performers (2001: 132, 140), cosmological features (151–54), and geographical locations (156), epic frame stories "link with other conventions and allusions to make the *whole appear Vedic*" (131, n2; emphasis in original).[3] James Hegarty refers to similar allusions to a Vedic past as providing such stories with a "Vedish" provenance, as "the Vedic past is mobilized in order to locate, and guarantee, teachings and practices" that are distinctly non-Vedic (2012: 117–18).[4]

This chapter surveys five instances of the Indra festival in classical Sanskrit texts that are clearly directed toward more pressing needs than reconstructing or repurposing the components—especially the sacrificial *yūpa*—of Vedic ritual. Composed in the second half of the first millennium of the Common Era, these texts locate the Indra pole in the royal capital cities and typify the literature composed in the wake of the second urbanization, which saw the rise of the heterodox dharmas to which Brahminical and early Hindu texts responded. This Brahminical literature strengthened the larger cultural move away from the language and performance of mobile Vedic rites and toward the stability of the royal capital city (Heitzmann 2009: 31). Rather than simply lumping these texts together, as some authors have done, I handle them individually, observing how they represent constituent pieces of the larger Indra festival tradition and noticing how authorial and ritual agents differently constructed, ordered, and interpreted the festival, innovating and adapting along the way.[5]

I connect each text to the larger theme around which it innovates: dharma in the *Mahābhārata*, drama in the *Nāṭyaśāstra*, royal power in the *Viṣṇudharmottara Purāṇa*, architecture in the *Samarāṅgana Sūtradhāra*, and devotion in the *Bhāgavata Purāṇa*. I conclude by considering how the contemporary case of Kathmandu's performance, the sole living example of the classical festival, builds on what we might refer to as an urban habitus: building on the structuring dispositions and organizing practices of the South Asian city presented in these much earlier classical texts, the reconstructed and revived Indra festival displays a rhetorical understanding of, appreciation for, and mastery amenable to the urban communities of the Kathmandu Valley.

These festival narratives, many of which are placed at the beginning (or near one of the beginnings) of their texts, operate innovatively as dynamic rhetorical framing devices that show the reader that something new is about to occur. Thus, just as the forty-foot pole in an urban center functions as the proverbial finger pointing at the moon, indicating the presence of the larger festival, so do these texts provide a ritual narrative that preemptively reorients their audience and immediately prepares them to think beyond the content of the text they are reading. Their authors reorder traditional South Asian ways of knowing and being, signaling to their audience some impending sociopolitical change.

This chapter's five texts use the Indra festival to architecturally restructure urban space—the theater, the temple, the palace, and the city—in its construction of a nascent early medieval Hinduism that recognizes "increasing sedentarization, the spread of agriculture and intensified urbanizanization," and foregrounds what Daud Ali refers to as "technologies of the self" (Ali 1998: 161). These technologies, detailed especially in Vatsyayana's *Kāmasūtra,* make up a "science of courtliness" that includes artifice, pleasure, and comportment, whose elaboration was prescribed "for a class of urban-dwelling men and women associated with the court of a king" (162). The urban Indra festival participates in these technologies, helping construct the public, exterior, and communal world of the city. Ali's assertion that "pleasure arose from the experience of the outer domains of the self; and courtly practices were thus pre-occupied with *exteriority*" (167) recalls those parts of the Indra festival—especially the pole's arrival into the royal capital city—that include agents explicitly concerned with aesthetic pursuits: priests, concubines, musicians, singers, actors, resident citizens, the king, his officials, and his family.

This annual performance of urbanization allows a further rethinking of the role of the city in classical and contemporary South Asia. Rather than restricting ourselves to Wendy Doniger's analysis of the mythic city, a metaphor for "the illusory body housing the (real) soul" that expresses "the unreality of the universe" (1984: 273), we might benefit from Anne Vergati's conclusions regarding the significance of the city in the practice and ideology of Nepalese festivals. Of the New Year's festival of Bhaktapur, she writes: "*Bisket Jātrā* is a mythical evocation of the founding of a town, the ancient capital of a kingdom, which, in a certain way, is the microcosmos of the entire territory of that kingdom. This foundation is 're-played' each year at the festival; the town is thus renewed at each New Year" (2002: 184). These Indra festival texts similarly signal to the reader not just the reality of an individual's self but the reality of the geographic space of the capital city. It is not only that "for the authors of the bulk of the classical kāvyas, the city had a *working* significance, rather than only a formal one," as Shonaleeka Kaul writes, but the city provides a setting for courtly practices, that, "pre-occupied with *exteriority*," highlight the public display of political power (2011: 16). Kathmandu's contemporary festival is one such event that, celebrated at the city's old palace, similarly evokes, replays, renews, and exteriorizes the dynamic life of early medieval South Asia.

Dharma in the *Mahābhārata*

Foreshadowing the contemporary Nepalese festival whose inaugural performance is placed against the violence of the *Mahābhārata* war, the authors of the Sanskrit epic used the Indra festival as a cipher for religious and cultural innovation. Chapter 57 of *Ādi Parvan,* the first of the *Mahābhārata*'s eighteen books, tells of the first performance of the Indra festival, that by Chedi king Uparicara Vasu, as a means of upholding dharma and retaining royal power. Establishing the themes of royalty, rivalry, and innovation that run throughout the entirety of the epic, the story of Vasu's performance of the Indra festival marks the very beginning of the epic.[6]

Vasu appears three times in the *Mahābhārata* (*MBh*), each time responsible for the performance of a ritual. In Book 1, he performs the Indra festival at the behest of Indra himself, providing a model for the ways this festival has been celebrated and understood by performers and audiences ever since. In Book 12, the authors construct an idealized and fantastical form of Vasu, who performs devotional rituals dedicated to Vishnu and lauded by *rishi*s. In Book 14, he incorrectly adjudicates the appropriateness of Yudhisthira's Vedic-style horse sacrifice by allowing the king to offer with "whatever materials are on hand" (*yathopanītair yaṣṭavyaṃ*, 14.94.21), for which he is sent directly to hell (*rasātalaṃ*).

Although van Buitenen asserts in his translation that the epic "begins in earnest with the tale of Uparicara Vasu [which] merely serves to introduce the miraculous birth of Satyavatī, matriarch of the Kauravas" (1973: 4), I argue that this narrative of Vasu is much more polyvalent and significant. Regularly connected with proper ritual performance, the cycle of stories that begins here establishes Vasu as a morally ambivalent character. His identity as a Chedi king allies him with the other wicked figures of Bṛhadratha, Jarāsaṃdha, and especially Chedi king Śiśupāla, whom Krishna kills in Book 2 and whose energy Krishna absorbs into himself. The eventual victory of Krishna and the Pāṇḍavas that defines the *MBh* is thus impossible without the prior eradication and absorption of Chedi, a kingdom ruled over by the ambivalent figure of Vasu.[7]

In our first encounter with Vasu in the opening verses of chapter 1.57, the authors immediately present their readers with the two conflicting sides of Vasu's royal dharma. We first read of Vasu's "brahminical" dharma: "There was a great lord of the earth named King Uparicara whose dharma was unwavering. One time, he was to go out hunting as one who was upholding a *vrata*. Vasu, the son of Pūru, grasped the pleasant area of Chedi at the behest of Indra. He took what was to be taken" (1.57.1–2). In this initial passage, he represents the dutiful, very martial, and very fertile brahminical king who wages war, hunts animals, has sex with his wives, honors his ancestors, and leaves descendants. But in the next two verses, Vasu is shown leaning toward a heterodox dharma: "Indra met Vasu in person; the king desired to lay down his arms, to perform acts of *tapas* [renunciation] and to live in an *ashrama* [monastery]. Considering his ability to achieve the quality of Indra through *tapas*, Indra gently addressed the king and immediately turned him away from *tapas*" (1.57.3–4).

This ambivalence in Vasu's character—containing both domestic and renunciatory dharmas—provides an example of the "double crisis of *dharma*" that James Fitzgerald puts forth (2004: 80). Arguing that the redaction of what we now have as the critical edition was produced in the immediate aftermath of the Mauryan dynasty, Fitzgerald refers to how the epic's brahmin authors first acknowledged the new heterodox and "universal" values, composed of elements of Jain, Ājīvaka, and especially what we now call Buddhist dharmas.[8] Patronized by Ashoka in the third century BCE, this dharma was suffused with the principles of yoga, valued harmonious relations between people, emphasized the practice of altruistic behaviors, and entailed the more interiorized virtues of nonviolence, respect, and social harmony, precisely those advocated by Vasu after his acquisition of Chedi (2004: 112–23).[9]

The textual imagining of an apocalyptic purge of extant kings and kingship made up the second part of the crisis. The epic itself—a "social and political parable" (Fitzgerald 2004: 100) born out of the resentment and self-loathing of disappointed brahmins—was the final result of this process, a document whose authors, editors, and redactors carefully integrated the increasingly popular heterodox values into a larger matrix of ethical norms, ritual practices, and patterns of patronage.[10] The figure at the center of this crisis is the person of Ashoka, best known for rock-cut inscriptions that promoted his vision of a Buddhist-inflected universal dharma that could unite his massive empire.[11] The very public form of his tall Pillar Edicts—"situated in places where people gathered so that ample publicity was given to them" (Thapar 2013: 218)—reifies the double crisis, providing a tangible form of these changing patterns of patronage. Fitzgerald is hardly the only scholar to make this argument, and the epic is not the only text to bear the weight of the Mauryan dynasty. Patrick Olivelle observes that *dharmaśāstra* texts like the Laws of Manu also "can best be understood as responses to the continuing effects and memory of the Aśokan reforms" (2010: 1, 2009: 20); Ashoka's attempt, Romila Thapar argues, was to "universalize a code focussed on social ethics and on the accommodation of diverse views" (2012: 19).[12]

Reflecting both Yudhiṣṭhira's renunciation of the nearly empty kingdom after the Pāṇḍavas' victory and King Ashoka's Buddhist missionizing after his victorious invasion of Kalinga, Vasu's performance of the Indra festival presents the opening salvo of the authors' adjudication of this "double crisis." Following his attempted renunciation, the Indra festival—performed by Vasu at the request (or demand) of Indra—refers to and critiques Ashoka's *dharma-stambha* via its central rite of raising Indra's pole.[13] Narrated after a longer dialogue as Indra tries to convince Vasu to remain king in Chedi and not renounce, the festival is handled in a mere four verses (1.57.17–20), nothing like the full chapters it receives in later ritual texts. This short passage focuses on the king's acts of bringing into the royal city and installing a single bamboo pole (*yaṣṭi*), an archaic and simplified version of the festival's most important public component.

> Indra, the destroyer of Vritra, gave to him a bamboo pole, this desired gift that signifies him as the ultimate protector of the people. In order to do *pūjā* to the pole of Indra, the Protector of the Earth (Vasu) brought [*praveśaṃ kārayāmāsa*] [the pole] to Earth [*bhūmau*] at the end of the year. And even today, the preparation and entrance [*prabhṛti ca . . . praveśaḥ*] of the *yaṣṭi* is similarly done by the best of kings, O King, just as it was done by him. On the following day, the *yaṣṭi* is raised [*ucchrayo*] by kings. Ornamentation with boxes, incense, garlands, and ornaments, and scatterings of flower garlands should be done according to injunction. (translation mine)

Drawing on the details of the classical festival and asserting that it is performed "according to injunction" (*vidhivat kriyate*), this narrative places the festival in a mythological time and place. Performed at the end of the year, the pole's classical entrance into the city in a grand royal procession (*praveśaṃ kārayāmāsa*) is replaced by its conveyance from an implied Indra's heaven, juxtaposed to Vasu's Earth (*bhūmau*) where it is installed.[14]

Indra's festival pole is here referred to as a "bamboo pole" (*vaiṇavīṃ yaṣṭiṃ*), the simplicity and singularity of which stands in surprisingly stark opposition to the massive wooden pole—the *dhvaja*, a term not used in this epic passage—and its several ancillary poles described in the early medieval texts (see figure 1.1).[15] In these later texts, installing the large wooden pole requires mobilizing complex hierarchies of religious and palace officials, accompanied by singers, dancers, musicians, courtesans, and citizens who all congregate to celebrate the festival against the background of the royal cityscape. But the *MBh* tells a different and very simple origin story here—the initial installation of a single bamboo pole by a single person at the direct behest of Indra—without the organized chaos that has come to define the festival over the past 1400 years.

Furthering this passage as an origin narrative, in the next few verses the authors relate this unknown festival to others with which the audience would have been familiar. Rather than drawing on the

Figure 1.1. Men from Kathmandu's Kendriya Manandhar Sangha (Central Manandhar Organization) (KMS) install Indra's pole on Bhadra 12. Photo by author.

existence of some original, primitive, or Vedic form of the Indra festival as Kuiper has argued, they construct an archetypal rite, giving it a proper name (actually, two or maybe even three names) that reinforces the king's central role.

> Those people who always celebrate the *utsavam* [festival] in honor of Śakra [Indra]—just as they are purified with the giving of land [*bhūmidāna*], etc., with the giving of boons [*varadāna*], or with a large sacrifice [*mahāyajña*], so also with the Śakrotsava.
>
> Then, Vasu, the lord of Chedi, he who is established in Chedi, having been honored by Maghavān [Indra], protected this Earth with dharma. Vasu, the lord of the Earth, who is dear to Indra [*indra-prītyā*], performed the Indramaha. (1.57.26–27)

This two-verse passage contains a two-part relative-correlative structure ensuring that we see explicit connections among its ritual components: the performers of the Indra festival are just like those who perform other royal rituals;[16] the Indra festival is just like these other established royal rituals; the benefits accrued (purification, *pūtā*) clearly mark the Indra festival as a royal installation rite; and Vasu is the instantiation of "those people," that is, the kings who perform and thus benefit from the festival. Again, rather than reflecting a Vedic precedent, this passage reflects the epic's concern with adjudicating conflicting dharmas and looks ahead to the set of court rituals that result in the construction and installation of kings in urban South Asia. The authors make clear that this is a process still in the making.

The festival only receives a proper name here, well into its description. Though the narrators approach a formal naming of the festival early in verse 26, referring to it as "the *utsavaṃ* of Śakra," they place significant distance between the two Sanskrit words describing the festival (*utsavaṃ kārayiṣyanti sadā śakrasya ye narāḥ*), rendering a more literal translation as "the festival which people regularly celebrate in honor of Śakra [Indra]."[17] The text gradually reifies the festival, properly naming it late in this section before moving onto other tales of Vasu—it is the *Śakrotsava* in verse 26 and the *Indramaha* in verse 27. By naming the festival only at the end of each verse, the structure maintains a consistent suspense as to the identity of this "new" festival. These two names build on the half-dozen uses of the verbal root √*pūj* in this section, placing Indra's rather intimate and alliterative reference to the festival as "my festival" (*mahaṃ mama*, v. 23) in the context of more established royal, devotional, and Vaishnava celebrations. Moving from the unknown and indecipherable, through a set of comparisons with more common royal rituals, and finally to a multiply named archetypal festival that is to be celebrated for all times, the final verse of this passage completes the reification of the festival by providing it with a new "facticity and independent existence" it previously lacked. Reminding the reader of Vasu's earthly nature and the local and domestic dharma he is to perform, this passage situates him twice in Chedi, the place whence he protects the Earth and where, as the section concludes, "Vasu performed the Indra festival" (*cakāra-indramahaṃ vasuḥ*).

The archaic, rustic, and archetypal nature of this story offers a number of options and opportunities for rethinking the role of the

Indra festival in *Ādi Parvan,* in the construction of the epic, and in its historical relationship to Ashoka and the Mauryan empire. First, by removing any allusion to the festival's Vedic provenance, the epic authors have been pushed the origins of the festival back into an unnamed and undetermined antiquity. Readers are left somewhat rudderless and forced to imagine the time *in illo tempore* when this festival was first performed. Such a mysterious narrative and festival ground the forthcoming readings of Yudhisthira's royal dharma in a new and previously unknown ideology.

Second, the epic authors have provided a sort of literary back formation by constructing a hypothetically simple version of a complex urban festival of which its readers would already have been aware, even from performances they had witnessed in their own city. This assertion presumes that the authors and editors were aware of the earliest *rājnīti* texts that prescribe the festival's performance (in the *Bṛhat Saṃhitā,* for example) and that they composed and interpolated Vasu's frame story into the *Mahābhārata* narrative at a later date, quite possibly at a much later date than is usually considered for the composition of the epic.[18]

Finally, and seemingly opposed to this previous option, the authors drew on the celebration of a small-scale autumnal village festival of which they and their audience were also already aware. Although such a festival may have involved the raising of a pole on the new year's day, thus using imagery also used in the *Rig Veda,* we need not consider that such a rural and rustic festival was in any way "Vedic."

These three options provide a compelling, plausible, and complex explanation for the content and form of Vasu's story. The third option—the plethora of pole-raising festivals in rural South Asia—provides a clear lens for understanding all three together. Anne Feldhaus (2003: 55) describes the installation of a bamboo pole in the contemporary Guḍhi Pāḍvā festival to Shiva in Maharashtra.[19] Kulchandra Koirala lists dozens of such festivals celebrated throughout urban and rural Nepal, many specifically raising bamboo poles (Nep. *bāṃs ko liṅgo*) and many of which are linked to the celebration of goddesses (1985: 118). Gérard Toffin describes how in the festival as celebrated in the Nepalese village of Pyangaon, two poles are fashioned from a pine tree—one male and the other female—but are not explicitly identified with Indra (Toffin 1978; 1992: 82–83).

The work of Jyotindra Jain on the art and music of the Rathva tribe of Gujarat and of their celebration of a festival to Bābo Ind might be the most insightful for analyzing the rustic nature of the epic festival.[20] Having cut nine branches from the trees in the forest, nine boys, each holding one branch, process up to a set of nine holes, planting the branches in a single row. A number of offerings are made to the tree, including goat sacrifices, and a number of ritual invocations are made. Though the Rathva festival to Bābo Ind "is basically an agricultural rite . . . in anticipation of agricultural prosperity," Jain clearly asserts its affinity with the Hindu festival of Indra and theorizes their connection (1984: 64). Dismissing the possibility that "the Rathvas adopted the cult of Ind only recently from the neighbouring Hindus who inherited it as a continuous tradition from the Vedic times onwards," Jain argues that "there were a variety of widespread agricultural deities and rituals from ancient times, including the cult of Indra, and that at different stages of history these merged and mingled with one another" (1984: 68).

In regard to all three options, I consider the epic festival to be an archaism, a ritual purposefully constructed to look as if it came straight out of an ancient village. Its unnamed and undetermined antiquity eschews a known Vedic past that a reader might expect, thus constructing an alternative narrative that anticipates, through its opposition, the classical urban festival of which its readers, I argue, were already aware. The rustic nature of the festival in this narrative focuses on the constructive ritual activity of Chedi King Vasu, placing the onus of ritual and moral responsibility squarely on one king rather than on the entire urban community that would participate in it. This singularity more clearly allows readers to consider and critique Vasu as a multiform of the *stambha*-raising Ashoka; Vasu's eventual fall from grace in Book 14 reinforces the religious shortcomings that authors saw in the Mauryan king and the new religious strand he sought to develop.

More than just an accusation of simplicity, the archaic Indra festival depicted in the epic is a ritual gone wrong. Its simplicity serves as a ritual-rhetorical device that highlights Vasu's improper ritualization by two oppositions. The festival's rural nature, signaled by its bamboo pole, is contrasted with the much more urban(e) festival as it is found in the texts and cities of early medieval India. Simultaneously, the festival's rustic nature also marks it as non-Vedic in preparation for

Yudhiṣṭhira's Vedic-style *aśvamedha* in Book 14, for whose improper adjudication Vasu will be sent to hell. By presenting the Indra festival as rustic and non-Vedic, the authors present Vasu as a ritually incompetent king who incorrectly performs the ritual because he fundamentally misunderstands the religiosity the epic advocates. Though seemingly a *brāhmaṇya rājā*, Vasu is actually the worst of both—neither brahminical nor properly royal—an identity that is meant to reflect poorly on Ashoka and his improper and non-Vedic *stambha*-raising.

Prescribed in a number of related *rājnīti* and other texts (as we will see in the next sections), the annual celebration of the Indra festival reinforces this ritual responsibility for powerful kings. The festival's narrative, written as a literary-performative back formation, thus alleviated the apparent contradiction of continuing a flawed festival associated with the narrative kings of Chedi and historical Mauryan king Ashoka. Despite their unique deconstruction of the Indra festival and its materials, the audience would be able to see its rural rhetoric as a critique of an outdated mode of ritual while celebrating their urban version of this festival, though now suffused with all of the socioeconomic trappings of urban life, with the presence of goddesses in multiple forms, and with a narrative that foregrounds and lauds the devotional figure of the god Viṣṇu.

Drama in the *Nāṭyaśāstra*

Similar to the *Mahābhārata*, the dramaturgical *Nāṭyaśāstra* (NS) uses the trope of the Indra festival as a means of cultural innovation. Although not as explicitly political as the epic or the rājadharmic *Viṣṇudharmottara Purāṇa* detailed in the next section, the opening chapters of the *NS* do similar work. Reflecting ongoing South Asian debates regarding orthopraxy, the text's opening passage draws on the sometimes violent contests for power inherent in the Indra festival to reframe and resituate *nāṭya* (drama) as a new, popular, yet accepted method of ritualization.

The first chapter of the *NS* resembles the opening frame of the *MBh* with the author Bharata relating the origins of *nāṭya* and using Vedic allusions to the Indra festival to signal sociopolitical change. As Indra indicated Vasu's worldly dharma (*lokyaṃ dharmaṃ*) by contrasting his own rule in heaven (*diviṣṭha*) with Vasu's on Earth (*bhuviṣṭha*), the

NS refers to *grāmya dharma*: performed in an earlier era, these actions left people "under the sway of desire and greed, affected with jealousy and anger, and whose happiness was mixed with sorrow." Bharata tells his audience what Indra desired as an antidote to this condition: "We want an object of diversion, which must be audible as well as visible. As the Vedas are not to be listened to by those born as Śūdras, be pleased to create another Veda which will belong [equally] to all the *varṇa*" (1.7–12). As a result, Brahmā constructs "the fifth Veda" (1.15) from available Vedic parts: "The recitations [*pāṭhya*] he took from the Ṛgveda, the songs from the Sāmaveda, the Histrionic Representation [*abhinaya*] from the Yajurveda, and Sentiments [*rasa*] from the Atharvaveda. Thus was created the Nāṭyaveda connected with the principal and subsidiary Vedas [*vedopaveda*]" (1.17–18).

Establishing the Vedic nature of this new performative system—*Nāṭyaveda* (1.53)—Brahmā situates the inaugural performance of *nāṭya* in a performance of the Indra festival. Reflecting the opening frame story in the Indra festival chapter of the *Bṛhat Saṃhitā*, this first performance of *nāṭya* depicts the victory of the gods over the demons, after which the god Brahmā declares the Indra festival to be "the proper occasion for a dramatic performance" (1.53). Indra makes a gift of the pole (*dhvaja*, 1.59), bequeathing it to the sons of Brahmā as one of a set of gifts given by attending gods and goddesses in the construction, ornamentation, and protection of the stage. Before the pole and the other gifts can be properly installed to ornament and protect the stage, the authors seem to account for the hesitation that certain Brahmins might have felt in admitting *nāṭya* into the Vedic fold; they have Indra take up the *dhvaja* (now called a *jarjara*, "the destroyer") with which he kills the demonic obstacles (*vighna*s) who attempted to obstruct the first performance of *nāṭya*, anticipating the opening forest rites in the classical and contemporary festival. Brahmā's choice of the Indra festival seems curious, until we recall the similarly innovative applications of the Indra festival and the political innovations at the heart of this text.[21] With these demons out of the way, *nāṭya* can begin, which it does with a set of rites that use Indra's *jarjara* as a ritual item: it is worshiped for the success of the performance (3.12); the director and two assistants carry it around the stage and recite the *jarjara-śloka* (4.78–81); and during the final series of opening rites, the director holds it across his navel before handing it off to his assistant, who carries it off stage (4.122).[22]

Before the authors of the *Nāṭyaśāstra* can simply assert that this unique mode of ritual performativity, *nāṭya*, can be a means of acquiring a higher spiritual state, they must contextualize it and counter prior arguments made against its religious value. This discussion of orthopraxy takes place around the Mahāvrata, another festival that exists at the margins of Vedic ritual. Reflecting the reference to *grāmya dharma* in the opening verses of the *NS*, the *Jaiminīya Brāhmaṇa* (*JB*) describes the incorporation of "popular" rites into the Mahāvrata through the defeat of Mṛtyu, the god of death, by Prajāpati, the Vedic god of life and creation. This divine dichotomy represents just one component of the many sets of opposites that suffuse this quasi-Vedic festival, which Pierre Rolland has described both as a "solemn Vedic ritual" and as a "puzzle of heterogeneous elements, without apparent unity" (1972: 55; translation mine). The "heterogeneous elements" that Rolland further describes as "bizarre" and "aberrant" came to be inserted on the penultimate day of the year-long Mahāvrata festival and include contests, a chariot race, target shooting, a tug-of-war, dancing, singing, drumming, swinging, lute playing, and ritual copulation. The *JB* refers to these rites as the ritual weapons (*yajñā-yuddhāni*) that Mṛtyu had used in his mythic combat with Prajāpati and provides a further opposition with the weapons of Prajāpati:

> In that ritual [hymns] were sung, [mantras] recited, and [rites] performed; these were the weapons of Prajāpati.
>
> On that *vīṇā* [songs] were sung, along with dancing and frivolous acting; these were the weapons of Mṛtyu. (*JB* 2.69–70)[23]

Jan Heesterman asserts that "this curious assembly of archaic nonstandard rites," inserted into an orthodox soma rite, represents the "remnants of a rowdy and orgiastic New Year festival" that serves as "no more than a curiously intriguing sideshow," noting also that these two sets of weapons are directly related to each other. Vedic singing (*√stu*) is related to "popular" singing (*√gai*); Vedic recitation (*√śas*) to dance (*√nṛt*); and Vedic acting (*pra+√car*) to "frivolous" acting (*vṛthā+√car*) (1993: 55). Even the parallel locatives that open these two lines (*yajñe* and *vīṇāyāṃ*) signal the analogous localization of these performances: whereas Prajāpati operates in the constructed space of an orthoprax Vedic enclosure, Mṛtyu organizes his heteroprax activities on the simple *vīṇā* (the lute).

To maintain its connection to the narrative of the Mahāvrata and reinforce the innovation that the authors of the *Nāṭyaśāstra* endorse, the defeated Mṛtyu and the equally inauspicious goddess Nirṛti are subdued and localized in the new performative space, placed on either side of the main door as protectors of the stage.[24] This theatrical display of transgressive deities recalls the ubiquity of Bhairav and fierce goddesses in Kathmandu's Indra festival and points to those formerly unorthodox, even transgressive techniques that now typify the science of drama and with which the *Nāṭyaśāstra* concludes.

> Recitation, dancing, singing, ornamentation, and musical instrumentation:
> These are *equal in value* to the recitation of Vedic mantras. (36.25)[25]

Negating the dualistic assertion made in the *JB* account of the Mahāvrata, the *NS* boldly asserts the victory of the festive and the unorthodox. Elevating these rites to the category of the Vedic, classical authors can now apply them to the popular core of the Indra festival, whose performance—as similarly quasi-Vedic as *nāṭya* and the Mahāvrata—represents a significant innovation in early medieval Hinduism.

Royal Power in the *Viṣṇudharmottara Purāṇa*

Replicating and physically expanding the performative space of the *NS*, the *Viṣṇudharmottara Purāṇa* (*VDhP*) and allied early medieval texts on *rājadharma* use the Indra festival to construct the space of the post-Vedic kingdom. In his work on the historical and symbolic construction of kingship, Ronald Inden reads these texts, datable to CE 700 to 1200, arguing that the royal installation rite (*abhiṣeka*) has a particular binary structure. In the first part of the ritual, the king is taken out of the kingdom and infused with royal authority; in the second part, he returns to the kingdom and "infuses the various constituents of the community with translvalued forms of the very things by which he himself was symbolically bathed" (1978: 43). This binary function establishes the king as "the immanent and microcosmic form of the transcendent, macrocosmic Puruṣa . . . [who] was treated as a human *axis mundi* and placed conceptually at the centre of his kingdom, the microcosm of the world" (1978: 47).

The Indra festival comes to supplement this larger series of *rājadharma* rites that also includes the *nīrājana* and *puṣyasnāna*. Through the *rājyābhiṣeka* installation, the most important of these rites, the king acquires the royal and quasi-divine power of the Cosmic Man—the late Vedic *Puruṣa*—on which his community was dependent. The public presence of singers, musicians, and courtesans who accompany and ornament the Indra pole's entrance into the city (*BS* 43.24–28) just as they celebrate the royal coronation (Inden 1978: 69) shows one of the significant valences of the material object of the Indra pole. As a temple replicates the space of the royal palace and as "the body of the god [in that temple] can be viewed as a double for the body of the king," so does the Indra pole represent a double of the king (Geslani 2018: 200).[26] The *rājadharma* texts of this era consistently attend to the public rites directed to this object—clearly royal and nascently Hindu.[27]

Among these texts—the *Kauśika Sūtra*; the *Atharva Veda Pariśiṣṭas*; the *Brahmā, Devī, Bhaviṣya,* and *Kālikā Purāṇa*s; and Varāhamihira's *Bṛhat Saṃhitā*—*VDhP* provides "the most extensive treatment of this subject [*rājadharma*] in early medieval India, especially in its elaborate description of the rituals to be performed by the king" (Inden 1978: 83, n9). Sponsored by King Lalitāditya of Kashmir, the *VDhP* is "inextricably bound up with the theology of the Pāñcarātra 'sect' of Vaiṣṇavas, on the one hand, and . . . an imperial political agenda, on the other" (Inden, Walters, and Ali 2000: 29). The politics of the *VDhP* are presented with a certain universality that will continue in many of these Indra festival texts. For example, Inden asserts innovations in the inclusive architecture it describes, its central structure, the Kashmiri Sarvatobhadra temple, which "appropriate[d] the temple style that princes recognized as emblematic of universal rule, that of the Gangetic plains, and combine[d] it with an elaboration of the local Kashmiri style"; this architectural reorientation was part of a larger project whose goal was to make Kashmir into "the center of the Indic earth" and transform "the Kashmiri imperial kingship into the paramount kingship of India" (Inden 2000: 84, 87). This universality, the eliding and implicit denial of details locating the content of the text in time and place, is taken up by court gurus of early modern Nepal for their revived performance of the Indra festival.

The significance of the Indra festival can be seen in its regular pairing with the texts of the *rājyābhiṣeka* and what amounts to the festival's annual replication of the components of this most important of all royal rites.[28] The *VDhP* became the standard source for the *rājyābhiṣeka* rituals that prescribed the ascension of the post-Vedic king, including those of the Marāṭha king Śivāji in 1674 and the Nepālī king Bīrendra in 1975 (Inden 1978: 56). The Indra festival, as an annual reinforcement of kingship, became a part of many texts in this genre, beginning with *Atharva Veda Pariṣiśṭa* (*AVPari*), whose chapter on the Indra festival draws attention to the intimacy between king and brahmin that influences future texts and performances (Bolling and von Negelein 1909: 120–21). The nineteenth *parisista* details the activities of these two performers on the night of Bhādra 11 and the morning of Bhādra 12 and the content of the mantras they chant.[29] In fact, the vast majority this text details the royal-brahminical chanting, never mentioning the process of producing the pole from a tree in the forest, always referring to the pole by the name of its presiding deity, Indra (or "the Indra"). *AVPari* begins and ends as follows:

> We will here describe the celebratory arrangements of the Indra festival of kings (1.1). [It takes place] during the bright half of Prauṣṭhapada [Bhādrapada] (1.2). Having arranged all of the ritual implements, these two skillful workers—the brahmin and the king—both bathe, put on new clothes, and adorn themselves with sweet-smelling *sujāta*, performing the *vrata* by fasting (1.3). On the following day, they recite the quarter-, half-, and full-verses of the *Shaṃnodevī*, having sipped the six-fold water (1.4).[30] Having arranged the *barhi*, [the brahmin] should make an offering, having taken the king from behind (1.5). . . . The next day, there is victory in his kingdom. On this entire earth, there is no king who will reach a more full old age. He who knows thus [*ya evam veda*], knows this about those who perform the *Indramaha*, thus it is stated in the *brāhmaṇa* (3.9). This is the conclusion of the Indra festival.[31]

The tree they are worshiping is carried to the city gate, where it will lie until the eighth day of the month of the bright half of Bhādrapada, when, along with the citizens, the king will approach the pole for the first time, decorate it, and have it brought into town (43.23–28).

But the Indra festival, like the *rājyābhiṣeka* to which it is related, quickly moves beyond these quasi-Vedic roots. Both the *VDhP* and

Varāhamihira's seventh-century *Bṛhat Saṃhitā* (*BS*) begin with similar stories about the battle between the gods and demons. In the opening verses of *BS* 43—the *indra-dhvaja-sampad* ("a description of the glory of Indra's banner")—the gods, kicked out of heaven by attacking demons, seek refuge in Viṣṇu, who provides them with the Indra pole (*ketuṃ* and *dhvajaṃ*). The pole's physical appearance—mounted on an eight-wheeled chariot and decorated with bells, garlands, and other ornaments—resembles that of the festival banner the king will soon raise. The mere sight of this decorated object puts the demons to flight and sends them to their death. Like other texts that tell a version of this story—the *Devī Māhātmya* with the goddess Durgā, and the *Kena Upaniṣad* with the universal impersonal principle, Brahman—the *BS* introduces the Indra pole as a unique and novel object whose mysterious appearance seems sufficient to defeat the demons. Unlike the *MBh* account of the Indra festival that provides a historical setting in which Indra gives the *dhvaja* to Vasu to constrain him to his terrestrial and urban kingdom of Chedi, the *BS* and *VDhP* begin with a story set solely among the gods.

Although this divine setting might appear standard, Viṣṇu's presence signals its own type of innovation. Despite Krishna's central role in the *Mahābhārata,* Viṣṇu is absent from Vasu's epic story, which Varāhamihira refers to at 43.9–10, and from the *Garga Saṃhitā,* on which the *BS* is largely based. Whereas the earlier *NS* also begins with the story and dramatic performance of the battle between gods and demons and defers to the quasi-Vedic Brahmā as the chief god who provides shelter to his quasi-divine refugees, here the semi-Vedic actors on the stage provide the Indra pole with which they achieve victory. The shift from Brahmā to Viṣṇu makes sense in the *rājadharma* texts of the early medieval period that set a new temple-based devotional Hindu path in a calendar that balances ritual warfare with pious public works (Geslani et al. 2017: 169–73).[32]

The role of Viṣṇu as the central deity within this genre of texts extends beyond his divine appearance and represents a reworking of the ritual system. Transcending an older Vedic notion of a local leadership, these early medieval texts effectively incorporated Vedic rites in a new concept of a universal Hindu kingship placing Viṣṇu, the Puruṣa, at the center of a set of new installation rites, of which the Indra festival is a constituent piece. This redesign was less an expansion of Vedic authority than a sectarian response to previous

South Asian dynasties that sponsored Buddhist monks and monasteries and whose installation rites focused on an icon of the Buddha. Inden writes:

> This change takes place in the eighth century and is marked by the building of the first monumental Hindu temples. . . . The Buddha was replaced as the supreme, imperial deity by one of the Hindu gods . . . [a] historical change [that] is precisely stated in the installation ceremony of the *VDhP*. The specific purpose of the rājyābhiṣeka in that text is to transform the recipient of the rite, an upholder of the vaidika tradition and devotee of the supreme god Viṣṇu, into a universal monarch and the earthly counterpart of his Cosmic Overlord, Viṣṇu. (1978: 55, 68)[33]

Although Inden refers to these initiation rites as one component of "the medieval forerunners of the later Navrātrī, Dasarā, and Divālī festivals" (1978: 82) that replicated the actions of the royal court in the setting of an urban temple, he never refers to the Indra festival that is found in all of these same texts—including the *VDhP*—and that is part of this same imperial project.

On a much broader scale, the Indra festival's consistent inclusion in those texts that construct Hindu kingship also connects it to their collective response to Buddhism, with the *VDhP*'s replacement of Buddhist icons and monasteries with Hindu icons and monolithic temples its most tangible form. Earlier, we saw how the *Mahābhārata* used the Indra festival in a similar way to establish the urban Hindu royalty of Vasu over against the strict nonviolence and renunciation advocated by the Buddhist-patronizing Mauryan dynasty. The Shah dynasty of Nepal similarly used consistently Hindu and Vaiṣṇava language to support their rule amid Buddhist and other non-Hindu populations, especially in the Kathmandu Valley. The coronation of Nepali King Birendra in 1975 was conducted according to the text of the *VDhP*, the political rhetoric of King Mahendra identified the citizens of Nepal as devotees of Vishnu who possess "an identical subtle substance that unites them within the subtle body of Vishnu in the form of Parbrahma" (Burghart 1984: 120), and the final Shah king Gyanendra received the support of Hindu nationalist groups from India (Hausner 2007: 128–29). Just like the authors of classical Sanskrit texts who consistently incorporated the Indra festival into their body of royal rites as a reaffirmation of the king's original coronation, the Shah dynasty revived the Indra festival in nineteenth-century Nepal to construct a unified Hindu kingship that survived until early twenty-first century. Ironically, the performance of the succession rites of King Gyanendra in 2001, following a palace massacre that left nearly all members of Nepali royalty dead, left his kingship "incompletely established and the institution of monarchy itself profoundly weakened" (Mocko 2016: 61).

Architecture in the *Samarāṅgana Sūtradhāra*

Bhojadeva's eleventh-century architectural text, *Samarāṅgana Sūtradhāra* (*SS*), picks up on the architectural innovations we see in the opening chapters of the *NS*, where Vedic spaces are re-formed into popular performative ones. The *SS* enlarges the performative space from the stage to the royal city as it prescribes the construction of the king's capital with all of its constituent buildings. As with the *NS*, the construction of the new performative space in the *SS* is keyed by the Indra festival, its central ritual pole, and its movement into the newly constructed space. Rather than signaling the text's innovations through the performance of the festival, as we saw with the *MBh* and *NS*, the authors focus on the construction of the space where the Indra pole is to be raised, almost completely bypassing the narrative and performative language we saw in these earlier texts.

As the seventeenth of the *SS*'s eighty-three chapters, the account of the Indradhvaja (the *Indradhvaja Nirūpaṇam*) occurs relatively early on. The chapters preceding this one are strictly introductory, in the sense that nothing properly architectural is described there. Rather, these chapters prepare the ground for the construction of the royal city by relating the construction of the space around the city: the formation of the worlds, humans, and the four social classes (*varṇa*) (chapters 1–7); the apportioning of land, standards of measurement, and the space of the city (chapters 8–10); and the preparation and planning of the site on which the city will be constructed (chapters 11–15). The physical processes of constructing a city begin only at chapter 16 with a series of preparatory rites that directly mirror those of the Indra festival: the *vana praveśa*, the trek to the forest to obtain the lumber for construction, a formal request that the *bhūta* spirits inhabiting the tree change their residence, the brahmin's recitation of an auspicious and welcoming *svasti* to the tree, and a final puja to the tree after its felling.[34]

Just as the Indra festival opens with the forest rites to obtain the festival's central object, so does the construction of a royal city—at least, its textual construction in the *SS*—begin with this trek. Circumscribed by similar rules as those in the *VDhP* and the *BS*, the *SS* includes sets of taboos enjoined on those who go to the forest, restrictions on the types of trees allowed, and requisite observations of the sacred fire. The only mention of the Indra festival is made at verse 190 of the 212-verse seventeenth chapter—and here referred to only as *utsavam*, "the festival"—but the authors clearly establish the innovative role of the Indra festival in the content and structure of the chapter. The bulk of chapter 17 details the intricate construction of the physical apparatus required for Indra's pole—its literal nuts and bolts—in difficult and technical language whose "elegant linguistic variation is more important than precision" (Hardy 2009: 42). The chapter's central structure is an Indra temple (*vajriṇo gṛhaṃ*, 17.31) inside of which is established a fantastic contraption that foreshadows the robots and flying machines of later chapters. One example of the technology that the authors describe is the *bhramapīṭhaṃ*, a word that Sharma translates as "revolving fulcrum" (17.26). This fulcrum makes up the main part of the pole's foundation—affixed with wooden poles (*dhvaja*), axles (*akṣa*), and a pedestal (*pīṭha*)—that allows the structure to move or turn. Although other ritual texts detail the anatomy of this space, such complex and fantastical architecture is unique to the *SS*.

This urban focus of the *SS* entails a shift in dharma that recalls the innovations we earlier saw in the *MBh*. The *SS* is part of a large and amorphous body of literature that prescribes a courtly culture for the *ārya*, the noble urban resident, of early medieval India. Daud Ali singles out the *Arthaśāstra* and *Kāmasūtra*, two of the earliest and most important texts in this genre, for the many relevant concerns they take up: the roles and titles of royal officers and elite citizens, beauty and refinement, courtly love, and, relevant to our purposes here, architecture.[35] Ali refers to the production of these two texts as constituting an "enunciative moment" as they "represent the culmination and refinement of previously existing traditions of knowledge" (2004: 71). The courtly ethos described in these texts reflects "a much wider transformation of ways of life in early India"; this transformation comprised a new "apparatus of rule" that refined and reoriented dharma on a number of different levels—social, political, economic, and religious—all while maintaining a focus on the three central and classical concepts of dharma, *artha,* and *kāma* (rectitude, acquisition, and pleasure) (Ali 2004: 29).

Architectural manuals such as the *SS* are among the most public and monumental parts of this reorientation and have served as much more than effective blueprints for the construction of cities. Reading these texts against the Nepalese city of Bhaktapur, Gutschow and Kölver affirm the "social and religious interpretations" that South Asian architects and town planners were required to consider, for example, the relationship between one's social status and the distance one resides from the center of town and the location of the royal palace (1975: 34). Ali goes even further, asserting:

> Contemporary and later "architectural manuals" . . . were concerned not only (or even chiefly) with architecture, but also with the entire material world which centred around the court and kingdom. They sought to develop a precise knowledge of the material world in relation to celestial and atmospheric powers or a divinely ordained cosmos—but in all cases this knowledge conceived of the physical and material world of the court as one calibrated along lines of political hierarchy. (Ali 2004: 43)

Thus, whereas the *NS* worked to eliminate hierarchy by allowing people from all ranks of society to perform the "Vedish" *nāṭya,* the *SS* works to forcefully reestablish hierarchy through all of the means available to its authors: the status of the *ārya* can be indicated through his use of official titles, beauty and refinement, courtly love, and architecture. This hierarchy operates inclusively as the text incorporates architectural models from all over India, a move whose political innovations reflect those that Inden asserted for the *VDhP* (Hardy 2009: 42). Along with the other innovations we see in the *SS*—the reorientation of dharma, the reestablishment of hierarchy, and the assumption of imperial rule—this political inclusivity is signaled by the presence, movement, and construction of the physical apparatus required for the Indra festival, a grand public spectacle whose content and structure place on these innovations the official royal seal.[36]

Devotion in the *Bhāgavata Purāṇa*

Whereas the previous texts celebrate the Indra festival as a means for constructing urban kingship, the devotional *Bhāgavata Purāṇa* (BhP), which focuses on the person of Krishna, completely reverses this polarity. Situated in the well-known cycle of Krishna tales in its tenth book, the famous Mount Govardhan story tells how Krishna protected his devotees in the land of Vraja from the onslaught of an irate Indra by lifting up the mountain, as he replicates Indra's *axis mundi* posture from the *Rig Veda*. Although the three main versions of the *govardhana dhara* story contain idiosyncrasies, all portray the underlying tension between Indra and Krishna that quickly boils over, as "Indra became enraged at Nanda and the gopas who had taken Krishna as their lord" (*BhP* 10.25.1).[37] The story makes clear why the people of Braj take Krishna as their lord—as an avatar of Vishnu, he saves them from certain destruction—but what often gets lost is the precise reason for his underlying conflict with Indra, Indra's roiling anger, and Krishna's salvific action.

The opening verses of the narrative set this all-but-pastoral scene against a tense ritual background: the performance of the festival of Indra. Bryant translates this passage (*BhP* 10.24.1–3) as follows: "As he was residing there in Vraj with Balarāma, *Bhagavān* Kṛṣṇa saw the gopas making preparations for Indra's sacrifice [*indra yāga*]. *Bhagavān* Kṛṣṇa is the seer of everything as well as the soul of everything; despite knowing all about it, he bowed down reverentially and inquired of the elders headed by Nanda: 'Tell me father, what is this bustle that has arisen? Why is this sacrifice [*makha*] being performed, from what incentive and by whom?' " (Bryant 2003:111–12). This series of apparently rhetorical questions cajoles Nanda into confessing his role in these inherently anti-Vaiṣṇava activities. He replies: "We people offer sacrifices to him as the husband-lord (*patiṃ īśvaraṃ*) of the clouds, my son, with offerings of substances that are products from his seed (*retas*)" (10.24.9).[38] Pointing up his ongoing rivalry with Indra, Krishna engages in a philosophical monologue the ultimate goal of which is to expose the utter powerlessness of Indra. Positing action (*karma*) and self-power (*svabhāva-tantra*) as the foundation of human nature and the three human qualities (*guṇa*)—*sattva, rajas,* and *tamas* (goodness, passion, and ignorance)—as the foundation of the natural world responsible for, respectively, the creation, stability, and destruction of the universe (*sthiti-utpatti-anta*), he associates Indra with *rajas* and asks, similarly rhetorically and rather sarcastically, "What will Indra do (*mahendraḥ kim kariṣyati*)?" (10.24.23).[39] Indra's conflict with Krishna is precipitated by the latter's rejection of Indra's festival: "Our people do not live in cities, regions, villages, or houses. There is always someone who lives in the woods or in the mountain forests. Therefore, initiate a festival [*makha*] to the cows, to the brahmins, and to the mountain. Perform *this* festival [*makha*] with the very puja items that had been dedicated for the Indra festival [*indra-yāga-sambhārās*] (10.24.24–25).[40]

Indra angrily and violently responds to the abandoning of his festival (*pūjāṃ vihitāṃ*) by calling down the *saṃvartaka* clouds with the intention of destroying his enemies: namely, Nanda and the *gopas* who had taken Krishna as their lord.[41] He accuses the forest-dwelling *gopas* of abandoning meditative knowledge and desiring "to cross over the ocean of material existence through the performance of rituals based on action [*karma*], which are like unstable boats. These gopas have sought refuge in him who is noisy, childish, obstinate, ignorant, and a mere mortal though whom they regard as wise; they now deem me an enemy [*apriyaṃ*]" (10.25.4–5) (see figure 1.2).[42]

All three major tellings of the festival end well for Krishna. After seven days, Indra withdraws his *saṃvartaka* clouds, apologizes to Krishna, and asserts the latter's lordship. He concludes by leading Krishna through an *abhiṣeka,* reflecting the Vedic-style coronations of kings in the *VDhP* and early medieval texts, coronating Krishna as Upendra—Indra himself is Mahendra—and bestows on him the name Govinda. Following his defeat, the groveling Indra engages in a lengthy dialogue in which he goes to Krishna for refuge (10.27.13); the victorious Krishna responds with a surprising and ahistorical reason for his ritual attack: "It was by way of my compassion and so that you will remember me always that your festival was broken (*makha-bhaṅgo*), Maghavan. Your glory, Indra, was excessive" (10.27.15). The cow Surabhi is given the final monologue and reasserts Krishna's ultimate supremacy over Indra, several times referring to Krishna as "our Indra" (10.27.19–21). Surabhi's assertion that Krishna "descended

Figure 1.2. Krishna lifting Mount Govardhan, with Indra riding his white elephant in the upper center (Rajasthani Miniature, nineteenth century). Public domain.

to Earth in order to relieve its burden" (21) not only identifies Krishna as an avatar of Vishnu whose function is to descend to Earth whenever trouble ensues, but also aligns Krishna with the matricidal axe-wielding Bhārgava warrior Paraśurāma and Indra with the murderous kings he was sent to remove.[43] The placement of Krishna's defeat of Indra in the *BhP* thus makes sense: appearing in the first part of Book 10, the *govardhan dhara* narrative places Indra among those demons, who, as "intruders into the Kṛṣṇa realm of play . . . disrupt Kṛṣṇa's carefree frolics in the groves of Vraj and hence are spontaneously killed by the

Lord" (Bryant 2003: xxiv). Pūtanā (chapter 6), the serpent Sudarśana (chapter 34), and the wicked King Kaṃsa (chapter 44) are killed, but the *rājasic* Indra (chapters 24–27) is chastised and readily dispatched much like the serpent Kāliya (chapter 16), who admits to being "full of wrath and *tāmasic* from birth" (Bryant 2003: 87–88).

The *Harivaṁśa* (*HV*) episode ends not with Indra's humiliation but with a surprising reconciliation. After bestowing of the names Govinda and Upendra on Krishna and before the *abhiṣeka*, Indra presents another gift to him. Indra says: "The four months of the rainy season have been established for me. But I will give you the second half, which is the autumn season [*śarat-kālaṃ*]" (*HV* 19.47). As an appendix to the *Mahābhārata* that frequently refers back to its parent text, the *Harivaṁśa* concludes its account of the *govardhana dhara* with a reference to the Indra festival that is absent from the other two accounts, as Indra suggests to Krishna a form of the celebrations that are by now quite familiar to us.[44]

> From this time onward, my people will honor me in these two months [Śrāvaṇa and Bhādra]. In this half-season, a flag [*dhvaja*] will [be raised] for me; then, you will commence with your puja. [The *dhvaja*] will be a reflection of the power of my rains. . . . O Krishna, just as is done in all of the divine worlds, people on Earth will celebrate you and me—Mahendra and Upendra—with the raising of flags and poles [*dhvaja-karāsu yaṣṭiṣu*]. Those who consistently worship the two of us together—Mahendra and Upendra—will never have difficulty come to them. (*HV* 19.48, 59–60)

This conclusion represents the only passage in the multiple accounts of the *govardhan dhara* that establishes a specific connection to the classical Indra festival, filling in the otherwise vague descriptions of Indra's festival as a *makha, pūjā, yajña,* or *yāga*. It makes no mention of the forests, trees, and poles that are central to Indra's festival and only vaguely refers to the ritual items that were then redirected to Krishna's festival for cows, brahmins, and the mountain.

This paucity of detail is deliberate, as readers feel encouraged to simply ignore a festival that the authors deem irrelevant, rather than being concerned with the burdensome chronological, geographic, and ritual details seen in prior texts. Whereas the extended account in the first book of the *MBh* allowed readers to follow elements of the material culture of Indra's festival—his pole, chariot, and indestructible flower garland—as they move from the people of Indra to the people of Krishna, the *govardhan dhara* narrative gives short shrift to Indra's festival by simply cutting-and-pasting Krishna's festival atop Indra's, essentially changing the name without getting caught up in any superfluous details. The change of name entails a change of purpose as well, and Krishna's elimination of Indra's festival tells us much about how Indra's festival came to be perceived, especially in a devotional context wherein the recitation, remembrance, and performance of the narrative was to inspire a feeling of devotion toward Krishna in the hearts of its audience.

In the introduction to his translation of chapter 10 of the *BhP*, Bryant asserts the transitional nature of the devotional text's central figure: "Kṛṣṇa appears at the end of one cultural age, and is pivotal to the inauguration of a new one" (Bryant 2003: xviii). It is not just the text of the *BhP* that marks this Krishna-centered chronological threshold, but the *govardhan dhara* narrative specifically does so wherever it appears. Crossing the threshold indicates the innovation that I have argued is a function of the Indra festival wherever we see it. By combining these two innovative narratives—of the *govardhan dhara* and the Indra festival—the authors multiply and intensify the innovation they seek to communicate. Taking it a step further, these narratives operate together by the theme of the archaism; a common trope of the Indra festival, van Buitenen also attributes this theme to the *BhP* as a whole, whose authors "consciously attempted to archaicize its language" (1966: 24).[45] Though the *govardhan dhara* narrative differs significantly from the ritual texts handled earlier in this chapter, especially the *VDhP*, it resembles the account in *MBh* 1.57: by juxtaposing the urban setting of the Indra festival to the bucolic setting of Mount Govardhan, it sets the Indra festival in a constructed folk heritage before rejecting it completely.[46]

The *govardhan dhara* narrative illustrates what Ronald Grimes refers to as a "ritual defeat," where "one ritual performance is accepted as invalidating another" and is "followed by ritual 'theft,' that is, the plundering of a conquered ritual system for its symbolic wealth" (1988: 115). Krishna's victory communicates more than just how the *BhP* "captur[es] and trumpet[s] the ascendence of the new avatāra over earlier forms of religious belief and practice . . . popularly celebrated in the Indramahotsava" (Austin 2015: 11–12). Inhabiting a textual lineage that uses the Indra festival to signal ritual innovation, it simultaneously plays on the notion of its archaism to reinforce what its readers already knew: the preclassical king of the mountain (Girirāj) has attained the status of an anointed universal king. Readers of this devotional literature would have been familiar with the annual Indra festival dominated by the installation of the king in full regalia and the forty-foot pole in their city's royal square and would now be able to imagine Krishna as the focal point of this festival. Following van Buitenen's notion of the archaic language of the tenth-century *BhP*—that "the Krishna legend has to *sound* Vedic because it *was* Vedic" (1966: 38)—we see the authors constructing a newly Vedicized Krishna in his singular moment of glory. Replicating the physical posture of the ancient demiurge Indra holding up the sky, the *govardhana dhara* Krishna now becomes "identical with the tree . . . [and] with the pillar at the moment of creation, when he himself literally *was* the world axis" (Kuiper 1975: 110).

The Urban Habitus in Kathmandu

The beneficiaries of this transition are Krishna and his people. Whereas the epic envisioned the very first Indra festival as a village performance that hearkened back to the beginning of an urban dharmic kingship, the authors of the *govardhan dhara* narrative reverse the trajectory, constructing a rural milieu in which Krishna's new devotional festival has been designed for "our people [who] do not live in cities, regions, villages, or houses." This shift renders the Indra festival outmoded, moribund, inappropriate, and therefore useless.[47]

The Indra festival is anything but useless in the urban environment of Nepal's Kathmandu Valley. Beginning with Gutschow and Kölver's 1975 study of Bhaktapur, much of the scholarship on the Kathmandu Valley has accounted for the uniquely urban nature of the religion and culture of the Newars and regularly attends to its urban habitus. In the first of his two volumes of the cultural psychology of Bhaktapur's Newars, Steven Parish writes that Newars turn "inward into the intricate and self-absorbing life of the city, to find meaning, splendor, images of transcendence" (1994: 19).

The Indra festival represents a significant component of this urban life. Combining Hindu, Buddhist, and Newar elements into a hybrid mix with pieces that do not always seem to fit, the narratives and corresponding rites of the Newar *yeṃ yāḥ* (*punhi*)—the (full-moon) festival of Kathmandu—delineate and reinforce the center, boundaries, and other powerful human and divine agents. Thus, while retaining the classical emphasis on the archaic Indra and the tall wooden pole that embodies the single central king, it supplements and sometimes overwhelms its focus on royalty with attention to peripheral goddesses and local protective deities and ancestors.

Organized around the *sāit* structure of the modern Nepalese festival, the next two chapters of this book detail the festival's five official events, accounting for its presence in contemporary Kathmandu, the urban milieu in which the festival's most significant innovations occurred. Kathmandu's local adaptations show how the Indra festival serves as a signal of innovation, alerting readers and audiences to seismic shifts in religious ideology, performance, and politics: the ad hoc nature of the Vedic Indra in his own festival, the perpetually archaic nature of the festival and its central pole, and the multiple narratives of origin that communicate a festival that is always out of time, always anachronistic, and never quite fits. Adapting to the classical Indradhvajotsava during the Shah imperium of the late eighteenth century, the local Newar *yeṃ yāḥ* (*punhi*)—a celebration *of* the city as much as it is *in* the city—celebrates the power of Kathmandu with overlapping components of multiple festivals celebrated separately yet always inseparably together.

Chapter Two

The Journey from the Forest

Sāit No. 1: The Ban Yātrā

The Ban Yātrā began at 9:09 a.m. on the morning of September 5 at the royal palace in the center of Kathmandu's old city. I arrived a bit earlier, giving myself a little extra time to ensure a good spot to see the rites that make up the opening event of the city's largest annual festival. Not knowing if I would return in three hours after the morning rites or in three days once the journey was completed—I returned after three days—I quickly stuffed a backpack with a single change of clothes, my new digital camera, and a flashlight. Accounting for the half-hour walk from the city's northeastern neighborhood of Handigaon where I lived, I left my apartment at 7 a.m. and arrived at the Nāsal Chowk courtyard immediately inside the palace around 7:30 a.m., where I met my two research assistants, Anil and Manoj, and a few of their friends. We quickly realized that we were the only ones in attendance.

The Sanskrit texts provide a brief description of these rites, quickly introducing their key personnel, ritual items, and physical spaces. This introduction typically lasts no more than one verse that has a priest (*purohita*), an astrologer (*daivajña* or *sāṃvatsara*), and a carpenter (*sutradhāra, takṣā,* or *varddhaki*) travel to the forest and select a proper tree that they will begin to consecrate as the festival pole.[1] Although the five Nepalese *sāīt* are not properly named in the Sanskrit ritual texts, an early passage from the *Viṣṇudharottara Purāṇa* comes close, asserting that the king should obtain the Indra pole "according to the rites of the Vana Praveśa"[2] (Entrance into the Forest)—providing a literary correlate to Kathmandu's ensuing Nagara Praveśa (Entrance into the City) performed one week later on Bhādra 8, as the pole is brought from the edge to the center of the city.

The contemporary ritual is similarly brief. In 2005, my first time seeing the festival, the Ban Yātrā lasted no more than fifteen minutes, garnering virtually no public notice and attended only by those who were active members of its performance. It consisted of a short procession presided over by the palace priest, a single government official, several soldiers in modern camoflage uniforms, and a deployment of six members of the Guruju ko Paltan (hereafter Paltan), a unit of the Nepalese military whose members dress in European-inspired uniforms. The Paltan is present during significant portions of all major royal festivals in the valley, in which they march, present arms, and perform a brief set of military drills. They are also present in many of the more public moments of the Indra festival, reminding their audience of the presence and authority of the Hindu Nepali state they represent. In a local newspaper article, Gautam Shakya, a member of the Indra Jatra Management Committee, somewhat regretfully asserts the centrality of the Paltan. "What is interesting is that when Prithvi Narayan Shah conquered the Valley, the soldiers were no doubt a source of intimidation and fear for the Valley's residents. . . . The fact that over time they too have been absorbed into Kathmandu's festivities speaks volumes of how the city truly is [a] melting pot, of how the Valley's culture has been built, layer upon layer, by the various forces and cultures that have come and gone over millennia."[3] The Paltan gathered in formation inside and soon marched out from Nāsal Chowk, passing by the image of Hanuman, who gives his name to the area—Hanumān Ḍhokā (Hanuman's Gate)—a distance of no more than fifty feet.

The Paltan was not the focal point of this brief introductory rite; instead, it was the *Rāj Khaṛga* (*kharga*) that they will protect during the festival. This ceremonial royal sword is never directly shown, always remaining wrapped in the same type of red-and-gold cloth *tās* that clothes and covers other key icons during this and other festivals.[4] Similar swords appear during other major festivals in the cities of the valley, their presence and procession serving as a cipher for the political and military dominance of the ruling dynasty in the traditionally Newar Kathmandu Valley. Referring to the political and cultural multivalence of the sword in Bhaktapur's new year Biskaḥ Jātrā (April 14), Levy writes: "Although the sword represents to the political authorities themselves and to other Nepalis the sign of the superordinate authority of the central [Hindu Shah] regime, to many local people in Bhaktapur this symbol, and many other such symbols still represent the traditional Malla kings; hence, the significance of the carrying and the handing over of the sword in this preliminary event becomes significantly altered in its local implications" (Levy and Rajopadhyaya 1990: 741, n14). The same kharga that appears during Kathmandu's Indrajatra appears even more prominently during the Pachalī Bhairav Jātrā. More than simply "handed over," as it is in Indrajatra and Biskah, it is taken out on a procession (*kharga yātrā*) from the palace and brought to Teku, where every twelve years the king of Nepal exchanges the sword—here not covered with the decorative *tās*—with that wielded by Bhairav or Bhadrakālī (Āju or Ajimā). In this exchange with the powerful and protective Newar grandparent gods, the sword "transfers power to the king of Nepal," the latter "provided with *śakti*, divine power" (van den Hoek 2004: 16, 94). Though no such transfer occurs during Indrajātrā, the presence of even the static royal sword communicates its potential and signals the royal identity of its bearer.

Anne Mocko (2016) argues for the independence of royalty and royal rites and festivals in Nepal's postmonarchical era. She asserts that the continued celebration of these rites despite the dismantling of the monarchy in 2006–2008 shows their power and pervasiveness. I agree with her, further arguing that these large city-wide festivals and many of their constituent rites are already multivalent, simultaneously pointing toward royalty and the ancestors, toward kingship and kinship. Despite recent and renewed concern over "how far a secular state should be involved in such rituals," for the 2017 Pachalī Bhairav Jātrā that represented the twelve-year performance when king and Bhairav exchange swords, the Malla community of the Teku neighborhood requested the presence of former King Gyanendra, who participated, offered puja, and exchanged swords with Bhairav (Ghimire 2016). Although the concern over state rituals had delayed the festival for three years—it was last performed in 2001, Gyanendra's first year as king—the presence of the former king signals the enduring and emotional relationships many Nepalis have retained for the Shah family and the specifically royal meanings they attribute to these rites.

While discussing the role of the kharga during the Indra festival, one local man posited to me that the kharga serves as the mark of the leadership of Indra the Great King ("Indra Maharāj ko netṛto garcha"), a divine power that transcends any particular historical dynasty. In 2005, the man who carried the kharga was the head of Guthi Samsthan, whose status as a central government official and whose public presence so early in the festival further indicated the state's desire to mark the Indrajatra as a royal Nepali and Hindu festival. Blessed by the palace priest, he carried the kharga to the military truck that would convey it to the forest later that day. Following the Paltan's brief display of military arms, the official party dispersed, meeting back at Hanuman Dhoka at about 2:30 in the afternoon. Accompanied by eleven soldiers in standard military fatigues and the goat that would be offered as sacrificial *bali* to the tree that evening, the Paltan secured the kharga, boarded the military transport truck, and set off for the forest.[5]

By 2014, the Paltan was not alone. Members of the Newar and nongovernmental Kendrīya Mānandhar Sangha (KMS, the Central Organization of Manandhars) had reasserted this prominent role, adding it to the many public roles they would come to fill in the festival, especially those that involve the three movements of the pole for which they are almost solely responsible. Though the soldiers and half-dozen members of the Paltan were still present, they were now outnumbered by tourists, local journalists and photographers, and most important the twenty-some members of the KMS, whose headman now carried the sword. The palace priest chanted mantras and provided a *ṭīkā* blessing to each KMS member present for this opening rite, each dressed casually though wearing a stark white turban. He also blessed the axe the headman carried that would be used to ritually cut the tree. After exiting the palace, they captured the moment by posing for photographs just outside of Hanuman Dhoka: the KMS, the Paltan, and the *tās*-covered *kharga* (see figure 2.1).

Given the virtual absence of literature on the subject and the growing interest in local culture among young Newars, we wanted to witness the whole process, from the rites at the palace to those in the forest. Getting to the forest was more difficult than we had imagined. Prevented from riding on the military truck from Kathmandu, we boarded a rickety public bus that took us to Bhaktapur and a second, its windows wide open during a driving monsoon rain, that dropped us off at Nala, a small town on the eastern rim of the Kathmandu Valley

Figure 2.1. Members of the Nepal army and the Kendriya Manandhar Sangha following the opening Ban Yatra rites inside the royal palace. The palace priest and *nayo* (leader) of the KMS carries the royal sword at the left. Photo by author.

most famous for its shrine to the Buddhist bodhisattva Karuṇāmaya. We traveled the final uphill mile on foot, on the unpaved roads of the steep hills that the September rains had turned to mud. Finally arriving at the Sallaghari Forest just outside the villages of Yosingu ("the village of the *yaḥsi* pole") and Khaṛgagauṃ ("the village of the royal sword"), we were greeted with a traditional Newar meal of potatoes, lentils, beaten rice, and buffalo meat, while seated on the ground floor of the temple of Ban Devī (or Ban Kālī), the protective goddess of the forest.

The process of setting out on a journey to convert a tree into a ritual pole is seen in other festivals as well, though it is more ritually marked when a new pole must be cut down rather than when an old pole is merely retrieved and reused. Thus, for the Indra festival in Pyangaon, Toffin describes how "in mid-day, a group of youths goes to look in the house of the religious association of the village, *guthi che*, for two poles, *yomsi*" (1978: 112). At the same time as the large new year's festival of Biskāḥ Jātrā in Bhaktapur, when a massive pole is raised there, on that same new year's day (April 14) the northeastern neighborhood of Handigaon celebrates its goddess Tunaldevi with the raising of poles at its two major intersections (Tiwari 2002: 3–6). These poles are obtained anew only when they need to be replaced; otherwise, they remain attached throughout the year to the outside of several houses on the main north-south street running through the neighborhood. Feldhaus describes how the Gudhi Parva festival in Maharashtra requires an annual trek from the village to the forest to obtain its central ritual bamboo pole (2003: 55).

We arrived at the forest at about 6:15 p.m., the weather having cleared up considerably, and heard that the selection of the *rāṇi-sālā* tree had taken place about forty-five minutes earlier. The classical transformation of the tree into Indra's pole begins with the disqualification of ineligible trees. According to the local tradition, the selection is made by the goat brought from Kathmandu, which is blindfolded and directed to a stand of trees, a choice that would have to be made by the humans in attendance.[6] The tree against which he would bump his head (or, some say, his rump) signifies the tree that he selects, and it would be cut down and fashioned into the pole (Anderson 1971: 129).[7] Most people I spoke with were aware of this method of the goat's selection and repeated it to me. Another version of this story adds the ascribed responsibility of a low-caste Newar man who is to perform additional rites: to supervise the goat in its selection of the tree, to offer puja and the goat as *bali* to the tree, and finally to tie a blue thread (New. *khā-jidūrī*; Nep. *pāsukā*; Skt. *pañcasūtraka*) around the chosen tree that remains until just before the tree is cut down the following morning.[8] When we inquired into this selection process, some of the old men present told us that although they were familiar with this story, not only was this procedure not followed this year, they had never seen it happen that way. The responsibility for selecting the tree had been, for as long as they could remember, the responsibility of the attending members of the various military, governmental, and organizational bodies present.

Sāit No. 2: Day One: Cutting the Tree

While eating dinner, some of the workers joked about not waiting until the appointed time of 7:51 p.m. for the festival's second *sāit*, *vṛkṣa-karttana* (the Cutting of the Tree), instead beginning and ending the work a bit early. Regardless, the night's work, which was the ritual cutting but not the actual felling of the tree—a job that requires several hours of work and sufficient daylight—was begun exactly at the designated time, as with each of the four other *sāit*. By 7:30 p.m., the sun had completely set; the only light that remained came from the candles the workers had brought with them, and by their light the ensuing rites were illuminated and observed. A non-Newar Parbatiya Brahmin *karmāchārya* priest from the Taleju temple at the palace in Kathmandu, also responsible for the Ban Yātrā earlier that day in the palace, performed a *kṣamā pūjā* (apologetic worship) to the tree (van den Hoek 2004: 39).

The main purpose of this puja is to exorcise from the tree those resident beings whose presence interferes with its transformation into Indra's pole. The priest informs the tree's denizens in no uncertain terms that they are to leave the tree and find a different place to live; Varāhamihira respectfully addresses them (*svasti namo*), before calling for their *vāsaparyayaḥ*—their change of domicile (*BS* 43.17–18). The *Kālikā Purāṇa* describes how, once the tree is selected, the priest touches it and recites mantras to it; while respectfully addressing the beings resident in the trees of the forest (*yāni vṛkṣeṣu bhūtāni tebhyaḥ namo 'stu vaḥ*), it changes Varāhamihira's *vāsaparyayaḥ* (change of domicile) to *vāsavadhvajaṃ* (Indra's pole), eliminating the exorcism while reinforcing the tree's transformation (87.12–13). The *Devī Purāṇa* draws attention to the tree's residents by creating something of a hierarchy in the two opposing types of worship in the *kṣamā pūjā*: after venerating the tree with *pūjā* (*pūjayitvā tato vṛkṣaṃ*), the priest makes a *bali* offering to the beings living in it (*baliṃ bhūteṣu dāpayet*, 12.13).[9]

For a festival whose primary purpose is to reinforce royal authority, this exorcism most clearly gets to the heart of the king's "conundrum" that Jan Heesterman recognizes. Impossible to get complete legitimation from the renunciatory and transcendent brahmins in their urban employ, the king "must . . . go out into the wilds to recuperate the strength that has left him" (1985: 123). Here in the forest, kings reauthorize their rule, accumulating merit and power by association with the forest's resident renouncers and by their military victories over its demonic denizens. The texts' constant urban references of the Indra festival tradition give way to their attention to the forest, allowing a resolution of the conundrum. As a member of the urban *grāma*, the king derives his authority from outside of this community, traveling to the forested *āraṇya* and exorcising and transforming the tree as a powerful ritual object with which he returns to the city.

We gain more insight into the contemporary forest rites by attending to the text of Nepali court scribe Śaktivallabh Arjyāl, whose significance in the modern Nepali Hindu tradition warrants his own chapter later in this book. In the *Indradhvajotsava Kathanam*, his early nineteenth-century text on the Indra festival, Śaktivallabh expands on the detail from the classical texts that he quotes and cites, spending considerable time with these apotropaic rites and the beings they are meant to eliminate, thus providing the model for the contemporary Nepalese rite. The *āchārya* (elsewhere, *purohit*) approaches the base of the tree (*vṛkṣa mūlaṃ*), the same place where Indra's royal icon will be placed once the pole is installed in the capital city. From this location, he conducts the following puja.

> Aligning himself to the east or south, he lights lamps. Obtaining kusha-grass, oil, yava-grass, and water, he makes a vow [*samkalpayet*]. He begins with the recitation of AUM, etc., at a sanctified place and time, on a specific day of Bhādra-shukla. [Then there is a recitation] of the lineage of [the king's] particular family [*gotra*]; the action of the king's country, region, and cities; the destruction of ghosts and *kuśmāṇḍas, piśhāchas, bhūta, pātanā, yoginī, gaṇa, śākini, vīra, betāl, rākṣas, janita, padravaśaman, sakala,* and *vyādhi*; and the pacification of the upper, lower, and middle spheres.

Śaktivallabh situates this exorcism within a larger puja to Ganesh, whose "massive crooked trunk shines forth like the light of a thousand suns" and who, as he reminds us, eliminates all obstacles (ff. 12a).[10]

> [The *purohit,* astrologer, and *sūtrādhara* go] to the forest and perform the worshipful-festival, which is accompanied by a Ganesh-*pūjā* with lights and a *kalash,* for the purpose of selecting the *dhvaja-daṇḍa;* for the performance of the Indradhvaja festival as it consists of all of its limbs of action; for the blessing of the attainment of the ascent to the world of Indra on a *vimāna* with an increased portion of *apsara-gaṇa,* with flutes and *vīṇā,* singing, and glorifications; and for the increase of his domain [*svacakra-vṛddhi*] at the expense of that of another. (ff. 11b)[11]

Śaktivallabh uses the Ganesh puja as a means for continuing to protect the tree from all sorts of demonic entities. With Ganesh's presence, a *prāṇ pratiṣṭhā*—presumably that of the icon of Indra that is yet to come—will effect "the pacification of *bhūt* . . . as well as of *vetāl, piśhāch, rākṣas,* and water-serpents." For those *bhūt* who have already crept in, the *purohit,* located at the base of the tree, touches it, chants mantras, and daubs it with red *kumkum* powder, performing a *dig-bandhana* (binding of the directions) that exorcises the supernatural forest- and tree-dwelling creatures that inhabit the tree as he continues its transformation into a royal pole.[12] With Śaktivallabh drawing on the classical Sanskrit rite, the *purohit*

> performs the necessary actions, with [two types of] ritual water in the four directions. Milk-rice and *bali* should be given to the *bhūt* in the four directions. To the east, "AUM to the *bhūt,* this milk-rice and *bali, namaḥ.*" Then it is to be placed in the south, to the west, and to the north. Then, the [five] auspicious *upachāra* are to be given as a puja to the tree. Having touched the tree, mantras are spoken. Then there is the recitation of a *svasti namo* [welcoming/farewell] to those *bhūt* living in the tree. Having received these gifts from the priests, [the *bhūt*] change their place of residence [*vāsaparyayaḥ*].

In his consideration of Varāhamihira's *Bṛhadyātrā,* Marko Geslani argues that the presentation of offerings (*balyupahāra*) to the Guhyakas or Pramathas—"hideous figures said to dwell in wild, secluded places . . . [who are] fierce and well armed" ensures the king's success in battle (2018: 136–37).

Whatever the historical trajectory between the king's journey into battle and his journey to the forest as part of the Indra festival, the fear and necessary harnessing of these dangerous beings is clear and extends beyond this small group of Sanskrit texts. In her study of south Indian villages, Diane Mines describes the occasionally unwitting transmission of fierce gods from the forest to the village during tree-cutting festivals. In one particular case where all of the tree cutters fell ill, a specialist determined that the ghosts and other fierce beings who had inhabited the tree possessed the men and made them ill. As a remedy, the men were instructed to deposit in their village a handful of earth from the place where they cut down the tree and "on those spots build permanent shrines to these fierce beings, adopting those gods into their lineage as lineage gods" (Mines 2005: 133–34). But Daniela Berti, in her description of the forest rites surrounding the cutting of the tree for the wooden *palkhi* of the Himalayan goddess Hiḍimbā, provides a slightly different interpretation of a similar puja, stating that the particular forest that is chosen is one that is "considered to be filled with the presence of *jogni*, powerful goddesses dwelling inside the trees" (2004: 91). These *jogni* must be pacified so that they will be willing to transform their power into that of the specific deity whose *palkhi* is being constructed.

These examples show not only the widespread phenomenon of using ritually obtained lumber from specially designated trees and forests but also the necessity of accounting for and redirecting the power of the tree's residents before the rites may continue. They also reflect the tantric underpinnings of the festival: not simply directed to a quasi-Vedic Indra, the festival accounts for the tantric power of deities like the Mother Goddesses, Bhairav, and lower-level *bhūt-pret* whose power is accessible to those who wield the proper knowledge. This Nepalese tantric foundation also incorporates Indra, who also, despite his relative independence from Tantric rites, has power over rains and ancestors that can be harnessed by Newars in several of Kathmandu's local neighborhoods, a topic taken up in the final chapters of this book.

The Nepalese puja concludes with a goat sacrifice, an element not seen in any textual descriptions of these rites. This *bali* is performed as a standard animal sacrifice: the goat is sprinkled with water and sacrificed only when he shakes it off, thus assenting to his own sacrificial beheading. Following his rather tentative assent, the goat's throat was cut with a regular *khukri,* the priest's assistant pulling the head back to direct the blood spray against the base of the tree and against the axe that would be used to cut down the tree the next morning, the same axe blessed by the palace priest earlier in the day. The goat's head was then completely removed from its body and placed facing the tree directly in front of it as an act of *darśan* to the increasingly sanctified tree. Although the kharga was conspicuous throughout the rite, wrapped in its red-and-gold *tās* cloth as it is at every major rite of the festival, its presence was of a purely symbolic nature: never used in any act of cutting, it was placed against the base of the tree, reinforcing the continued presence of the Nepali state. Five or six cuts were made into the tree with the bloodied axe at the proper time, completing the day's work. The entire rite lasted about ten minutes and concluded with firing two shots from the rifles of the two attending Paltan soldiers: one shot was said to be for Ban Devī, the other for Indra Maharāj.[13] The evening's cutting, in other words, was of a purely ritual nature, the nonritual "felling" beginning the next morning.

Many people refer to Indra in Nepali as *pāni ko devatā* (the god of the rains), and, as if on cue, it began to pour as soon as the evening's activities were finished. All of the puja items were quickly scooped up, and the religious and military officials quickly piled into the waiting truck to be taken back to Kathmandu, while the remaining locals and researchers were left to their own devices. Approximately twenty of us walked back down from the jungle, trudging by candlelight along a dirt-and-gravel track that quickly turned to mud in the monsoon rains. After nearly forty minutes of crossing rice fields and streams in the dark and rain, we arrived at a farmhouse in the village of Tāthalī, where we were given another meal of potatoes, lentils, beaten rice, and buffalo meat, this time with a glass of *thoṅ* rice beer.

Day Two: Felling the Poles

Traveling back from Tāthalī by tractor in a ride that was only slightly shorter and slightly more comfortable than our walk the previous night, we arrived back at the forest at about 7 a.m. Whereas the activities of the previous day were largely performative—the Ban Yātrā, the display of the *kharga*, the ritual cutting of the tree, the exorcism of *bhūt*, and the sacrifice of a goat—the morning activities of the second day were characterized by brute physical labor: felling trees and transporting them back to Kathmandu. In all, three trees would be cut down—one thick tree for Indra that had been selected and ritually cut the previous evening and two thinner trees that, cut into eight equal parts, represent the Aṣṭamātṛkā (the Eight Mothers). The Indra festival is suffused with the rhetoric, ritual, and iconography of goddess worship; even the *Devī Purāṇa* begins its forest rituals "according to the rites of establishing the goddess" (*devī pratiṣṭhā-vidhinā,* 12.4). Moving from under the watchful eye of the forest goddess Ban Devī, Indra continues to be surrounded and protected by feminine power as he approaches the city: eventually installed around Indra's central pole in Kathmandu, the eight Mother Goddesses function like those in their shrines around Newar cities, as they "ward off the danger of that other world" (Pickett 2005: 250).

The two trees are opposed to Indra's in a number of clear and symbolically significant ways. While the tree-cutters assert that their choice of the thinner trees was based solely on expediency and efficiency, their selection displays a particular adherence to a ritual and hierarchical paradigm, one in which the primary (male) shows a physical superiority to the secondary (female): as the Aṣṭamātṛkā trees are each cut into four pieces, Indra's pole becomes eight times taller than each. Moreover, the bark of the goddesses will be left on, leaving them more raw, more natural, and more like trees, whereas Indra's will lose all of its bark, marking his pole as a consciously constructed ritual object. Finally, Indra's pole will be pulled to the city by hand and raised in the palace area during one of the high points of the festival, whereas the goddess poles will be transported by truck and installed around Indra's central pole only after the festivities and crowds have largely abated.

I was given several accounts of who was responsible for this forest work.[14] Representatives from the governmental office of Guthi Samsthan in Kathmandu told me that it was people from the Daṅgol and Manandhar (New. Saḥmi [Sahmi]; oil presser) castes who performed all of the work. Later, I was told more specifically that the Manandhars do nearly all of the work, and a single member of the Daṅgol caste is responsible only for measuring the pole with an iron chain, ensuring that it meets the height requirement of thirty-six "hands" (cubits, the length from elbow to tip of middle finger). This system, however, has since passed out of circulation, mainly due to the new official way of handling this set of jobs. From its inception in 1964, Guthi Samsthan replaced the traditional Manandhar-governed system with one that is referred to by the English phrase "tender system," which is treated as a government contract. That is, individuals offer bids to Guthi Samsthan, which then offers the contract or tender to the lowest bidder. This person, according to some of the officials I spoke with at Guthi Samsthan, has no formal ritual duties and does not even have a proper title—most people referred to him as the *tender manche* (the tender man)—though I refer to him as the project's foreman.[15] As the foreman, his goal is to successfully complete the project and turn a profit for himself, while paying his workers an acceptable wage.[16]

Hardly to my surprise, the lowest bidder and foreman for the project in 2005 turned out to be Ratna Bahadur Manandhar, a member of the caste traditionally responsible for this work, who offered to do the job for "one lakh rupee" (100,000 Nepali rupees, approximately US$1,000). Ratna Bahadur, a man in his sixties, supervised the several days of events in alternating shifts with his son.

All of the activities surrounding the pole traditionally involved the Manandhars, and despite Guthi Samsthan's assumption of these roles, the Manandhars and the KMS have recently made a successful bid at retaking them. The KMS is now in charge of gathering and paying the workers, most of whom come from Bhaktapur's Sūrya Binãyak neighborhood on the Arniko Highway, the route the pole will travel over several days. Ratna Bahadur's bid stands as one of several successful steps in reasserting Manandhar and Newar identity in the face of a government that is often perceived as being anti-Newar. The regular presence of the KMS headman at these forest rituals of the first day points not only to the traditional ties between the festival and the Manandhar caste but also to the festival's increased Manandhar presence via the KMS.[17]

Cutting the trees began as soon as everybody arrived that morning. Two loosely organized teams of four to six people worked simultaneously, one team working on Indra's tree and the other team first on one Mātṛkā tree, then on the other. All trees were felled by 9:30 a.m., and then the real labor began. This morning—more of a "functional" as opposed to "ritual" day—also saw the participation of the villagers in the area. Many women were observing the annual activities in their forest on their way to and from the nearby Śiva temple as they celebrated the festival of Tij. Others came closer to do some gleaning. In a use of ritual leftovers that is repeated several times throughout the festival, several people from the village used the resources made available by the tree cutting: two children came by to collect armloads of branches taken from the top of the felled tree, and two women collected the wood chips left over from the cutting.

Conveying the Pole

The unnamed yet extraordinarily difficult labor of conveying the forty-foot pole some twenty miles from forest to city, work that is almost completely ignored in scholarship on the festival, recalls questions regarding the archetypal nature and chronology of the festival. Many Nepalese assert that the Indra festival begins only when the pole is raised in Kathmandu's royal square on the twelfth lunar day of Bhādra, an event that occurs ten full days after the Ban Yātrā, the festival's first *sāit*—thus ignoring the festival's first three *sāit* and its first ten days. Omissions of the pole's conveyance are reproduced in the secondary literature as well. In his study of the set of Kathmandu's autumnal festivals, van den Hoek provides only two paragraphs covering the entire six-day period from the arrival of the royal coterie in the forest to the pole's formal arrival in the city (2004: 39–40). Pradhan includes the forest journey as the first of the festival's "Preliminary Rituals," stating blandly in his table 1: "About one week before the festival: cutting the pine tree to be used as the ceremonial pole" (1986: 386).[18] Toffin recapitulates the brevity and content of the classical Sanskrit texts, saying that the pole is "carried to the capital accompanied by singers and dancers" (2010: 46). Although the textual sources detail the preliminary rites in the forest, the pole's subsequent installation in the capital city, and its disposal marking the festival's end, they virtually ignore the pole's conveyance from forest to city, describing the event in a single verse or even less: it is conveyed "by men or by a cart" (*BS* 43.21b), "by cart or bull" (*DP* 12.22b), or "by bullock cart or by people" (*VDhP* 2.155.5).

Rather than assuming that the conveyance simply provides nothing of substance for these classical authors to write about, I am asserting rather that they inserted this silence into the texts to gloss over activities that simply did not fit their agenda. By paying attention to these texts as consciously constructed documents whose authors wanted to adhere to a greater sense of orthodoxy in support of their royal patron, I hope to better account for how the Indra festival's rite of conveyance contributes to a dynamic understanding of religious, political, and social life in modern Nepal. Although the Indra festival has traditionally supported the monarch who sponsored these royal texts, and whose aura continues to permeate this festival, the lack of attention devoted to the liminal conveyance of the pole communicates the danger inherent in this ritual's performance and geography, much like the danger physically inherent in the tree in the forest whose resident *bhūt* must be exorcised before the pole's arrival in the city.

This liminality provides a vacuum of power and authority that workers will readily fill with a certain raucousness that fits the situation.

Conveying the poles to the city immediately follows the felling of the three trees. The two goddess trees are heaved down the side of the hill onto the road below, loaded onto a tractor (the same tractor on which we rode to the forest), driven down the hill, and reloaded onto a military truck that will take them to Darbar Square in Kathmandu.[19] The Indra pole, once it is cut down and its branches cleared off, will have its top end cut straight across, leaving a flat surface, and its base end will be cut into a wedge. The texts prescribe that this part of the tree, and another small section removed from the base, be thrown into a body of water, mirroring the festival's concluding *visarjana* when the pole, having served its function, will be disposed of into a nearby body of water. About one foot from the tip of this wedge, an approximately six-inch-wide and four-inch-deep ridge is cut, running the circumference of the pole, into which the pulling ropes will be fixed; once this occurs, the pulling will commence (see figure 2.2). This wedge resembles the

Figure 2.2. Pulling the pole from the forests near Nala. Photo by author.

head of a penis to some and the head of a snake to others, thus introducing the phallic and serpentine imagery that reappears in the festival.

Immediately after cutting and fashioning the pole, the work of the pulling began. As with most of the work on this day, little ritual or fanfare accompanied the predominant theme of labor. The route followed by the pole was simply the most efficient one possible, with no organized puja performed at any place along the route. Thus, from a ritual standpoint, this part of the Ban Yatra was relatively uneventful. Most people told me that its route went from Nala to Bhaktapur to Thimi, then to Kathmandu, and finally to Bhotahiti. Though references to the cities of Bhaktapur and Thimi might appear to give some sort of significance to these places and some of their more prominent temples, the only major stop the pole made was for a late afternoon lunch break (3:15 p.m.) in the parking lot of Barahi Cinema Hall, on Bhaktapur's southwest side. The lunch was a traditional Newar meal of *baji, kerāu,* and *chuelā* (beaten rice, beans, and fried buffalo meat), with a leaf-plate of lunch also set atop the *lingo* and left in the middle of the highway for Indra's consumption.

In fact, none of these place names that are nearly universally mentioned by people in describing the route of the *lingo* refer to anything more than the cities it passes through as it makes its way from the jungle to the neighborhood of Bhotahiti on the east side of Kathmandu's old city. Yet this geographical irrelevance was not always the case, and the persistence of these place names, like the persistence of the story of the goat's selection of the tree, reflects a continuity of local tradition. In years gone by, as several *guthi* documents show, it was the Manandhars of each of these places—Kathmandu, Thimi, and Bhaktapur—who would travel from their respective city to retrieve the *lingo* from the jungle. In a more specific story I have heard, Manandhars traveled to the city immediately to the east of their own, pulling the tree into their own city, and eventually on to Kathmandu. Mary Anderson describes the Manandhars of Thimi as pulling it directly from Bhaktapur to Kathmandu, in a simplistically functional yet astute comment regarding this tradition win the Indrajātrā, and she remarks: "This practice of men from various villages participating in certain important festivals is very ancient and seems to enhance unity among the people" (1971: 129).

Though the Manandhars, via the organization of the KMS, have reasserted their authority in the festival, especially by their performances of rites surrounding the Indra pole, changes in the administration of the festival has changed the nature and identity of the region itself. Feldhaus describes how obtaining, pulling, and installing the *kavad* poles provides workers with

> an opportunity to dramatize various geographical units, and to express and strengthen their own identification with some of these units. The large kavads and poles serve, first of all, as a focal point for bringing together the villages and towns that they come from. . . . The journeys of these large kavads and poles bring the places they come from together with the places they pass through. The Pancakrosi kavad unites the five Pancakrosi villages into a small region. . . . Finally, the pilgrimage as a whole enacts the unity of a region that many of the participants identify as "Maharashtra." (2003: 71)

Just as the *kavad*-carriers in Maharashtra bring together and strengthen their identification with the cities they came from, so can Manandhars from these different towns performing the individual segments of this task enact the unity of the region of the Kathmandu Valley. Despite the lack of significant change in the precise route of the pole, the tender system initiated by Guthi Samsthan in the mid- to late twentieth century threatened the unity of the Newar Kathmandu Valley by eliminating these intermediate municipal nodes.[20] Viewing local ethnic groups and their regions as divisive to the coherence of the Nepalese nation, the state's administration of the festival removed the Kathmandu Valley as a ritually coherent region, and these Newar cities and their attending groups of Manandhars are no longer strung together by this progress.[21] The attempted replacement of the progresses between these valley urban sites with a single processional route from the jungle to the national capital city would relocate the geographical emphasis of the festival. No longer celebrating the local and ethnically Newar site of the Kathmandu Valley, the festival would become a national festival celebrated by and for people of all ethnicites, its focus squarely on the modern Nepali nation-state headed by its elected prime minister and hereditary Hindu king. But the Manandhars' expansion of their roles is reasserting this traditional geography.

Ritual Security, Ritual Violence, Ritual Death

Of those I asked along the way, and in a theme that recurs throughout the festival, most agreed that the role the various military forces play in the course of the festival is *surakṣā* (security, protection), specifically the protection of the pole. The Paltan is present near the tree at two dangerously liminal times: first, after the tree is selected but before it is cut down; and second, once the procession of the tree has commenced and is in the hands of the nonroyal participants. In Nepal in 2005, the main enemies of the king—of whom the pole is a cipher—were the Maoist rebels. Though it seemed fairly unlikely that Maoists would try to harm the pole or any of its pullers during the conveyance, all of its activity occurring in the relatively safe confines of the Kathmandu Valley, the Maoist threat resulted in the pole's overnight abandonment in the hills.

The protection offered by the royal soldiers was never intended to be against armed Maoist rebels. Rather, as with their presence in the opening rites inside the palace in Kathmandu, they are there to provide a royal and military presence to an otherwise mundane rite reminding the public of the connection the Indra festival has with the militarized Nepali state. The military also performs the supernatural correlate of this royal function, keeping away the cosmological forces of evil and the fomenters of multifarious obstacles, like those *bhūt-pret* expelled from the tree at its transformation in the jungle, presided over by Ganesh, the remover of obstacles. The presence of the military provides for the ongoing identity of the wooden pole as a royal-divine object.

Their protection also signaled the presence of conflict and danger. Each step in the conveyance of the pole is fraught with great danger, a precariousness that is conveyed in the earliest textual sources. The dangers inherent in this rite contribute to a practical logic to which transgressive behaviors performed at the festival's most liminal times and places serve as a ritually logical response. The *Bṛhat Saṃhitā* refers to the many omens portending fateful ends to the king, his family, and his ministers. The king should be on guard when encountering an imperfect tree, a creaking axe, a broken cart, fighting animals, and a sputtering ritual fire. Such omens, as Marko Geslani has carefully attended to, mark irregularities and abnormalities in nature that "signify a negative and inauspicious outcome" (2018: 203). The several days of the Ban Yātrā represent the most intense period of physical contact with the pole and thus the highest degree of ritual violence, at least until the festival's third day.

The conveyance of the pole was continually accompanied—some would say marred—by acts of violence—some incidental, some overt—that helped define not just the identity of the pole but also of the workers in charge of its conveyance. It is at the festival's most dangerous and liminal time, during the pole's travel from forest to city, that the texts maintain their nearly absolute silence. In classical Sanskrit texts, the forest is the location for destroying demonic enemies, performing austerities and Vedic rites, and reciting royal narratives, whereas the city, though an enclave secured by its king, is a place where enlightenment could never be achieved. Just as with the vacuum of power that allowed the leadership of the Newar KMS into the Ban Yātrā, the symbolic vacuum of Sanskritic textual authority in regard to the conveyance was filled by those workers responsible for the nonarchetypal work of pulling the pole.

The violence of the festival is inherent in the category of *jātrā,* a word that translates as "festival" but often denotes, especially for the Indra festival, the violence that frequently accompies it.[22] Though I have witnessed late-night drunken brawls in other festivals (e.g., the Dasain festival of Bhaktapur), the energy of Kathmandu's Indra festival seems to be inherent in a festival that has historically been connected with kingship, power, and victory. Well attended by the city's residents, the festival draws thousands of additional people into the city from the surrounding villages, especially on the valley-wide holiday celebrated on the festival's third day (Indrajātrā Day on Bhādra 14). With people congregating in tightly packed crowds in various neighborhoods, incidents of pickpocketing, drunkenness, and fighting—and violent police responses—increase dramatically. Male festival-goers, it is said, save up all of the personal slights and offenses suffered throughout the year and use this opportunity—a festival that includes feasting, drinking, urban anonymity, and the cover of darkness—to exact revenge on their enemies. Referring to the festival as fight *jātrā* and revenge *jātrā,* a friend of mine, when young, was warned by her parents not to go too late to the city during the festival—especially to Hanuman Dhoka especially on this day—as it was just *guṇḍas* who were pulling the chariots. After these processions, she was told to return home to avoid the fighting and general raucousness in the center of the city.

Violence was also present in various forms during the pole's conveyance from the jungle. While the pole symbolizes state violence against its enemies, this large, heavy object is a sheer physical menace to those attempting to wield it. These difficulties are noted in the textual record, evidenced by the list of problems resulting from the breakdown of any part of the cart that carries the pole: the breaking of the spokes leads to the destruction of the king's power; of the rim, the king's army; of the axle, the king's wealth; and of the axle pin, the carpenter (*BS* 43.22).[23] Although no similar results are listed for the breakdown of the men who perform this heavy labor, I witnessed several injuries along the way. In one incident on the afternoon of the second pulling day, the son of the foreman, who filled in for his father when he was away, tried to grab one of the short wheel pipes that had fallen out from underneath the pole; he did not move his hand away quickly enough, and the pole pinned it to the ground, breaking it instantly. Another worker had his foot broken in the same incident, and both were rushed to the hospital.

The physical difficulties of the pole's conveyance across the valley were quickly overshadowed by the difficulties of pulling it five miles down the Arniko Highway, the main two- to three-lane highway, during the middle of Tuesday afternoon rush hour, a tactical nightmare for which little municipal preparation had been made.[24] Tension was evident throughout the five-hour ordeal; workers and drivers regularly engaged in verbal and rather violent physical altercations, many of which stemmed from a perception by the workers that drivers were taking too much liberty as to the path allowed them by the pole. It was their duty to get the pole to Kathmandu, and the vehicles on the highway all too closely resembled the demonic obstacles they had just exorcised in the forest. For the next few hours, until the job was complete, the road was theirs. During its highway journey, the back portion of the pole struck the tires and bodies of innumerable cars, trucks, and buses and tipped over several motorcycles and their riders. While many onlookers appeared amused at this sight, many drivers of the struck vehicles were not as patient, and many verbally sparred with the workers. The attitude on the part of the workers seemed to be not one of sympathy but of entitlement. After one vehicle lost a piece of its front bumper after being struck by the pole's back end, the driver got out of his car to complain to the workers and to the accompanying security personnel, to no avail. The only thing that prevented him from being physically assaulted himself was the physical evidence, the piece of his car's bumper that he held in his hand. Although the workers' guilt was evident, the driver was offered no recompense and was urged to move along. In another incident that curiously reflected the greater political tension in Nepal at the time, one pedestrian loudly suggested that the workers resembled a group of Maoists. Approaching their destination after twelve consecutive hours of work late on the second day, and after several breaks for beer and liquor, the workers did not take this accusation lightly. As one of the workers began to shove his accuser, those who had not yet encircled the two combatants dropped the pole and rushed to the side of their fellow worker. Finally realizing that he was about to become the victim of a lynch mob, the man got back into his taxi and, as the mob pounded and kicked the vehicle, sped away, nearly careening into oncoming traffic. This incident is only one of many that pointed up the tensions inherent in this physical labor as well as the political rhetoric that many people used to comprehend this public act of walking.

The political situation that was on everybody's mind in 2005 was further elicited by the various chants—more like call-and-response work songs—used by the workers while pulling. The first, most general, and most-used chant consisted of a call of "Hos te," called either by one of the supervisors or by the team on the first rope, with the response of, "haiṅ se," the Nepali equivalent of "Heave ho!," shouted by the men on the second rope. This chant is used in various other festivals, especially those that involve the difficult pulling of old and rickety chariots, propelled along by large wooden wheels and laden with a many related caste members. While pulling the pole through midday traffic on the Arniko Highway, the call and response changed to various related Nepali-language complaints regarding the task at hand: "hāmī lāī gāhro" ("it is difficult for us") and "tānne gāhro" ("the pulling is difficult").[25] In Nepal in 2005, these chants immediately brought to mind something a bit more dangerous, especially for those who could hear the chanting but could neither discern the content therein nor see the source of the noise. In Bhaktapur district, two little boys stopped in their tracks as they heard the workers' chants, the older warning the younger of the approaching *julus*, the political rally that has the potential to turn into real and uncontrolled violence. The boys turned and ran back in the direction from which they came. This same thing happened again, nearly a week later as the pole was being pulled toward the palace area from Bhotahiti; hearing the chants emanating from the eastern part of the old city, shopowners near the palace quickly closed their shutters, clearly anticipating a *julus* and the possibility of their windows being smashed and their shops ransacked. When they finally saw the source of the chanting and the pole being dragged down the street, their fear turned to relief, and many saw a bit of the humor in the situation. A political rally led by student leaders and party politicians was more worrisome than the symbol of military power and the destructive potential of the god Indra.

The transgressive behavior of the workers was as sexual as it was violent, appropriate in a festival whose central object—a tree whose leaves, branches, and bark have been removed—is glossed as *lingo* in Nepali, readily translated as "penis." Several times during the day, the response to the usual call of "Hos te" changed to the slighly naughty "lyāse" (young girl), evoking the smirks of many onlookers. More memorable, however, were those chants that referred to Indra and the pole being dragged down the road. These chants, frequently repeated, consisted of the call of "Indra ko lāḍo" and were met with the response of "Kathmandu chiryo." The rather literal translation of this phrase is, "Indra's cock . . . will penetrate Kathmandu." This use of public obscenity has no clear sympathy with the classical festival or any royal valence. Though maintaining the festival's classical focus on royalty, this chant blatantly mocks both king and Indra; whereas the classical pole serves as a beacon to display the universal rule of the king or a sword directed toward the city of the king's enemy, the obscene pole is set to militarily and sexually destroy the capital city of Nepal. These transgressive acts of violence and obscenity that move so far from the festival's classical focus on royalty allow us to consider this act of conveyance specifically and the Indra festival as a whole as participating in the ritual genre of the South Asian funeral procession.

This relevance of ancestry in the festival's rite of conveyance becomes clearer as we observe similar uses of obscenity in South Asian funerary rites. Four examples of such transgressive behavior should suffice. The Gathe Mugaḥ festival is celebrated during the agriculturally risky late summertime in Nepal when the first monsoon rains are expected, when the Mother Goddesses are absent, when members of the low Gāthā caste are said to search for human skullcaps to use as drinking vessels, and when human sacrifices are said to have once taken place. During this festival, when the obscene Gathe Mugaḥ causes women "go into their houses 'to avoid being insulted' and watch through the windows" (Levy and Rajopadhyaya 1990: 515–17, 521), young men loudly shout "grossly sexual" obscenities to young women; these obscenities climax and conclude when the search for skullcaps concludes and Gathe Mugaḥ is expelled from the town.

Kathmandu's Trishuljatra (Festival of the Trident) celebrated at Pashupatinath, the temple complex that includes the city's primary cremation grounds, contains narratives that involve human sacrifice, demonic threats, and blood-thirsty goddesses. During the main procession, in which children are symbolically impaled on spears sticking up from portable goddess shrines, the bearers of these shrines "start to shout loudly, in the direction of Kathmandu." Michaels writes, "The words they utter at this point are so vulgar and pornographic that we must limit ourselves here to the mere hint that they are aimed principally at Kathmandu's girls" (2008: 116).

Jonathan Parry describes the transgressive celebration at funerals in Benares of those who has lived a full life and thus whose passing constitutes a "good death": "As for more distant male mourners, they are free from the outset to express the joyous triumph of a 'good death'. While the women wail, the young men dance in a burlesque of female sexuality—gyrating hips, upturned thumbs held in front of the chest to suggest breasts, and sometimes a woman's shawl draped over the head" (1994: 155).

Finally, late at night on the third day of the Indra festival after (and following the exact path of) Kumari's chariot procession, Manandhars bear through the streets of the old city of Kathmandu the insults of onlookers as they carry the *baumata,* a serpentine/phallic bamboo structure whose oil lamps guide the path for the souls of the recently deceased. Functionally unrelated to Kumari, *baumata* follows her procession and that of Indra's mother, the demoness Dagi, accompanied by a group of white-clad citizens of Kathmandu mourning recent losses of family members.[26]

Each example of ritual obscenity is performed as part of a larger ritual context that focuses on death and the elimination of its more negative psychological components, whether in the context of high-risk agriculture (Levy), narratives of dangerous divinities (Trishuljatra), an actual funeral (Parry), or a rite of remembrance (the Indrajatra's *baumata*). The obscene chants shouted during the pole's conveyance from the jungle fit into the larger Indra festival, already suffused with images and performances of danger and death. By asserting the funerary and ancestral nature of the liminal conveyance of Indra's pole—and the entire festival—we can begin to see the replacement of the festival's universal and royal valence with that of the local and ancestral. This foregrounding of death and kinship, over the Hindu focus on power and kingship, represents one of many ways that the Newar *yeṃ yāḥ* replaces the Hindu Indrajātrā, even during the physical handling of Indra's pole, the central object of the Sanskritic textual tradition.

The conveyance ended nearly three days later at approximately 2 a.m. Thursday morning. Some sixty tired workers rather unceremoniously dropped the pole against a curb in Kathmandu's Bhotahiti neighborhood after having pulled it by hand for approximately thirteen hours that day through the forest, down and around the hills of the valley, and on the Arniko Highway during rush-hour traffic, covering approximately twenty-five miles. Several gunshots from the accompanying soldiers marked the end of the conveyance, and all parties returned wearily home.

Conclusion

The pair of contending symbol systems underlying the Indra festival—royal and funereal—simultaneously celebrated by multiple populations in Nepal, represents what Toffin refers to as the "heart of the festival's ambiguity." "Before the allegiance of actual authority, the indigenous inhabitants celebrate the Indrajatra in their own way and also find the elements for reaffirming the irreducible originality of their culture. Nevertheless, it is as if the Newars have interiorized their defeat and the point of view of the powerful. For the Indo-Nepalese and the reigning dynasty, this is certainly the most important message of the festival" (2006: 70). Despite Toffin's contention that the Indrajatra's repeated celebration of "*processions funéraires* . . . supports the identity of the Newars in general and of the Newars of the city of Kathmandu in particular" (2006: 69), the regular juxtaposition and frequent simultaneity of these symbol systems does more than simply support and reaffirm Newar identity. Even less, I argue, do these funerary rites require the Newars to voluntarily celebrate their 1768 defeat at the hands of Prithivi Narayan Shah. Despite the precise historicity of these funerary rites, their current celebration actively subverts the dominant royal meaning, which they acknowledge but have not completely interiorized through the festival's focus on the city's ancestors.

Their surrogation of these apparently dominant royal rites, a move made more possible through the aniconic form of Indra's pole, is performatively parallelled in its nonarchetypal conveyance to the city. The physical danger the pole presents, the obscenities the workers repeatedly shout, and the violence they display to the general public occur within geographically and chronologically liminal frames: between forest and city, outside of the framework of the festival's widely accepted eight-day duration, and in the lacuna of silence constructed by the authors of the classical Sanskrit texts.

The funerary rites performed in the contemporary Nepalese rite point to their successful replacement of the festival's solely royal focus as we see it in the classical texts. I argue that the raucous and funereal Ban Yātrā does not simply represent a degree of harmless performative resistance in the vacuum of textual authority but a rejection of the texts' conservative maintenance of kingship, where the human king was identified with the divine Indra. This concern with death and royalty extends far beyond the performative, however, especially considering "the realities and structures of everyday life in particular times and places." The 2005 performance of the Indrajatra subverted more than just the 1768 invasion of the Shah dynasty; it also reflected the most significant issue in the political lives of most of this generation of performer: the potential—for some, the desired—death of the contemporary Nepalese monarchy, a death ritualized in the popular symbolic funerals performed after King Gyanendra's removal from power. The second Janandolan (people's movement) of 2006, in which hundreds of thousands of Nepalis took to the streets in protest of the monarchy, represented the most public repudiation of the 240-year-old Shah dynasty, and the conveyances of Indra's pole several times reminded people of the power that such urban processions can have.

More than simply signaling the festival's ancestral theme, the rite of conveyance and the transgressive behaviors that accompany it allow for more dynamic understandings of religious, political, and social life in contemporary Nepal. It is only when we consider the classical textual record as just one contributing element to the habitus of contemporary Nepalese life that we can properly focus on how the festival of Indra continues to be a relevant and contested performance in twenty-first century Nepal. By asserting that the textual silence represents a deliberate authorial strategy to preserve a religio-political orthodoxy, we can view the liminal setting of the conveyance as an ambiguous time/space in which ritualists and scholars might improvise their approaches to ritual performance. Local ritualists can, more or less clandestinely, subversively, and successfully, replace a universal with a locally accepted meaning. Scholars may invert traditional approaches to the study of religion and ritual as I have attempted to do here, using contemporary performances as ways to assist in interpreting the content of and gaps in a classical textual record, rather than the other way around.

Chapter Three

Preparing, Entering, and Establishing the City

For four days, the pole sits in the bustling, commercial area of Bhotahiti on the eastern edge of the old city, directly across from Rāṇi Pokharī, the Queen's Lake that houses the Lakṣmī-Nārāyaṇa temple, open only during the Tihār festival in November. While not much happens during the intervening four days after its arrival and before its conveyance to the royal palace, the pole remains an attraction, a sort of oddity and sidelight despite being the Indra festival's central object. During these four days, a Manandhar member of the KMS sits on a small stool at the base of the pole—the end that will be put into the ground—and performs multiple functions. As frustrated tour guide, he repeats a summary of the festival's highlights to those Nepalis—mostly non-Newars originally from outside of the city and valley—unaware of the nature of the object being displayed, its destination, and its purpose. To this end, he posted two identical signs, one at either end of the pole about thirty feet apart from each other, that informed people of the identity of the object and on the proper ritual etiquette they were to display toward it. The Nepali-language signs read in full: "This is Shiva's lingo. Please [respectfully] touch your head to it. It is the deity of the Indrajātrā. Please do not [disrespectfully] step over it."[1]

As priest, he maintained the base of the pole as a temporary ritual site. Having constructed an approximately one-foot-square brick enclosure on the pole's arrival and exposed a stone mandala slightly beneath the street level, he kept eight incense sticks constantly burning around its perimeter in a form that would mimic the eight Mother Goddess poles installed around the central Indra pole and the eight Mother Goddess shrines that encompass the city. Those who made an offering of money onto the mandala would then apply to their foreheads the red and yellow *tika* from the powder he kept supplied atop the pole. As a sort of shaman, and as one example of the use of parts of the pole as a relic or for more pragmatic purposes, he provided healing services by breaking slivers from the pole into smaller splinters; devotees would take these home with them in a small satchel or plastic bag, tying them to their arm or placing them in a locket around their necks to alleviate a common cold.[2]

These several days in the interim lead to the event that opened the classical festival, the *nagara praveśa* (the entrance into the city). In Kathmandu, this event represents the third of the festival's five *sāit*, preceding the pole's grand installation (the Nepalese festival's fourth *sāit*) and its final *visarjan* (its fifth and final *sāit*). Building onto my argument from chapter 2, this chapter details how the Indra festival, especially with its movements of people, goods, and gods through Kathmandu's streets, simultaneously draws on and actively subverts the dominant royal meaning of the classical texts as it memorializes the city's ancestors. Moving onto the second half of ths festival, this chapter shows how the king, the city, and local ancestors become conflated through this contemporary performance as it uses Indra's tall pole—the focus of the classical festival—as a material object that furthers this symbolic conflation.

Sāit No. 3: The Entrance of the Pole

The entrance of Indra's pole into the city represents one of many examples of the concept of the *praveśa*. Rather than a single term prescribing a single practice, the *praveśa* operates as part of a habitus that "makes possible the achievement of infinitely diversified tasks, thanks to analogical transfers of schemes permitting the solution of similarly shaped problems" (Bourdieu 1990: 83). The concept of entrance has proven to be a flexible and effective tool in many genres of Hindu literature whose authors describe the penetration of one physical body by another.

Indicating many types of "transfer of essence" that frequently begin or conclude a ritual or narrative event and seen most dramatically in possession events, the *praveśa* marks an boundary crossing in which a ritual actor or literary character transitions from one place and one state of being to another (Smith 2006: 67). Among the many examples of the *praveśa* that effect an intimate relationship between otherwise discrete (quasi-)physical objects: creation stories tell of the creator entering his creation; domestic texts describe how a new homeowner enters his new house; the epics tell of women becoming a *satī* by entering a funeral pyre; architectural texts set the precise rules for ensuring that in the ritual of *prāṇ pratiṣṭhā*, the essence of the deity enters the newly constructed icon; Vedic texts allow for internalizing one's Vedic fires; devotional texts describe the descent of an avatar into the realm of humans; and the Upaniṣads elaborate on the intimate relationship between the individual *ātman* soul and the universal *brahman*. Each entrance event is premised on the presence of a powerful being who moves through physical space, a matrix whose outer edge it penetrates, a vehicle by which the object enters and pervades this matrix, and outward signs that the matrix has been penetrated.

Most directly relevant to the Indra festival, the Sanskrit epics narrate the grand and dramatic entrance of a king into his city. The epics elaborately describe these victory processions: those of Yudhiṣṭhira into Hāstinapura in *Mahābhārata* 12.38.30 and of Rāma in several chapters of book 2 of the *Rāmāyaṇa*. Despite the differences in these narratives—namely, of Yudhiṣṭhira's consecration becoming official while Rāma's is interrupted—these *praveśa* events consistently display the themes of social inclusion and urban adornment that highlight the public celebration of victory, power, and heritage that precedes the ensuing coronation. Analogous to the physical actions of a person that denote deity possession, for example, the public and cacophonous gathering of masses of people welcoming a victorious king into his city indicate a successful entrance and the final formalization of that power.

A significant part of the Indra festival in its own right, Kathmandu's *nagara praveśa* prepares the city for the event with which most people say the festival actually begins: the pole's installation in the royal square. This preparation is performative and aesthetic, as the city begins to take on a new appearance through a series of adornments: beer pots and wooden poles are installed throughout the city streets, icons of Indra are raised in a few Jyāpu neighborhoods, centuries-old icons (most noticeably that of the menacing Kal Bhairav) are repainted, and temples have their red and gold *tās* bunting replaced.

The language of *praveśa* and these urban adornments place meaning onto the aniconic pole. Entering the city from the forest, the pole is likened to a conquering king about to be enthroned, and through the descriptions of the pole's elaborate decorations it is likened to the city in which it is established.[3] The sixth-century *Bṛhat Saṃhitā* uses much of the same language as did the epic coronation passages, showing how the decoration of Indra's pole reiterates how "the body of the god can be viewed as a double for the body of the king" and, I would add, of the city as well (Geslani 2018: 200).

> On the eighth day of the bright half of Bhadrapada, the king, along with his well-dressed citizens, astrologers, ministers, chamberlains and prominent Brahmans, should have the Indra pole brought [*praveśayet*] into the city by his citizens.[4] [The *yaṣṭi*] is dressed in a new cloth and ornamented with flower garlands, perfumes and incense, and is accompanied by the citizens of the city playing conches and musical instruments. [The city is] decorated with beautiful flags, triumphal arches and garlands of forest flowers. Its people are happy; its roads are clean and orderly; its courtesans are well-dressed; its shops are well-kept; and its crossroads are filled with actors, dancers and singers. Here, the Puṇyāha and Vedic chants are loudly chanted. (*BS* 43.23–26)[5]

Though describing the pole's ensuing installation, the Tamil epic *Silappadikaram* (*SK*), whose *Indiravilavureduttakadai* chapter, named after the festival, focuses primarily on a description of the city of Madurai. The text describes the city's layout, the organization of its inhabitants by caste and occupation, the surburban dwellings of its defending warriors, and the healing lake where the "lepers, hunchbanks and cripples" gather to partake of its waters. In this urban setting, the Indra festival begins.

> On the verandas of the big mansions were to be seen artistic planks set with emeralds and diamonds whereon stood coral pillars. At the entrance of these mansions were

> suspended ornamental hangings having the shape of the *makara* fish from whose teeth (horns), carved with symbols representing auspicious things and adorned with *kimpuri*, hung strings of pearls in series. The streets were further beautified by golden pitchers filled with water, maidens, golden flags, pure white feather fans, fragrant pastes and many other ornamentations. (Dikshitar 1939: 116–17)

Both functional and technical, such descriptions heighten the already aestheticized urban ideal of the *nagara varṇana* (descriptions of the city); placing such a festival in the boundaries of the city multiplies the affective and sensory perceptions of the intense and diverse attending crowds (Kaul 2010: 49–51). The aesthetics of such urban accounts point toward the festival's central point; in the Indra festival, it is the central pole that—having moved several times through and across the city's boundaries and becoming the glorified and ornamented center of the city's attention—replicates the movement of a king who, as Inden writes, "by articulating the sovereignties of the earth, was supposed to bring about an ordered, prosperous world. The procession of the image of the god whom he had taken as cosmic overlord was the completion of a successful imperial progress. . . . Performing these practices, a paramount king claimed to reiterate the embodiment of his god and kingdom" (2006: 268, 270). These accounts of the beautification projects carried out elsewhere clarify how the Indra festival is not merely a private and royal puja annually performed by the king and his ministers to Indra, as argued especially in the *Atharva Veda Pariṣiśṭa*, but a major civic festival that engulfs and overwhelms an urban space, as it projects its central object to a status beyond its appearance as a simple wooden pole but as a representative of the city itself and of its ruling king.

Kathmandu's *Nagara Praveśa*

Kathmandu's *nagara praveśa* picks up, literally, where the first left off a few days earlier. At 1:30 p.m. of Bhādra 8, the motorcycles parked against the *lingo* were removed, and the Paltan playing fife and drums and carrying two Nepalese standards approached the *lingo* lying in Bhotahiti, circled it, and then stood off to the side until the *sāit* (1:45

p.m.) arrived (see figure 3.1). On each of the previous days since the *lingo* had arrived, Manandhars perform a relatively simple puja on site, and on the previous day, thirty-one red circles were painted on the *lingo*, at roughly equidistant intervals, thus dividing the pole into thirty-two sections. The number thirty-two is of great significance in South Asian architecture, as Holle, Toffin, and Rimal (1993) and Toffin (1994) argue. Hindu temples are grounded on a thirty-two-part Vāstupuruṣamaṇḍala; homa altars are made up of thirty-two bricks; and the foundational Ākāśa lotus contains thirty-two petals. The city of Kathmandu is even more connected to this particular number, as its resident Maharjan families are said to reside in thirty-two neighborhoods,[6] and the city is composed of thirty-two gates. This number is used "to represent the universe on a reduced scale" (Holle, Toffin,

Figure 3.1. Preparing the decorated pole for its entrance into the city. Photo by author.

and Rimal 1993: 22) and "elevates Kathmandu out of the realm of [the] ordinary world" (Toffin 1994: 435). The application of this number to the pole—an object that metonymically highlights the city through its origins outside, its travels through, and its final dispersal outside the city—offers a further reduced model of the universe, elevating the pole to the status of the city itself.

The ropes that were used to pull the pole from the Salagarhi Forest were retied to the grooved head of the pole, whose semi-divine nature was further highlighted with offerings of coconuts, garlands of marigold flowers, fruit, and offerings of Nepali rupees. Another man from the KMS, with shaved head and crisp white *dhoti*, acted as priest, applying *tika* to those who came by to venerate the pole for a final time in its current position and witness its grand entrance into the city. Instead of the project's foreman and his tendered workers, who finished their work as soon as they dropped the pole at Bhotahiti three days earlier, this day's pulling was performed by members of the KMS. As with many of the jobs connected to the heavy labor of the Indra festival, this one has recently passed from the police and military recruits. By 2014, Manandhars managed the security of and performed the puja to the pole after it arrived at Bhotahiti, though some military recruits still were present to help out. During the *nagara praveśa*, Manandhars from a *sanāḥ guthi* even walked ahead of the pole, publicly declaring their identity by displaying a large sign that clearly identified, in ascending order, the urban geographical locations where they lived and worked: Dhālāsikva, Asan Tyoḥ, and the Newar name of Kathmandu, Yeṃ.[7] Young Manandhar members of the Thahiti Manandhar Guthi accompanied the procession on flute. A series of gunshots from the attending Paltan signaled the *sāit*, and the pole was on the move.

Upon entering Durbar Square from the northeast, the pole was pulled to the left behind the Kākeśwar Temple and passed in front of the doors of the Taleju Temple and then straight up to the hole in which it would be raised. As on its short journey there, once it was laid down many of those gathered came forward to touch their heads to it, make offerings of money, and take powder from the base and tip to place a *tika* on their foreheads (see figure 3.2).[8] The pole was once again measured, and mirroring the four gunshots fired at the start of the day's pulling, four more were fired, signaling the end of the day's work and the end of the *praveśa*. The pole lies in Darbar Square for the

Figure 3.2. Honoring the pole upon its entrance into the royal square. Photo by author.

following four days, until the fourth *sāit*, the *Indra-dhvajotthāna*, when amid a throng of people the pole would be raised and, according to most people, the festival would officially begin.[9]

Sāit No. 4: Installing the Pole

The royal preparations for the festival begin three days later on Bhādra 11, when the king remains awake for the whole night and, together with his *purohita* dressed in white clothes and turban, recites mantras to Indra and Viṣṇu and maintains his sacred fire.[10] The king recites a four-verse set of mantras (*BS* 43.52–55) when the pole "is decorated, installed, brought into town, bathed, bedecked with garlands, and disposed of," including an abridged version of the *trātāraṃ indraṃ* passage from *Rig Veda* 6.47.11 that identifies Indra as a rescuer, helper, and hero. The passage from the *BS* adds a concluding half-verse

(43.55b) that extends Indra's power to the terrestrial world: "May our heroes be crowned with success!"[11] On Bhādra 12, the BS has the pole installed [*utthāpyo*] "while offering molasses [*guḍa*], bread [*pūpa*], and milk-sweets [*payas*], as well as *dakṣiṇa* [donations] to brahmins [*viprān*]" (*BS* 43.38).

While poles are raised for many Nepalese festivals, rarely is the raising the primary rite, and rarely is the pole the central object as it is here. Typically, a pole is simply a signal to those who pass by that a festival is currently in progress. The spring new year's festival of Handigaon in northeast Kathmandu focuses on the chariot of the area's goddess Tunaldevi, who is carried from her temple in the town center to Gahana Pokharī (Jewelry Lake), while two poles, raised at the neighborhood's main intersections, stand virtually unattended.[12] The situation in Bhaktapur for Biskaḥ Jātrā is a bit different, where the pole is raised on the last day of the solar New Year's Eve (April 13) and lowered on the next day. This ritual of the pole lasts only one day—New Year's Day—while the complete festival is a nine-day affair. Though the installation of the pole is an important element of this festival, other rites are arguably more significant to its operations: the processions of the chariots of Bhairav and Bhadrakālī, the two tug-of-war matches involving the Bhairav chariot, and the processions of many of the city's deities to the temple of Taleju.

Despite the centrality of the pole in the contemporary Indra festival, it is clear that many other rites supercede those surrounding the standing pole. The classical textual record, however, beginning with the *Mahābhārata*, devotes all of its attention to the pole, describing its lavish adoration and adornment. The classical pole is treated as the central ritual object, the thing to which all attention is directed—especially, given the nature of the texts, the attention of the king and his officials. What we do not see is the plethora of rites that we might presume were part and parcel of the classical festival that were performed independently of the pole. Reflecting my argument about the absence of textual attention to the journey from the forest in the previous chapter, whereas in the Nepalese performance the pole serves merely as a signal to the important rituals that are being performed nearby (especially those dedicated to Bhairav and Kumari), the textual record is devoted almost solely to this cipher, looking at the proverbial finger pointing at the moon. This differential attention clues us in to the careful textual construction of the classical festival that avoided "popular" rites not supportive of the single central king and to the revival of the classical festival in contemporary Nepal, superimposed as it seems over the myriad local rites to the ancestors, Bhairav, and various goddesses.

During the four days that the pole was horizontal in Hanuman Dhoka, a five-foot staff with a green fruit (Nep. *salā phal*, New. *bhagatyā*) and an approximately three-foot-long red flag are attached to its top end.[13] Before the installation, Devi Pyakha from Kilagal Tol dances with a somber musical accompaniment. Counting their performance in Kilagal Tol on Bhādra 10, they will dance five times during the course of the festival, continually reenacting Kumari's defeat of Daitya, the latter initially victorious over Kumari's companions, Chaṇḍī and Bhairav. Following the troupe's performance at the installation, a Mānandhar woodwind band will play until about ten minutes before the installation, with a military brass band playing for the final five minutes.[14]

Gathered together for the spectacle in Darbar Square are large numbers of tourists, local spectators, and reporters from local media. The ritual work is done, as it had been done for some years prior, by Manandhars of the KMS, all of whom wear paper badges announcing their affiliation.[15] Up until 2006, also in attendance in an official capacity were approximately a dozen court officials, each wearing a button with a photograph of the then politically beleagered king and queen; the head of national security who carried the Rāj Khaṛgā on his right shoulder as he did at the *nagara praveśa*; the Paltan, adorned in their traditional uniforms; and the military brass band that played before and after the event.

The raising of the pole is conducted with traditional machinery. Approximately twenty pairs of bamboo poles, tied together in V-shapes of different sizes, are wielded by members of the KMS, used as fulcrums to progressively raise the pole and maintain its stability throughout the process.[16] As the pole is successfully raised higher and higher, the tallest bamboo supports used in the back are discarded, the workers taking up smaller ones waiting on the side and rushing toward the base of the pole. Ropes attached to the top of the pole are handled by individuals stationed on the bracketing Jagannāth and Indrapur temples; these ropes are used not so much to pull the pole into place but to stabilize it once it stands straight up but is not yet fully stable.[17] Once the pole is completely vertical, workers wedge about a dozen wooden boards all around the pole, securing it against the walls of the pit in which it is dropped.

A certain element of danger is inherent in such a risky enterprise and possibly even required. Inevitably, the massive pole will begin to sway to one side, or the upward progress halts and begins to regress. These relatively sudden movements are met with collective gasps from the crowd, easily heard over and between the gunshots fired by the soldiers stationed on the steps of nearby temples. In the four raisings I have seen, the event has gone off without a hitch and the work is completed within twenty minutes, but this is not always the case. The Indra pole fell in 2012 and in 2016, causing several injuries and even one death.[18] Parish (1996: 154) witnessed a similar event as the pole at Bhaktapur's Biskaḥ Jātrā was being lowered and noted how, in addition to this result being inauspicious and potentially deadly, higher castes placed the blame on the untouchable participants who had attempted to exceed their allowed involvement.[19] The *Bṛhat Saṃhitā* was aware of such a risk, including a series of verses describing the results from such ritual disasters: once the pole is raised, dangers arise from carnivorous birds alighting atop it and the pole being struck by lightning, meteor, or earthquake; a resulting danger occurs to citizens, court officials, or the king himself, should the pole break at the base, middle, or tip, respectively (43.64b).[20] The *Rāmāyaṇa* uses the simile of the crashing of Indra's pole to show Bharata's expression of grief at hearing the news of his father Daśaratha's death, reinforcing the festival's association with risk, danger, violence, and death.[21]

Following the (typically) successful raising, the Manandhar and military bands—together with another Newar band whose members play *shennai* horn and *dhime* drum—simultaneously play, circling the pole three times.[22] All interested onlookers follow the bands and the king's officials, circumambulating the pole, touching their heads to it, and pulling off pieces of the pole, shredded from its forest journey to the city, to take with them as *prasad*, a sacred memento. The military band reorganizes itself into a parade-like formation, plays the national anthem, displays arms, attaches bayonets, and disperses. Also in attendance is a white horse led by two men clad in red military uniforms who serve as the collective witness for the king who no longer attends. Following the dispersal of the military band and the Paltan, the general public also departs.

The *Kālikā Purāṇa* refers to this final space as the "Indra mandala," a useful term that relates this new space to the city at whose center it stands (*KP* 87.35). In Gregory Grieve's study of the relationship of mandala paintings to the city of Bhaktapur, he quotes Paul Mus, who argues that "*mandalas* are not symbols that represent an ontological essence, but are rather a type of prototypical god whose ceremonies produce the lived territory of the city" (Grieve 2006: 18). Despite the Indra mandala garnering relatively little attention—people strolling by will throw a coin toward base of the pole, touch their hands to their heads and hearts in a respectful gesture, or simply admire the size of this annual intrusion into the urban landscape—with the city's attention drawn to other and more mobile objects, deities, and people, the Indra mandala functions in a similar way. As Devī or Śiva is said to be the *bindu* residing at the center of a *yantra,* so also "the ceremonial pole symbolizes the centre of the city and of the ritual activities" (Pradhan 1986: 392).

Even more so, I assert that the Indra mandala represents and reconstructs the city of Kathmandu, attracting attention to this urban microcosm via a number of its ancillary objects. Installed at the base of the pole is an icon of Indra, seated cross-legged in *rāja-lalita-āsana* (a position of royal repose) atop his elephant Airāvata. Like aniconic *rudrākṣa* beads that have "no obvious iconographic traits that would connect them with a particular god" (Granoff and Shinohara 2004: 27), the juxtaposition of Indra's anthropomorphic image to the aniconic object serves as a visual argument that the tall wooden pole, by itself unidentifiable, is intended to be seen as Indra.[23] Brought out in an old metal box by brahmins from the Taleju Mandir, the icon is given over to local Jyāpus and placed in a cage at the base of the pole. By rotation, one Jyāpu man and one armed member of the Paltan military troupe stay together all day and all night through the course of the festival for the protection, it is said of this small and hence easily stolen image, purportedly made of solid gold.

Indra's flag, kept during the year inside the palace, is then attached to the top of the pole. Hanging down to within approximately six feet of the ground, the flag resembles that of a metal *patākā* flag that hangs from the top of many Nepalese temples.[24] The nineteen symbols that adorn the flag recall the eight auspicious Newar symbols, the *aṣṭa maṅgala,* that appear together on similar but smaller flags destined for domestic space or carved in stone on temple facades, as well as to the fourteen objects that emerged from the *samudra-manthana*, the story of the combative and creative churning of the ocean between the gods and *asuras*.[25] Finally, adorning these representations of auspiciousness and creation, the Indra mandala is completed with the installation of eight subsidiary poles; the Jyāpu man on duty told me that the eight poles represented the "sons of Indra," an interesting parallel to the "daughters of Indra," the *śakra-kumārī* of the *Bṛhat Samhitā*.[26] Each a one-quarter portion of a tree felled in Salagarhi Forest topped with a colored flag, these poles collectively protect Indra's central pole and the entire Indra mandala while constructing yet another microcosmic image of the city, that of the eight Mother Goddesses (New. *Ajimā* [the Grandmothers]) who surround, support, and protect the single and central male figure, alternately identified as the Hindu Indra, the mildly Sanskritized Bhairav, or the Newar Grandfather Aju.

The *Upāku* Procession

The microcosm of the city displayed in the festival's central mandala speaks to a broader connection of the Indra festival with the city of Kathmandu and with the themes of death and the ancestors. In his study of the significance of agriculture and the ancestors within Newar ritual life, Bal Gopal Shrestha addresses the various socioeconomic foundations of the five-day Newar Svānti festival that occurs toward the end of the *chaturmasa* period. More commonly known as Diwali throughout South Asia (Nep. Tihār, Skt. Dīpāvalī), Svānti is also called Yamapañchaka, "the five days devoted to Yama, the god of death." Celebrating the many animals associated with the ancestors, especially crows, dogs, and cows, this festival focuses on "remembering, worshipping and appeasing deceased ancestors (*pitṛ*) [that] are dominant feature[s] of Newar ritual life" (Shrestha 2006: 215). More specifically, by venerating Yama and these animal messengers to the under/other world, "people try to subjugate the power of death. . . . Hence we can consider the festival of Svanti as the celebration of the victory of life over death . . . [and] also the renewal of the ritual cycle in Nepal" (218).

The main ancestral rite in the Indra festival is the ritual of the *upāku vanegu* (*upaku*), "walking the boundaries" of the old city. Celebrating the ties between kingship, kinship, and the founding of the capital city on the first night of the Indrajātrā, the *upaku* draws on the founding of Kathmandu by King Guṇakāmadeva and on larger thematic ways that festivals celebrate the founding of Newar cities. In her work on the city of Bhaktapur, Anne Vergati asserts that "all three Newar festivals of the Valley aim at ensuring the prosperity of the Valley. . . . All include processions of divinities taking place inside town-limits, displaying in this manner the hierarchy of the gods among themselves and also the relationship beween the gods and the inhabitants of the territory. These processions celebrate the foundation of the king's capital and the regeneration of the social and religious order" (2002: 25). The city of Bhaktapur and the spring festival that celebrates its founding, Biskaḥ Jātrā, were established by King Ānanda Malla in the twelfth century at the behest of Śaiva goddess Bhadrakālī, who provided the king with the gift of a sword (*khaḍga*), the symbol of Nepalese kingship, with which he would slay the snakes who continually threatened the local princess. Following his success, he established the city of Bhaktapur and its 12,000 houses, installed the goddess Tripurasundarī at the center of the city, and inaugurated the Biskaḥ Jātrā festival.

Kathmandu's story of origin mirrors this narrative pattern (Vergati 2002: 171). Coming to Guṇakāmadeva in a dream, the goddess Mahālakṣmī commanded the king to build the city at the confluence of the Bāgmatī and Viṣṇumatī Rivers in the form of the sword (*kharga*) of Kālī, a fierce goddess who lends military assistance to kings. At the center of the king's sword-shaped city resides the deity Kāntīśvara, a small street-set stone that is still visible immediately outside the Akash Bhairav temple in the central neighborhood of Indra Chowk. The shrines of the eight Mother Goddesses on the city's periphery become nodes on the *upaku* funeral procession for the city's recent ancestors and on King Guṇakāmadeva's sword that models the shape of the city. His instituting of the Indra festival annually brings all of these places together.

The *upaku* procession also points toward yet another of the festival's many chronologies, that of the sixteen-day *sohra śrāddha*, the sixteen (*sorha*) days for ancestor rites (*śrāddha*).[27] Beginning several days later on the *pūrṇimā* (full moon day) of Bhādra—the final day of the classical festival and the day of the Newar *yeṃ yā* (*punhi*)—the sixteen-day duration continues until the first day of the bright half of Asoj, the first day of the Dasain festival.[28] Van den Hoek describes this period as "marked by the centrality of death and sacrifice . . . when the deceased of the previous year are collectively mourned and the gates of heaven open" and asserts for the Indra festival specifically that its "composite character . . . is the unifying notion of sacrificial death" (2004: 18, 60).

During the *upaku*, thousands of people process the city's streets, walking in a clockwise direction around the sword-shaped perimeter of the old city, visiting the decorated shrines (mostly of one or another goddess) that lie on its borders.[29] These shrines are adorned with large piles of prominently displayed *samay bajī* festival food, often with a fresh fish or a buffalo head placed atop it, and often with local Jyāpu drummers and musicians playing near their entrances (see figure 3.3).

Figure 3.3. A pile of *samay baji* arranged for the *upaku* procession outside a temple at Chhetrapati Chowk. Photo by author.

Samay bajī in Kathmandu was traditionally distributed on the *pūrṇimā* to children who went from house to house singing a special song: "lā chaku wayka / samay bajī" (Give me one piece of meat / for my *samay baji*), a song that ended with the announcement of the arrival of Indra's elephant Pulukisi ("wala wala Pulukisi!"), who makes a prominent appearance during the contemporary *upaku*, either leading or interrupting the procession.[30] Some householders would respond to the children's song with a generous splash of beer poured directly into their mouths, and others have the children sit on the common ground floor of their home and provide a small feast with *samay baji*.

Most participants carry lit incense during this three-hour procession, and many of the attending women place hundreds of small clay lamps (Nep. *batti;* New. *mata*) along the sides of the path, marking their progress. Each head of household, clad in white as a sign of mourning, also walks the interior of the city behind Indra's mother, Dagi, two days later on Bhādra 14, following the procession of Kumari.

Although the *upaku* procession is sometimes said to instantiate Guṇakāmadeva's founding of Kathmandu in the tenth century, it is also multiple and contested, contrasting sharply with the other major procession in the Indra festival, the Sanskritic *praveśa* that we saw at the beginning of this chapter. The *praveśa* has as its goal the conveyance and presentation of Indra as the center of the city, ensconced as he is at the center of the Indra mandala surrounded by the eight goddesses whose poles surround Indra's, just as their shrines surround the city. The *upaku*'s central deity to whom the Ajimā refer—the transgressive grandfather Āju, also known as Bhailu, Bhailadyaḥ, or Bhairav, and a local rival to the Hindu god Krishna—bears no immediate relationship to Indra or his classical festival and thus carves out for the festival a strictly local meaning on a parallel geographical plane. Thus, the Indra mandala's representation of the city changes depending on which set of goddesses one follows. Whereas the Hindu Mātṛkā surround and protect the Vedic Indra, the Newar Ajimā instead surround the central Āju, thus slightly shifting the center of town from the royal Darbar in the center to the neighborhood of Wanghaḥ and the temple of Bhairav-Āju about one-quarter mile to the northeast. The differences in meaning between these two urban processions extend to their very core: whereas the Sanskritic *praveśa* highlights the king's singular violent and hegemonic penetration of the center of the city, a theme continued from the Ban Yātrā and the epic *praveśa* of Rama and Yudhisthira, the *upaku* communicates an embracing of the city from the periphery by thousands who seek to reestablish a relationship with their city after the rupture and trauma experienced following the death of a loved one.

Local Ancestral Poles

The kingship-kinship duality of the Indra festival comes together in local neighborhoods as multiple smaller pots, poles, and posts are installed around the city. Installed by families and *guthi* organizations, the pots are *hāthu dyaḥ*, pipe gods in the form of brass pitchers or Bhairav masks behind which is contained a reservoir of beer and that refer to the larger Seto and Akash Bhairav masks that distribute beer to the public.

The posts are topped by icons of Indra, Bhairav, Narayan, Indrayani, or Ganesh, deities all related to some narrative of the Indra festival. In the neighborhood of Thahiti Tol, Triratna Manandhar—the *thakali* of his *phuki* (the head of his lineage)—has been responsible for raising a six-foot-tall wooden pole in his ancestral neighborhood about a half-mile north of Darbar Square. Manandhar leads the puja at this pole that, previously topped by an image of Ganesh before it was stolen some years ago, is tied with rope to an electrical pole, located near tea stalls, *thangka* shops, and the Buddhist *stupa* that dominates the center of the neighborhood square. Resembling the raising of similar poles during the festival in Gūḍhi Paṛvā in Maharashtra, as described in chapter 1, this domestic ritual may represent one of the most ancient strata of Kathmandu's festival and may have presented a model for the revival of the installation of the classical Indra pole.[31] Situated directly on the *upaku* funeral procession route, Manandhar's family pole resembles that of Indra's single central pole only in its wooden material; otherwise eschewing any contact with Hindu royalty, these peripheral poles contribute instead to the local festival's focus on the city's ancestors.

Sāit No. 5: Visarjan

The Indra festival concludes with the *visarjan*, the fifth and final *sāit*, that sees the pole come crashing to the ground, pulled by hand in yet one more of the pole's movements through urban space, and finally disposed of. The disposal of Indra's pole is predicated on a principle similar to that which underlies the treatment of the more famous unfired clay images of Durgā constructed for the Durgā Pūjā festival in Bengal or of the images of Ganesh in his festival of Ganesh Chaturthi in Maharashtra. Having never received one of the rituals that establishes him as a deity—*prāṇ pratiṣṭhā, nyās pūjā*, or, for a more typically Nepalese example, the serial reception of the *daśa-saṃskāra* rites of passage such as the processional image of Avalokiteśvara annually receives—Indra's pole is never completely transformed into a deity. Such temporary and liminal manifestations of the divinity hardly preclude its reception of public veneration, and the *visarjana* provides a final opportunity for Kathmandu's residents to bid farewell to the pole and to the festival as a whole.[32]

The *visarjan* begins with the *indra-dhvaja-pātana* (*patana* for short). Referring to the "falling/dropping" of the pole, this event initiates the larger process of pulling the pole to the river and immersing it in water. This series of events not only represents the elimination of an unconsecrated ritual object but is also a dangerous task due to the pole's royal connections. The Nepalese *Kathanam* prescribes the king's activities at the event of the *visarjana*, namely, reciting auspicious mantras and maintaining an overnight vigil.[33] The *Kālikā Purāṇa* provides the following prescription: "At night during the last *pada* of Bharaṇi, the *visarjana* of the pole should be done. While all the worlds are asleep, the king is not to look at it. Were the king to see the *visarjana*, O king, he would surely die within six months" (87.43b–44b).[34] This *visarjan* provides a stark contrast with other components of the festival. Unlike the previous movements of the pole where the king is ritually involved—via his palace priest, officials, horse, and royal sword—the pole's final disposal requires that the king should, for his own protection, steer clear of this concluding ritual.

The danger and darkness associated with the classical *visarjan* reinforces the Indra pole as a mortuary marker—as with Triratna Manandhar raising his family's pole in Kathmandu's Thahiti neighborhood—and the Indra festival as a celebration of both kingship and kinship. Always performed at night, Kathmandu's *visarjan* reinforces the festival's funereal theme with its presence of bundles of dried grass. Placed on the steps of the adjacent Indrapur temple when the pole was installed, these bundles were then spread out on the ground where the pole will drop. Also produced at Vedic ritual sites to provide the gods with a comfortable place to sit, grass bundles are more commonly seen at cremation grounds throughout South Asia, as they provide the initial kindling for the piles of wood for cremation fires; such bundles are also sometimes attached to the pillars of cremation structures, appearing as symbols of the ritual activities performed within. These bundles are prominently displayed in certain *shrāddha* rites for the recently deceased, serving as a sort of placemat on top of which banana leaf bowls of food are displayed and left out to feed the ancestors. It is the responsibility of street dogs—local manifestations of Saramā, the guardian dog of Yamarāj, the king of the underworld—to eat this food and thus convey it to the ancestors.

The *visarjan* begins with dismantling the ritual site: the ropes connecting the pole to the two adjacent temples are released, the bamboo cage around the main pole is removed, the ancillary Mother Goddess poles are assertively tipped over, and all of the wooden planks that had been wedged into the hole to keep the pole upright are removed and nonchalantly tossed to the side. It takes little more than a gentle push to send the pole to its demise, striking the grass-strewn ground with a loud crash to the resounding shouts of the gathered crowd. Following the pole's crash, a crowd of boys and young men rushed the prone pole, made a final farewell to it, and engaged in a furious mock battle using as weapons the bunches of grass that now represent the physical mechanism for the expression of the resultant chaos in a kingdom without a king, where, according to traditional chronology, the old year has finished but the new one has not yet begun.

Tying ropes the tip of the pole, members of the KMS and others pulled the pole to the Bagmati River at the city's southern border. Members of the military armed with automatic weapons and members of the ceremonial Paltan with their old rifles accompanied the procession, firing their weapons upon the pole's arrival at the river. The smooth paved stones of Darbar Square ensured a speedy procession; moving much more quickly than at the Ban Yatra sixteen days before, the group reached their final destination, approximately one kilometer away, in little more than thirty minutes. Just as in the pole's route from the jungle, the only logic underlying the particular route taken was expediency, tracing a path that was as close to a straight line as possible.

After the procession had reached the northern bank of the Bagmati, they removed the ropes that had been used to pull the pole, the headman of the KMS performed a very brief puja on the head of the pole with uncooked rice, flowers, and red *sindūr* powder, and the pole was abandoned on the marshy bank of the river, without being fully submerged. Although I cannot know exactly what happens to the pole after its *visarjan,* I can relate the various stories that I have heard and read. After being "immersed" in the Bagmati River at the *visarjana,* one of the following occurs:

- The pole will be taken by the Poḍe (untouchable sweeper) caste and repurchased from them by the Manandhars (the KMS) who will use the wood in their local oil presses.
- The Poḍe will use the wood from the pole for their building projects. In different versions of this story, they must purchase the lingo from either Guthi Samsthan or the KMS.
- According to van den Hoek: "In 1993 it was collected by members of a Rana religious association to repair a temple under their custody—they are doing so for several years already" (2004: 42).
- According to Chalier-Visuvalingam: when the Indra pole is lowered, a funeral procession of Manandhars carries it to the southern cremation ground to be thrown in the Bagmati river. Then the pole is hacked into pieces which are used to feed the perpetual fire of the *pitha* of Pachali Bhairava (Chalier-Visuvalingam 2004: 147).
- Members of the KMS told me that "rishi-muni" renouncers at the temple of Pachalī Bhairav take a piece of the pole as it lies in state at the cremation grounds at Teku Doban, burn it, and cover themselves with the ashes as an "antibiotic."

All of these accounts acknowledge the pole's lack of complete submersion and continue the narrative of the pole's instrumentality: just as the villagers living near the jungle gleaned the branches and wood chips of the tree after its felling, as the Manandhar on duty at Bhotahiti prescribed medicinal applications of slivers of the pole, and as particpants removed pieces of the freshly installed pole at its installation, the wood of the pole is seen to be auspicious and its subsequent and practical use advantageous.

Significant also was their destination: the neighborhood of Teku Doban. The location of the cremation *ghat*s used by the Jyāpus of the lower half of the city, the neighborhood is synonymous with death and the ancestors, somewhat like Manikarnika Ghat is for Benaras (Toffin 1994: 451). In the first two accounts of the pole's fate, slight variations of which many different people related to me, the Poḍe reprise their ritual role as beggars at Hindu funerals and other death rites, where they take up the cast-off clothing and goods of the deceased. By allowing themselves to receive the "deceased" pole, they reassert their inferior social position vis-à-vis the bearers of the pole (the Manandhars), the king, and the city of Kathmandu, all of which the pole represents to varying degrees. The activity of the the "rishi-muni" who cover themselves in ash from the pole further reinforces the dangerous and tantric nature of the place.

The festival pole's final destination at Teku and the presence of Pachali Bhairav challenge the festival's singular classical focus on the central ruling king. Initially "a deity of the cremation ground where he was identified as the lord of the demonic spirits of the dead," and a subordinate, multiple, and protective deity in the service of the goddess, Bhairav emerged as the object of his own devotional cult who "moved to the center of many meditative and territorial *maṇḍala*s" (White 2009: 485). Pachali Bhairav specifically draws on all of these identites as he reflects a concentration of the many Bhairavs who will come to overshadow Indra in his own festival. Celebrated some twenty days later, Pachali's festival—replete with imagery of, possession by, and sacrifice to Ganesh, Bhairav, and the goddess Taleju—bears such a close relationship to Indra's that van den Hoek considered it an "extension" of Indrajatra (2004: 61).[35]

Pachali's location at the cremation grounds of Teku, his similar narratives of thieving, womanizing, transgression, and captivity, and his multiple connections to royalty and the palace draw on classical and contemporary themes of the Indra festival but diffuse them with a focus on the ancestors venerated with the *upaku* procession and the installation of small family poles. Facilitated by the people's movement in the early 2000s, Bhairav's multiple connections with royalty and the ancestors sparked a new rhetoric of ancient connections of Nepalese kings with Bhairav, specifically with Pachalī Bhairav and his putative connections to an ancient palace in the village of Pharping in the southern reaches of the valley. Following the assassination of much of the Shah family in 2001 and Gyanendra's authoritarian power grab in 2005, several Newar people asserted that Bhairav, rather than the Vedic Indra or the classical Vishnu, was "our first king."

Regardless of the particular locus of royalty in Kathmandu and despite the absence of the king of Nepal, the rhetoric and pomp of royalty continue to represent a significant valence of the Indra festival. The next two chapters continue the theme of ritual innovation but will shift to the agents of the Nepali Shah dynasty. Focusing on the production of two Nepali- and Sanskrit-language texts produced in the early Shah period, these chapters will reinforce themes central to the Indra festival, moving away from Indra's local connections to Bhairav and the ancestors and toward the ways the Shah dynasty drew on the festival's classical and pan-Hindu rhetoric of the Indra pole, the classical object frequently overshadowed by the local focus on Bhairav, the ancestors, and the living royal goddess Kumari.

Chapter Four

Nepali Chronicles and the Living Goddess Kumari

The Nepali-language newspaper *Gorkhāpatra*, founded in 1901 during the heart of the Rāṇa era, is well known for its conservative, nationalist, and, after the return of official royal Shah rule in 1951, royalist leanings.[1] Like the classical Sanskrit texts in chapter 1, early *Gorkhāpatra* issues reveal the careful construction of an equally conservative version of the Indra festival for public consumption.[2] Among its descriptions of the festival, a 1927 article spends much of its attention describing the presence of soldiers and officers on horseback (*ghoḍa-caṛhī afisarharu*), directly naming the Śārdūla Jaṅga Palṭan and the Jaṅgī Nijāmati, several of the various branches of the military that maintain a public presence in the celebration. But, signaled by their titles being underlined in the newspaper text, the high ritual moment of the festival is the joint arrival of the Shah king and the Rāṇa prime minister: as part of the royal *savārī* procession, Śrī 5 Mahārājādhirāj and Śrī 3 Mahārāj arrive in a "four-horse buggy" (*cau-ghoḍe bugghī*). Following them is the *śrī chief saheb* in his own *bugghī* accompanied by his general *sahebs*; the *mahā-nāike* who arrives with the *dhvaja-patāka* (flagpole); and finally, only after this significant military presence, the divine siblings Ganesh, Bhairav, and Kumari, living deities who begin their first and most important *rath yātrā* urban chariot journey on the festival's main day.[3]

The description of the festival's constituent rites is also highly conservative. Consistently using the Sanskritized Indrayātrā rather than the common Nepali Indrajātrā, the paper draws considerable attention to the multiple actions of the *lingo* and is careful to state, "according to the textual tradition" (*śāstrokta vidhi-vidhān le*). When discussing local Newar rites, on the other hand, infrequently as it does, the paper remains rather elusive. Its description of the *upāku vanegu* never mentions this urban ancestral procession by name, simply stating: "According to practice, men and women will circumambulate the city carrying sweet-smelling incense and oil lamps."[4] Descriptions of other local practices remain equally vague; though stating how "in many neighborhoods, images of ancient gods and goddesses will be placed," the paper never mentions the proper names of these Newar gods (the Āju and Ajimā grandfather and grandmother deities), the specific neighborhoods where they are installed, or the Newar caste groups responsible for them. Moreover, the articles routinely assert that these local rites are performed "according to tradition" (*rīti-sthiti bamojim*) preserving the textual tradition (*śāstrokta*) only for those Hindu rites that surround the festival's central pole.[5] Only the article from 1927 details the chariot procession of the Kumari, arguably the singular highlight that occurs on the festival's third day, the valley-wide holiday officially called Indrajātrā. Despite *Gorkhāpatra*'s many references to the Gaddi Darbār (Gaddi Baiṭhak)—the porch on the west side of the royal palace where Kumari's chariot procession begins and ends and from which the king or his representative throws gold coins to an eager crowd—these articles never refer to the blessing that Kumari gives to the reigning king, and afterward to all Nepalis, typically seen as the festival's high ritual moment that ensures the safety of the kingdom for the following year. Circulating among the general public since the early twentieth century, *Gorkhāpatra* reflects the deeper conservative and political leanings of the power brokers of the era, and the Indra festival represents a significant component of the period's increased nationalism. It is hardly the only text in service of maintaining that particular status quo, however.

The next two chapters will consider two Nepalese texts produced in early nineteenth-century Kathmandu. Like the issues of *Gorkhāpatra,* these texts assist in constructing a particularly Hindu version of the Indra festival in support of a new and stable political center. Though drawing heavily on Nepal's robust and diverse goddess tradition, the Shah dynasty differed significantly from the Newar Malla kingdom it replaced: with the Indra festival at its core, it sought to promote an *asal Hindustān* (a true Hindu kingdom) that, divorced from the culture of the local Newars, allied itself instead with its Hindu neighbors to the south.[6] The expressly Hindu values put forth in these texts—their identification of particular goddesses, financial support of particular temples, and performance of particular rituals—reinforces the explicitly Hindu identity of the Indra festival seen in the early medieval textual manuals they draw from. Continuing a relative antipathy toward other religions and cultures, these two Nepalese texts provide a foundation for the subsequent Rana prime ministers and final Shah kings when, as Gellner writes, the "stress on Hinduism meant that it became harder to practice the easy ambiguity of multivalent symbolisms" (2005: 767).[7]

This chapter focuses on the narrative of the Nepali-language text frequently referred to as the *Wright Vaṃśāvalī* (*WV*)—retranslated and published as the *Nepālikabhūpa Vaṃśāvalī* (*NBhV*, History of Kings of Nepal)—and the role of goddesses, especially Kumari, in the Indra festival. The next chapter attends to the royal (*rājnīti*) and Sanskrit-language *Indradhvajotsava Kathanam* of Śaktivallabh Arjyāl, a court poet and guru of the Shah royal family. The chapters will analyze the primary political use to which the Indra festival has been put since early modern Nepal: namely, for the production of a Hindu kingship in the presence of non-Hindu Others. These two texts were produced in the decades after the Shah victory of 1768 as they looked back on a reconstructed and revived Indra festival as the starting point of a rule that was to be steeped in a more recognizably pan–South Asian Hinduism predicated on introducing classical texts to a new Nepalese audience. Unmooring the archaic Indra festival from the complex of Hindu royal reinforcement rituals and installation rites adopted from the texts of the early medieval period, these Nepalese texts reflect the same imperial logic and maintain the same themes—power, innovation, and rivarly—that have underlain the festival's appearances in texts throughout its South Asian history.

More than simply taking up residence in the Malla palace in Kathmandu's royal square, Shah kings and scribes rooted their Indra festival texts in the Newar goddess tradition, seen in the earliest manuscript evidence. The earliest noted reference to the Indra festival appears in a passage from the *Gopālarāja Vaṃśāvalī* (CE 1379 [VS 1436]), in which King Stithimalla and Queen Rājalladevī celebrate the rite of the Mahālakṣmī Vrat along with the Indrajātrā (New. *endyāta*) in the city of Patan.[8] Although Vajracharya states that it is impossible to be sure about the connection between these two rituals, he notes that their overlap in the festival calendar (Bhādra śukla 2) highlights the relationship between Mahālakṣmī—whose role in the narrative construction of Kathmandu in a narrative of Bhairav we will see—and Kumari, whose presence dominates the contemporary festival tradition (1976: 172, 177).[9]

These texts anticipate the central role that Kumari, in her various names and forms, plays in the contemporary festival as they detail the many narrative, human, and material forms she takes. This focus on the goddess will provide much of the structural support to this chapter, as Indra—as is fairly typical in this festival that bears his name—gets pushed to the side in favor of deities who are more dynamic, devotional, local, and relevant to modern Nepalese life. This political focus on the goddess and her powerful *śakti* is hardly unusual in Hindu settings. As royal dynasties have done periodically throughout South Asian history, the Nepali Shah dynasty textualized its power and simultaneously politicized its texts, infusing them with a power that supported its rule. Like the *Gorkhāpatra,* these Nepali-language and Hindu-oriented texts often drew on the performance of local rituals and festivals as strategic foils against which they could communicate, display, and assert royal power throughout the expanding and increasingly unified Nepal of the late eighteenth and early nineteenth centuries, a bulwark against the British imperial threat to the immediate south in India.

Nepālikabhūpa Vaṃśāvalī

The *NBhV*—especially in its earlier publication as the *WV*—represents one of the most widely available texts of the entire genre of the *vaṃśāvalī*—the genealogy or chronicle—many of which were composed, compiled, and popularized in the early Shah era.[10] Their veracity dubious at best, *vaṃśāvalī* purport to relate a history that goes back to a much earlier time, even to the mythological origins of the Kathmandu Valley. Hasrat begins his history of Nepal with a descrption of the *vaṃśāvalī* genre:

> The *Vaṃśāvalīs* are genealogical lists—imperfect chronicles furnishing bare dynastic lists of kings and their regnal years, intermixed with mythological, religious and legendary tales

> [. . . whose] authenticity as a source of historical material is often challenged. . . . A common feature of these compositions appears to be their semi-historical character and dependence on traditional mythology and Nepalese lore; they deal with profusion the pious observances and religious acts of the monarchs rather than the scant political happenings of the time. (1970: xv)

Despite the genre of the *vaṃśāvalī* representing a "major source for the writing of Nepalese history" and their "unquestioned value as historical documents," Riccardi asserts that they "have created as much confusion as they have illumination," due in part to "the general failure to look at the *vaṃśāvalī* as anything more than general receptacles of historical and mythological information" (1986: 247). Regarding the *WV* specifically, Riccardi asserts that though "only a translation of a traditional chronicle, it is often cited as if it were a work of sober critical history" (1986: 247).[11]

Published in 1877, the *WV* has become "the most often reprinted and thus one of the most influential texts on Nepalese history" (Zotter 2013: 139). Its translation "from the Parbatiyā" (i.e., Nepali) rather than Sanskrit, as translator and surgeon of the British Residency Daniel Wright writes on the text's frontispiece, serves as a signal that its authorship (or at least final editorship) is apposite to the new Shah court. Though its Nepali authors/editors might have translated older sections from the original Newar, its narrative terminus in 1829 means that they wrote newly appended sections in Nepali that narrate recent events connected to their court. Its publication in English signals a moment of contact between Nepal and a British and larger Western audience, while this combination of Newar and Nepali elements signals "a moment of crisis for the Newars . . . [who] needed to persuade the new rulers of the validity and antiquity of their traditions [and] . . . to respect, and not appropriate or abolish, their long-established temples, endowments, and customs" (Gellner 1999: 7, 8).[12]

Accounting for the many warnings regarding the historicity of these texts and their application in determining key aspects of the history of Nepal, Bajracharya and Michaels refer to the "emplotment" of the *NBhV* and of the entire genre of the *vaṃśāvalī*, as its narrative use of human and nonhuman agents produce "wonder and religio-aesthetic appreciation" (2012: 94, 95). By situating itself amid the multiple languages, ethnicities, and religions of Nepal and by consistently drawing on religious narratives, persons, deities, and rituals to further their narratives—not to mention the assuredly historical events that affected the cultural foundation of these narratives (fires, earthquakes, landslides, and temple repairs; Bajracharya, Michaels, and Gutschow 2015: viii)—the *vaṃśāvalī* produce an imaginary world that establishes the religious significance of Nepali kings and by extension the people and places over which they rule, set against "a soteriological concept of time that is not interested in temporality and historicity but in eternity and immortality" (2012: 95).

In this new translation, the authors attend most closely to "publicly known and verifiable monument[s]" to show how "all forms of locality [are] interwoven into a synchronous perspective of places" (Bajracharya, Michaels, and Gutschow 2015: 221–22). In a similar way, I wish to use the text's several references to the "publicly known and verifiable" Indra festival to show how it also supports the historiography of the *NBhV*. Rather than historically verifying the truth of particular performances of the Indra festival, especially of the 1768 performance on which the text and the history of the Shah dynasty turn, I hope to do the inverse. By looking at its gradual construction of a narrative of the Indra festival, of the semi-divine agency of kings, and of the co-presence of the goddess, we can more closely see how the text furthers the narrative construction of religious and political power at the dawn of "modern Nepal."

The Royal Kumari

Its notion of Hindu kingship rooted in the early medieval Hindu textual tradition, the Shah monarchy of Nepal came to associate its kings with the god Vishnu, though they were only vaguely identified as portions of him and never seen as fully fledged avatars (Burghart 1984; Mocko 2016: 1–6).[13] Covering nearly one millennium of Nepali history, the *NBhV* emphasizes the perennial connections of its Shah kings with divinity, although the text associates kings with goddesses rather than with Vishnu. These connections are made in stories in virtually every royal generation, most frequently invoking the "living goddess" Kumari, the human, juvenile, and female manifestation of the Malla tutelary goddess Taleju (Tuljā).[14] In the *NBhV*, the goddess (most often Kumari) appeared to Chandraketu Deva in "the form of a child" in a story that introduces Matsyendranath and Gorakhnath (Bajracharya, Michaels, and Gutschow 2015: 48; further citations of the *NBhV* are to this edition); King Lakshmikamadeva, in honor of his grandfather Gunakamadeva, "regarded a neighboring girl as Kumārī, established her as Kumārī, and initiated the tradition of worshipping Kumārī" (60).[15] Harisimhadeva built a temple to Taleju (78); Jagatjyoti Malla played dice with Taleju (91); and Jaya Prakash Malla, the final Newar Malla king of Kathmandu (1734–1747, 1752–1769), built a house for the royal Kumari in 1757, instituted her chariot festival, and even fought his last battle against Prithvi Narayan inside the Taleju temple (115, 118).[16]

Despite historical and literary evidence that traces the royal cult of Kumari to Jaya Prakāsh Malla in the mid-eighteenth century, the *NBhV* innovates around this history, placing the agency behind the construction of her ritual complex into the hands of the tenth-century Thakuri king Gunakamadeva, whose story set the standard for the intimate relationship with Kumari seen in the long list above.[17] Seen as a distant but key royal ancestor of the valley's Newar people, Gunakamadeva, in response to a dream, followed the command of the goddess Mahālakṣmī to establish the city at the junction of the Bāgmati and Vishnumati Rivers in the shape of her *kharga* sword. As another common element of this narrative bundle of king, city, goddess, and festival, the *NBhV* says that Gunakamadeva "arranged the procession of Indrajātrā accompanied by the Kumārī Group" (59).[18] Placing Kumari in the Indra festival and attributing agency to Gunakamadeva some seven centuries earlier, the *NBhV* masks the local Newar culture that underlies this festival as well as the later Shah revival of the festival, placing it in a legendary past that supports the Shah composition of this document.

The significance of this story is multifaceted. The city that Gunakamadeva founds is often said to be in the shape of the sword of Mahalakṣmī—or Durgā, Kālī, or Taleju—at whose points are placed the shrines of the eight Mātṛkā (Mother Goddesses) and at whose center is the stone-god Kāntīśvar, the god from whom the city takes one of its many names, Kāntipur. A striking variability in the names ascribed to the goddess results from the bicultural nature of these goddesses, a now untraceable process of Sanskritization, and the imperfect overlap between the eight Hindu Mātṛkā (Mothers) and the many Newar Ajimā (Grandmothers).[19] Whatever the sequence, the eight Hindu goddesses are based on the seven mother goddesses who assist Durgā in slaying her enemies in the text of the *Devī Māhātmya*, a narrative replicated during the Dasain festival at the Taleju temple at the royal palace.

An alternative conception of the city is that it is in the shape of Bhairav's triangular sword, with the temple of Akash Bhairav (New. Ājudyaḥ) at the southern tip, Lucumaru and Asammaru Ajimā in the east, and Hyātamaru and Kulamyamaru Ajimā in the west (Juju 2003: 22). This focus on Akash Bhairav challenges Gunakamadeva's story in a number of ways, most importantly by connecting to one of the most important Newar stories of the founding of the Indra festival. This story refers to Mahalakṣmī's appearance but replaces it with that of the tribal king Yalambar who appears not to a king but to a local Jyāpu farmer, who similarly establishes the city's urban core at Bhairav's temple after a tribal king's assassination by Krishna. Amid this local narrativizing, citizens of Kathmandu walk the *upaku* in remembrance of their ancestors in a rite that (though mentioned in the *Gorkhāpatra* news articles) has no textual reference.

The narrative material that is a part of Gunakamadeva's dream—Indra's presence, royal agency, goddess worship, and the urban setting of Kathmandu—extends beyond the text's clearly mythological material to its culminating moment: the historical events surrounding Prithvi Narayan Shah's 1768 invasion of Kathmandu. Marking the conclusion to the text's narrative section (chapter 5), this story tells of Prithvi Narayan Shah's victory over Jaya Prakash Malla, the Newar king of Kathmandu, during that year's Indra festival, and as such serves as the origin story of the Shah dynasty in Kathmandu and one of the most famous stories about Nepal's Indra festival. This story seems to first appear in the *NBhV*, although with the composition of a number of *vaṃśāvalī* around the same time and a strict sequence of such texts nearly impossible to determine, it should suffice to say that the connection of the invasion with the Indra festival could not have appeared much before the early nineteenth century. The festival's narrative framing of the invasion heightens the tension inherent in the Shah invasion, and its attending ritual, politics, and rivalry—themes that have always served as the festival's engine—provide the story with the "credibility and authority" that Bruce Lincoln asserts is required for a "myth" (2014: 24).

Reinforcing the *NBhV*'s mythological dimension of this event, the Indra festival appears not to represent such a sigificant narrative in other *vaṃśāvalī*. In his analysis of many texts of this genre, Hasrat refers to the Shah invasion many times but only once mentions—from the *Gorkha Vaṃśāvalī*—its setting in that year's Indra festival (1970: 164). Other accounts of the Kumari also differ significantly from that of the *NBhV*; though Hasrat asserts from these texts that Jaya Prakash Malla fortified the central role of the Kumari during the final years of his reign, he places her annual festival and the blessing she provides to the king in the "annual *yātrā* of Hāthikhāl of Kāṅgeśvarī"—a local festival of the Newar goddess Kaṅgā Ajimā whose shrine sits on Kathmandu's western edge—rather than the Indra festival (1970: 90–91).

The *NBhV*, however, ensures the centrality of the goddess's power by emplotting Prithvi Narayan Shah into a millennium of Nepalese kings through his veneration of Kumari and—and within—his grand military entrance during the Indra festival of 1768. Before returning to his complex story, however, we attend to Kumari's central presence in the contemporary Indra festival, assessing its role in Nepalese religion and its literary and religious effect on the historicity of the Shah military invasion of Kathmandu in 1768.

The Royal Kumari in the Indra Festival

Goddesses are omnipresent in the contemporary Indra festival, their *śakti* power frequently juxtaposed to the power of the equally dangerous Bhairav. Icons of both are set up throughout the city during the festival: in a *pati* resting place in the heart of Darbar Square, icons of Svachhandra Bhairav and Vishvarūp Mahālaxmī are placed together, protected around the clock by two armed guards, while an icon of Chandesvarī Mahālakṣmī Bhagavatī is set up in an adjacent space, now a Tibetan Buddhist *thangka* shop, with a small mask of Bhairav on the floor next to her.[20] More dynamically, masked dance troupes (New. *pyākha*) from different parts of the valley repeatedly display the power of the goddess, recalling the central *mahiṣāsura-mardinī* story of the *Devī Māhātmya*: when the gods, Bhairav included, are unable to vanquish the demonic Daitya, the virginal and powerful Kumari becomes the agent of his ultimate defeat (see figure 4.1).[21] These appearances of the goddess make public the power of protective deities, with devotees

Figure 4.1. Three members of Devi Pyakha (Nep. Devi Nach, the goddess dance troupe), dance on a stage at the southern neighborhood of Nhu Ghah (Nep. Jaisi Deval) during Kumari's first chariot procession. Photo by author.

responding to them in all sorts of ways: from the simple devotional act of touching the icon or mask and then touching their own head and heart; to simple offerings of lights, coins, and fruit; to more elaborate and organized blood offerings of chickens, goats, and buffalo that such powerful deities require; to attaining a more direct relationship with the deity in different degrees of trance and possession.

Though painted and sacralized masks depicting the gods represent the most regular forms of venerated deities, the royal and living goddess Kumari is one of the most visible, recognized, and marketable images of the Indra festival.[22] Typical for religion in the Kathmandu Valley, she has different identites vis-à-vis diverse communities. She is the incarnation of the Buddhist Vajradevī or the tantric Guhyeśvarī; of the Hindu goddess Durgā; and of Taleju, the originally Newar tutelary goddess of the Malla dynasty.[23] There are approximately eleven different Kumaris throughout the cities of the Kathmandu Valley, most of whom make their primary appearance during the subsequent autumnal festival of Dasain (Skt. Durgā Pūjā). The Raj Kumari of Kathmandu, however, makes her grand appearance during Indrajātrā, about three weeks earlier, in a series of chariot processions with her brothers Bhairav and Ganesh, occuring on the third, fourth, and eighth (and final) days of the festival (Bhādra śukla 14 and 15 and Asoj kṛṣna 4).[24] In the week leading up to these jatras, their three large wooden chariots are displayed in the Basantapur area immediately south of the palace, in the open space near Kumari's House (New. *Kumārī Chen;* Nep. *Kumārī Ghar*) where the Rāj Kumari lives during her several-year term (see figure 4.2).[25] Kumari's relationship to Nepal's king—supported largely through the chronological and geographic proximity of the Indra festival—is "manifested in the very architectural logic" of the royal square and, by extension, the capital city itself (Mocko 2016: 127).

Figure 4.2. The three chariots of Kumari, Ganesh, and Bhairav in the Basantapur neighborhood immediately outside the palace. Photo by author.

Her chariot processions represent something of a microcosm of the Indra festival. Preceded by Ganesh and Bhairav in their wooden chariots, each of which carries some twenty of their fellow Śākya caste members, Kumari is accompanied on the ground by the festival's complete cast of characters: Indra's elephant, Pulukisi; the quasi-demonic Lakhe; the masked dance troupe of Sava Bhaku; the city's five Buddhist Bajrāchārya priests (the *pañcha buddha*); numerous Newar musical bands from all over the city; and a military band playing the national anthem.[26] The chariots, traveling approximately fifteen minutes apart from each other, stop at the same locations where they will receive items of puja from the general public and will return flowers (and sometimes local alcohol). They also stop at important temples and monasteries where they exchange puja items and allow prominent deities, religious officials, and local community members to come into contact with each other and exchange *darshan*. These chariot processions also demarcate the three regions of the city—lower, upper, and center—a geographical scheme in all Newar cities.[27]

Kumari's first chariot procession, that to the lower part of town, is celebrated on the afternoon of Bhādra 14, the day the *NBhV* gives for the Gorkha invasion. The festival's high ritual moment and now a valley-wide holiday, this event is referred to on contemporary Nepali calendars as "Indrajātrā." On this day, Durbar Square fills up by 2 p.m., as Nepalis from outside of the city and valley arrive nearly three hours before the procession begins, and men, women, press, and tourists are assigned to stand and watch from the steps of four temples. Reprising his role from the classical *rājyābhiṣeka* coronation, the head of state—formerly the king, now the prime minister or president—is attended by numerous foreign dignitaries and "distribut[es] a large quantity of coins . . . symbolic, of course, of the prosperity meant to flow from the newly established king" (Inden 1978: 76–77).

As is the case for all three of her processions, the Devi Pyakha dance troupe dances at a nearby stage for the duration, emphasizing the conflict between its constituent parties. Bhairav's dancer fights with the demonic Daitya as Bhairav's chariot approaches, and Kumari's dancer takes center stage when Kumari's chariot approaches. While the chariots are out of view in another neighborhood, individual deities will dance, as will the group of three *bhūt-pret*. As the chariots exit the neighborhood, the dancers perform the climactic scene. Daitya rolls around on the ground for several minutes as Kumari ritually stabs him with her sword; as he gathers up his last bit of energy, he and

Kumari dance rapidly in a circle around the stage for several seconds, and Daitya, defeated, exits through an opening in the crowd, not to be seen again. His defeat is followed by several victory dances, by Kumari alone and with her *bhūt-pret* assistants. Although Daitya is soundly defeated, he is not killed, his death being performed only once every twelve years.

Kumari's first two processions neatly travel the boundaries of the lower town on the third day and the upper town on the fourth day, respectively. Her third and final procession takes a "middle" route through the Kilagal Tol neighborhood, still technically part of the upper town. Referred to as the *nānichā yāḥ* (the procession for *nānichā*), this procession's origin story admits its relatively late interpolation: Jaya Prakash Malla (eighteenth century) added it when his wife or concubine (named Nānichā) missed the upper-city procession.[28] Regardless of the veracity of this story, Kilagal Tol receives significant attention on this day. Kumari stops there for an extended period of time, and Devi Pyakha, which has danced elsewhere throughout the festival already, now dances on the stage in its home neighborhood.[29] Amid this overwhelming concentration of the divine power of the goddess, the Kumari dancer is said to take *darshan* of the living goddess, as her powerful gaze is trained on and empowers her vehicle for defeating demonic evil.

Women now play a more significant role on this day that is, as one man told me, "especially for the ladies."[30] Though referring to this procession's narrative of origin, his description is now truer than ever. Just as Patan's Rāto Macchendranāth festival has long had women pull the chariot of "the Red God" through a portion of the city, the Indra festival has recently followed suit, as women now pull Kumari's chariot the whole route of the Nanichaya. The inclusion of women on this day reflects a larger place for women in the Indra festival. Women and girls have been given the sixth day of the festival when they drink rice beer from the mask of Seto Bhairav in Darbar Square. Without the rather violent intervention of men and boys, the more reserved behavior of women and girls ensures that each gets a much longer drink from Bhairav's beer pipe. The descent of the mask of Akash Bhairav in Indra Chowk early in the morning on the second festival day now has the women of the *guthi* present who, dressed all in red, hold lit *sukunda* lamps in a semi-circular ring around the perimeter.

The chariots return to their starting places to face the small metal mask of Bhairav installed in a small shrine directly in front of the the Maju Dega temple, unfortunately ruined in the 2015 earthquakes. Following the Nanichaya, a tired Kumari reenters her house to bestow her blessing on the king, the festival's central rite that is most explicitly concerned with the king's divine right to rule and the event around which the *NBhV* fixes its narrative of a changing Nepali polity. Reinforcing the classical coronation rite, in which "the king's pūjā of the gods installed in his city's temples . . . 'awakens' them for the benefit of himself and his kingdom" (Inden 1978: 77), the Indra festival and the literary relationship between kings and goddesses evident throughout the *NBhV*, the king enters Kumari's house and receives her blessing. After the king, the citizenry of Nepal ascends to the upper floor of her house, receiving "the prosperity meant to flow from" the living incarnation of the goddess. In replicating the blessing of the Nepali head of state for the common people, Kumari extends to them a portion of the royal power she possesses, allowing them to participate in the ongoing power of the king, of the Kumari, and now of the Federal Democratic Republic of Nepal.

The Royal Kumari in the *NBhV*

The *NBhV* makes much of Prithvi Narayan Shah's reception of Kumari's blessing, in a dual narrative that brings the text's millennium-long narrative full circle. The first of these two narratives, also the first appearance of Prithvi Narayan in the *NBhV*, is set in Bhaktapur in the 1740s. His visit to Raṇjīt Malla there introduces the theme of the "misplaced blessing" that demonstrates the power of the Kumari. The passage reads as follows.

> When Prithvi Narayan came of age he went to see Nepāl, living in Bhaktapur with Rājā Raṇjīt Malla, who, being pleased with his guest, promoted a friendship between him and his son Bīrnarsingh Malla. In this way, Prithvi Narayan lived three years in Nepāl, with the object of acquainting himself with everything regarding the country. On the Vijayā Daśamī [the final day of the October Dasain festival], when the Navadurgā troupe was being taken to Mūl Chok, Rājā Raṇjīt Malla and Prithvi Narayan Sāha stood together at the door of the Kumārī Chok. Passing by,

> Bhairav gave the prasāda to Prithvi Narayan instead of to Raṇjīt Malla. Similarly, Kumārī presented him with a blue lotus. A few days after this Pṛthvīnārāyaṇa took leave and returned to Gorkha.[31]

Connecting religious ritual with political power, this story is set on the tenth and final day of Dasain (New. Mohani, Skt. Durgā Pūjā), the goddess festival that begins a half-month after Indrajātrā. Through the many buffalo sacrifices performed during the festival, especially those that represent the buffalo demon Mahiṣāsura, "deities, king, priests, and householders all participate in Devi's battle, and in so doing partake in Devi's victorious—and necessary—power. . . . Through their active participation in Devi's battles people *become,* in a sense, Devī" (Levy and Rajopadhyaya 1990: 562–63).

Placing Prithvi Narayan in the text's set of goddess rituals, the story of his reception of Kumari's (misplaced) blessing establishes him as a worthy Hindu king and Kumari's blessing as the signal of the Shah invasion as successful, the full transfer of ritual and political power complete. Another manuscript of the *NBhV* that Bajracharya, Michaels, and Gutschow footnote reinforces this point; following her misplaced blessing, "Raṇajit Malla of [Bhaktapur] thought: 'The *prasāda* went first to the king of Gorkhā. Our reign has now come to an end' " (2015: 97, n33).

By approaching the *NBhV,* and by extension the *vaṃśāvalī* genre, as a mythic narrative rather than a historical account provides the opportunity to emplot its famous story of the Indra festival atop the burgeoning Shah political regime and within the many goddess narratives of the *NBhV,* especially that of Kumari. After its account of the Newar king Jaya Prakash Malla and his renewal of the foundations of the temple of "glorious Taleju," the replacement of the central shaft inside, and the repair of the Buddhist Svayambhu *stupa,* the text shifts back to Gorkha king Prithvi Narayan Shah, a passage that I provide in full.

> Adhering to the fortune of Kumārī's *prasāda* which Prithvi Narayan had received during his youth in Bhaktapur, glorious Paśupatinātha summoned him to Devapattana. The king, together with his troops, arrived . . . and paid *darśana* to Paśupati. A voice was heard, saying: "Victory, victory."

> During those days, Prithvi Narayan heard that the *pūjā* at glorious Paśupatinātha had been carried out with *pañcāmṛta*. He made a solemn decision and established the *pañcāmṛta guṭhī* for regular worship. This was the only religious endownment made by Prithvi Narayan Shāha to the temple of glorious Paśupatinātha.
>
> Eight months after this, on the 14th of Bhādra, N.S. 888 (A.D. 1768), Prithvi Narayan Sāha and his troops entered Kāntipur. Jayaprakāśa entered the Taleju temple, and his troops fought for an hour or two.[32] He hid a lot of explosives in the basement (of the palace) and fled to Pāṭan, taking the king of that place, Tej Narsingh, with him, and then taking refuge at Bhaktapur. The Gorkhālīs entered the palace, and went to the temple of Taleju to celebrate. Tulārām Pāṇḍe was killed by the explosion of the gunpowder, as were number of troops along with him.
>
> Because of the *prasād* he received from Kumārī, Prithvi Narayan Sāha celebrated the "festival of the full moon's day," and obtained the right to rule.[33]

Beginning by reiterating his initial reception of Kumari's blessing, this extended passage shows the number of different ways the *NBhV* authors contextualized Prithvi Narayan's military victory. In a theme that runs throughout much of the *vaṃśāvalī* genre, kings are shown to be ritual innovators. Here, Prithvi Narayan Shah creates the new ritual of the bathing of images at the important Shaiva Pashupatinath temple on the Bagmati River.[34] The text juxtaposes these rituals with descriptions of his military exploits, as he and his troops receive the blessings of Paśupati, who grants them "victory" (*jay jay*), and then more actively celebrate (*baḍhāī garnu*) in the temple of Taleju as they are attacking the city. Finally, this passage highlights the prominent role of Hindu goddesses, especially Kumari/Taleju, whose primary role is the ritual support and protection of Nepali kings.

A brief tangent on the final sentence of this passage shows this final point, and by extension the others, quite clearly. In Nepālī, this final sentence reads: *kaumārīkā prasād pāīyākā phal le pūrṇimākā jātrā garī hukum calāyā*. Wright translates it as, "Prithwīnārāyana Sāh obtained prasāda of Kumārī on the 14th of Bhādon Sudi, and by his order the Jātrā was continued" (2000: 231–22). Bajracharya, Michaels, and Gutschow translate it as: "After celebrating the festival of the full moon's day, Pṛthvīnārāyaṇa could rule (over Kāntipura) because of the *prasāda* granted to him by Kumārī" (2015: 118). By clearing up the chronology and moving the date to the full moon day (*pūrṇimā*, Bhādra 15) from Bhādra 14, which was given in the previous paragraph but not in this one, and naming the Indra festival as the "festival of the full moon's day," it provides a word-for-word translation of the festival's Newar name, *yeṃ yāḥ punhi*.[35]

More important, the latter translation attributes causation to Kumari's blessing—since she blessed Prithvi Narayan, now he can rule Nepal—whereas the former attributes no such result to it. The Nepālī clearly asserts this causation: *phal le* means "from the fruits" of Kumari's blessing, with a wording that again echoes the story of Gunakamadeva, who "had immensely honoured the goddess Kumārī by establishing her and by arranging her procession so that *as a consequence* [*phal le*] of his devotion to Kumārī [*kumārīkā pūjābhāv garyākā*], he could defeat (the kings) in four directions, obtain much wealth, perform many virtuous acts and reign [over] the kingdom happily" (Bajracharya, Michaels, and Gutschow 2015: 59–60). Such a passage brings the *NBhV* full circle, emplotting the new non-Newar Gorkha king in the many genealogies the text provides. Replicating the story of Mahīndra Malla who went to Bhaktapur, lived with Rājā Trailokya Malla, and daily worshiped Taleju who ordered him to build a temple for her in Kathmandu (Bajracharya, Michaels, and Gutschow 2015: 102; Wright 2000: 207), this story directly connects Prithvi Narayan Shah to his now-attributed ancestor, the Ṭhakurī king Gunakamadeva. Whereas the earlier king established the Indrajatra and placed Kumari's processions in that new festival, the later king fulfilled his destiny, as it were, by achieving victory as a result of his continued veneration of Kumari, during the Indra festival, at the Taleju temple of Kathmandu.

It is unclear whether Prithvi Narayan received a second blessing from Kumari during the later Indra festival in 1768 or whether his initial reception from Bhaktapur's Vijayā Daśamī in the 1740s was deemed sufficient and is the one the authors refer to in that final sentence. Perhaps they are being purposefully ambiguous. Though certainly apochryphal, the text's double reference to this event, and the many mythic multiforms of kings who build the temples and receive the blessings of powerful goddesses in the *NBhV* unambiguously point to the sheer power of goddesses in Nepalese traditions. But the stories of Kumari's misplaced blessings did not end in the eighteenth century, lending continued credibility to these older stories, to Kumari's enduring ritual power, and to the ritual setting of the Indrajātrā when they occur. In 1955, the Kumari is said to have given the royal *tika* not to the reigning King Tribhuvan but to Crown Prince Mahendra; within eight months, Tribhuvan was dead and Mahendra was the king (Anderson 1971: 135). In 2007, when she conferred the *tika* twice—first and officially to Prime Minister Koirala, the first time such a ritual was directed toward a nonroyal head of state, and second and rather unofficially to King Gyanendra amid the gradual removal of his royal powers—the state ensured that such a dual blessing would not be repeated (Mocko 2016: 139–41) (see figure 4.3). These

Figure 4.3. Kumari in her chariot on the final day of the festival. Photo by author.

stories of the multiple or misplaced blessings of the Kumari convey a similar message about Nepali royalty: its veracity and power are ritually determined by the royal Kumari, and her powerful blessing can only properly be given once. As Mocko notes, the "bond between the king and the Kumari has thus been central to the construction and reproduction of the monarchy," a bond that is more clearly seen in these moments when her blessing is improperly, accidentally, or multiply given (2016: 130).

The 1768 Shah Invasion

The narrative of Prithvi Narayan's invasion during the 1768 Indra festival is standard, well known, and powerful. Its veracity is rarely questioned, but the dubious nature of this story lends the Indra festival its narrative power. After describing "every kind of absurd and grotesque buffoonery" that the Newars perform every evening of the festival—namely, masked dances and urban processions—Oldfield asserts this direct connection between the Shah military victory and the Indra festival. "The only part the Gorkhas take in the Indrajatra is in the erection of a triumphal flagstaff in front of the Darbar, to commemorate the anniversary of their conquest of the Valley. . . . To commemorate this important event, every year at the Indrajatra a flagstaff . . . is raised at night-time, and the salute fired the same time, to record the exact hour when the city fell into the power of the Gorkhas" (1974: 319–20). A brief look at other accounts from the same era as the *NBhV*, whose narrative ends in 1829, will problematize this otherwise clear narrative. Historical accounts of the 1768 invasion all revolve around the stunning lack of opposition that Prithvi Narayan and his troops faced. Historian Percival Landon identifies the cause of this absence of opposition to Jaya Prakash Malla. His contentedness with his power in the valley, his disregard for Prithvi Narayan's repeated attacks against and siege of the Kathmandu Valley, and his unwillingness or inability to protect the valley led Jaya Prakash to be "hated by the head men of the Valley [who] bound themselves by an oath to kill him, even at the cost of their own lives" (Landon 1976: 59–61).[36] After his victory, according to the *NBhV*, Prithvi Narayan executed five of the six Pradhan leaders of Patan, who just a few years earlier had handed over the throne of that city to Prithvi Narayan's brother, Dalmardan Shah. He then "confirmed the acts of charity performed" by the sixth, who escaped to Benaras, and "now lived and ruled quietly" (Bajracharya, Michaels, and Gutschow 2015: 118, 130).

Landon's account of the attack draws heavily on Wright's translation of the *NBhV*. Beyond the local antipathy toward Jaya Prakash Malla, the Indra festival becomes the setting that allows Prithvi Narayan to more easily conquer the city. Landon attributes the ease with which Prithvi Narayan enters the city to the "the Indra-Jatra [which] seduced from their military duties nearly all the garrison of the town. The Gurkhas entered the city almost without opposition. . . . Prithwi Narayan, once in possession of Kathmandu, ordered the orgies connected with the festival to continue" (1976: 63).[37] Landon's account, like many others, projects the relative chaos of the festival as the opportunity that Prithvi Narayan fully understood and took advantage of, while the intoxication that permeated the festival precluded any opposition and provided sufficient cover for the Shah army to march through the center of the royal square, overcoming the drunken troops mustered for the celebration.[38] Landon's concluding flourish ("ordered the orgies . . . to continue") signals his explicit dependence on the *WV* ("by his order the Jātrā was continued"), though his derogatory language ("orgies") alludes to a similar value judgment in Oldfield's 1880 *Sketches of Nepal*. Oldfield's description of the festival clearly distinguishes, as do the *Gorkhāpatra* accounts, the orthodox Hindu from the playful Newar festival, clearly preferring the former to the latter. Independent of the content of the Indra festival, the theme of betrayal becomes narrativized as part of that year's festival: the "active" betrayal by Prithvi Narayan's brahmins trickles down to a "passive" betrayal by the citizens and soldiers of Kathmandu who were sufficiently inebriated or otherwise occupied with local festivities that they were unable to defend their city: thus, not only is the Indra festival the setting for the Shah military victory, it also becomes its cause.

Prithvi Narayan's victory could hardly have been a complete surprise, however, as the Gorkhas had been acquiring territory in, launching attacks into, and overthrowing kings of the Kathmandu Valley nearly continuously for a decade—hence the credibility and authority of the narrative of Prithvi Narayan's ad hoc blessing by Kumari a decade before his invasion. The *NBhV* situates their 1768 invasion in the Indra festival and thus adds an ideological component to the militarism that supports their Hindu identity, affirming for the Indra festival what Bajracharya and Michaels say about ritual in the *NBhV* more generally, that it "celebrat[es] the unchangeable that always remains as it was from the beginning; it is therefore never simply repeated but always enacted again as before; in this way it remains the original" (2012: 95).

The absence of the setting of the Indra festival in the earliest Western account of Prithvi Narayan's invasion further helps us understand the narrative construction of this event. The Asiatic Society published Father Giuseppe de Rovato's *Account of the Kingdom of Nepal*, the brief historical account he wrote in 1801 after his four years as a Capuchin missionary in the Kathmandu Valley. Although he was in Nepal from 1767 to 1771 and thus present for the Shah victory, de Rovato's account, preceding Wright's publication by nearly sixty years, includes no reference to the Indra festival; his account is one of the political gamesmanship, treachery, and the local betrayal of Jaya Prakash Malla by his citizens and officials that led to Prithvi Narayan's ability to enter the city "without opposition" (ff. 14), a theme continued in the accounts of Landon and Oldfield, whose reference to the Indra festival must have come from the *WV*.[39]

Colonel William Kirkpatrick's 1811 *Account of the Kingdom of Nepaul* provides the inverse of de Rovato's account. Rather than Prithvi Narayan's invasion occurring without reference to the Indra festival, Kirkpatrick details the Indra festival without the invasion. His text, the account he left of his expedition of Nepal in 1793 some eighteen years earlier, is the first Western account of the Nepalese performance of the Indra festival.[40] Kirkpatrick's comprehensive study was commissioned by the British East India Company, the ruling body to the south of Nepal that had very little idea of what lay north of the trading city of Patna. His stated purpose was to "present the public with a general idea of a country and people, particularly interesting to an English reader, on account of their vicinity to the principal settlement of the British Nation in India" (Kirkpatrick 1969: xv). Given the utter failure of the previous year's more explicitly military mission by Captain Kinloch—a failure attributed mainly to the presence of an unknown and quite virulent form of malaria in the southern Tarai that he was forced to cross to get to the valley—it is easy for a reader to presume a more tactical purpose behind Kirkpatrick's visit. Divided into nine chapters, Kirkpatrick's study provides a broad gazetteer-like study of Nepal's geography, agriculture, history, peoples, and religious and domestic spaces and places, as well as a section on religious festivals, which briefly describes each of a relatively full complement of Nepalese celebrations. His complete entry on the Indrajatra runs as follows:

> Indra-jātra, takes place in Srawren (July, August); it is a holy progress from Deh-choak (one of the mountains forming the western limits of the valley) to the temple consecrated to Bhowani by the name of Bālkoomāri, and situated in Tumi; in the course of the procession, the shrines of many Deotas occur, at some of which the pilgrims stop to worship. Tumi is a town of considerable note lying between Khatmanda and Bhatgong, and at present annexed to the fief of Behadur Shah. (Kirkpatrick 1969: 195)

The highly flawed nature of Kirkpatrick's description of the Indra festival might be attributed to his brief residence in Nepal from February 13 to April 3, 1793, when he would have been unable to attend that year's autumnal festival.[41] Given that Prithvi Narayan Shah's successful invasion occurred only twenty-five years before and that Kirkpatrick's mission was supported by the East India Company, one might expect that his informants would have highlighted the significant political import of this otherwise religious festival. Instead, Kirkpatrick's presentation of the Indra festival as a purely religious festival with no political valence whatsoever strikes me as odd, given the attention that such a connection receives in later literature. I surmise that the invasion and the festival are connected only in the later literature, especially in the *NBhV*, which folds his reception of Kumari's blessing at the Indrajātrā into the story of his prior blessing during the Dasain festival some years previously. More than an opportune occasion to launch an attack, and certainly more than reinforcing the status quo, the *NBhV* avails itself of the themes and resources that the Indra festival has long provided and has the narrative turn on its account of the festival, furthering the innovative role the authors have ascribed to the festival since the *Mahābhārata*. Asserting that the Indrajatra represents a revival requires us to consider what precisely the Indra festival *is*, how it could be an archetypal festival, and how Prithvi Narayan Shah could have invaded the city during a festival that only came to exist several decades later.

Leaving virtually unstated the intercultural conflict at the heart of its story of a transfer of real power from Newar Malla to Hindu Shah dynasty, the *NBhV* attributes significant responsibility to the figure of Pratap Singh Shah, the second Shah king of Kathmandu. Widely regarded as an ecumenical figure, his peaceful disposition toward the Newars resulted in his reception of a Tantric initiation from a local Newar priest (Toffin 1999: 191) as well as his marriage to a local Newar woman (Shaha 1990: 42). Though having reigned for only a few years (1775–1778), Pratap Singh "was engaged in constructive activities [and] had renounced war to undertake a plan of rehabilitation" (Regmi 1975: 104). More than merely supporting local culture, one of the most consistent and lasting impressions that we have is of Pratap Singh credited with Sanskritizing many cultural elements, bending them toward a unified and Hindu Nepal, the long-term project of the Shah dynasty. Under his direction, for example, many local neighborhoods adopted Sanskrit names: the neighborhood of Vaṃgha—the location of the Akash Bhairav temple, of the urban processions that make up the Indra festival, and of the street-set stone of Kantipur that gives Kathmandu one of its earliest names and where Indra and the gods came to worship Bhairav—became known as "Indra Chowk."

The *NBhV* has one paragraph on Pratap Singh, and it is devoted almost entirely to his connection with the related topics of Hindu goddesses and the Indra festival.

> Prithvi Narayan's son Pratāp Singh Shah reigned three years. This king, regarding Guhyeshvarī as the lord of Nepal, made 125,000 sacrifices to her and offered wealth to the pit. He brought the linga of Nuvākoṭa to the Kathmandu palace in a procession, and assigned a *guṭhī* to organize an annual festival in which the pole is installed and then pulled down.[42] This king followed the customs of Nepal. He performed all the ceremonies in the worship of the goddess Taleju, assisted by *āchāra* priests, and died in NS 898 (CE 1778).[43]

Although the *NBhV* presents the Indra festival as long predating Pratap Singh, this single paragraph provides a thematic continuity with the tenth-century King Gunakamadeva, as the Shah dynasty is made to maintain its focus on goddess devotion and the Indra festival, while as Prithvi Narayan Shāh did with the *pañcāmṛta* ritual at Pashupati, establishing a local *guthi* to manage the ritual. In a point that cannot be overstated, the Shah revival of this Hindu festival culminates in the nineteenth-century figure of Pratap Singh, who introduced the raising of Indra's pole into a festival classically known precisely for this singular event.[44] The centrality of Indra's pole recalls the festival's consistent attention to urban geography, especially to those places where the gods regularly came, as well as its centrality to the classical festival. A clear innovation that plays on the archaism of the classical festival, Pratap Singh's transformation reorients the Indra festival around the central *darbar* of Kathmandu and thus around the Shah king and his veneration of the goddess Kumari, the human manifestation of Taleju.

Regardless of the historicity of Kumari's eighteenth-century blessing stories, or even of the setting of the 1768 Indrajatra for the Shah victory, the use of the Kumari narrative in the *NBhV* represents part of a larger strategy that supported a Hinduizing and Sanskritizing cultural campaign that tried to construct a single Nepali nation at the expense of the local languages and cultures. All the while, this campaign drew on the extant cultural cache of the resident Buddhist Newars—"their long-established temples, endowments, and customs," as Gellner notes—with the Indra festival serving as the cultural background for the smooth dynastic transition that these powerful stories attempt to effect (1999: 7, 8).

It cannot be overstated that the *NBhV*'s account of Prithvi Narayan's invasion focuses almost solely on Kumari while completely ignoring Indra's pole, a near-impossibility for any contemporary person—local or tourist, Hindu or Newar, young or old—who pays any attention to the festival. That the pole is virtually ignored by this earliest generation of authors on Nepal—de Rovato, Kirkpatrick, and the *NBhV*—lends more credence to the idea that the rites surrounding Indra's pole are a revival of the Sanskritic Indra festival tradition. Set only during the relatively recent reign of Pratap Singh since the late eighteenth century (and only included in texts written several decades after that), this revival was not yet deemed significant enough for inclusion into their texts or, what is more likely, had not yet occurred. While Michaels et al. support the typically Nepali position that the culture of Nepal is both Hindu and Buddhist—three of the five manuscripts they base their translation on are Buddhist (Bajracharya, Michaels, and Gutschow 2015: xiv–xix)—the appropriation of the Indra festival belies the text's interests: the presence of the royal Kumari and other goddesses whose connections to generations of Nepali kings, despite seeming to transcend any sectarian background, are written into the *NBhV* to support the Hindu Shah dynasty. Michael Witzel's "rather obvious" point regarding the *vaṃśāvalī* in general—that "they are lists containing the *vaṃśa* of *one* particular dynasty" (1990: 19)—applies also to the *NBhV* specifically. By narrativizing the Indra festival as the founding event of their rule in the Kathmandu Valley, the authors of the *NBhV* assert the explicitly Hindu identity of the Shah dynasty and argue for the ancient Hindu identity of Nepal, whose kings venerated the Kumari and celebrated the same ancient festival of Indra.

This argument for the festival's revival, and its emphasis on its continuity with the Hindu goddess tradition, is reinforced in the next chapter with an analysis of a second textualization of the Indra festival from the same period as the *NBhV*. Like the *NBhV*, Śaktivallabh's *Kathanam* reinforces the festival's focus on the Indra pole, its associations with the Newar goddess Taleju, and the processions that convey her human representative, the Kumari, throughout the city. The authors of these texts undermine the festival's Newar heritage, however, to the best of their ability, just as the passages in *Gorkhāpatra* did, and they do this most effectively through their focus on Pratap Singh's revived installation of Indra's pole. But their renaming of the festival is equally effective; by shifting from the Newar *yeṃ yāḥ* (*punhi*) ("the [full-moon] festival of Kathmandu") to the Sanskritic Indrajātrā, the Shah monarchy eliminated any mention of the Newars and the specific locality where the festival occurs, arguing instead for the unbroken Nepali and Hindu history of a single pole-raising festival. In Śaktivallabh's text, whose production is also inextricably linked to the reign of these early Shah kings, the application of the Indra festival serves as a key strategy for Sanskritizing the Newar culture of the Kathmandu Valley and thus establishing Hindu rule. Despite the author's laser-like focus on the newly instituted and freshly installed Indra pole, whose revival he was at least partially responsible for, he found such strict boundaries very difficult to maintain.

Chapter Five

The Construction of the Indra Festival in Nineteenth-Century Kathmandu

Performing similar Hinduizing and Sanskritizing work as the *Nepālikabhūpa Vaṃśāvalī* (*NBhV*), Śaktivallabh Arjyāl's nineteenth-century *Indradhvajotsava Kathanam* revives and textualizes the Indra festival for the Nepali Shah dynasty at the expense the multicultural ambiguity in which it had previously been celebrated.

Śaktivallabh Arjyāl (1724–1806; VS 1781–1863) served as the *rāj purohit* (royal priest) for the first four Shah kings of united Nepal between the late eighteenth and early nineteenth centuries. His origins have been debated, as Hara Prasad Sastri refers to Śaktivallabh as "a Bengali Paṇḍita, settled in Nepal" (1915: 191). This brief note appears to consider him one of the cultural resources of Tirhut—Mithila, Bengal, Bihar, and Benaras—on which the previous Newar Malla dynasty had depended for their royal and biological descent and whose Brahmans had supplied the Kathmandu Valley with its Brahminical agents of Hindu authority. Sastri might also be placing him in the Mishra family of Varanasi that were the hereditary Hindu gurus of the Shahs in seventeenth-century Gorkha. Although these gurus operated at the same time as the Arjyal clan, they were never admitted to full commensality as were the Arjyal *purohits* (Whelpton 1991: 25).[1]

Most accounts of Śaktivallabh provide a more local accounting of his origins. Nepali historian Baburam Acharya writes of how, in the absence of Sanskrit scholars from the mid-eighteenth-century Shah home of Gorkha, scholars from Kaski, a region just to the west of

Gorkha that Prithvi Narayan Shah subdued via negotiation, bribery, and numerous military campaigns from 1752 to 1766, accompanied the king to Kathmandu (1975b: 145).[2] In a process that Acharya implicates in the cultural expansion that accompanied Prithvi Narayan's territorial expansion, these scholars from Kaski taught and wrote in Sanskrit and the nascent Nepali, the latter soon to be supported as Nepal's national language.

Śaktivallabh has acquired a nearly mythical status in the centuries since his death. Rāmjīprasād Aryāl locates the family name Arjyāl amid a lengthy series of genealogies he traces back to the Gupta period in India. He associates the name with King Narasiṃha, whose mother Brāhmāṇī lived in the Nepali village of Arjī (or Arjayī); with the beginning of the reign of her son there, he writes, the Ārjyāl family began (*thar śurū bhaecha*) (Aryāl 1990: 7).[3] In the fourth generation after Narasiṃha, Nārāyandās Arjyāl assisted in establishing Dravya Shah's rule in 1559 (VS 1616), making him the first Shah king of Gorkha; from this time the Arjyal clan entered the service of the Shah royal family.[4] The Arjyal family held the position of *rajpurohit* until the Kot massacre in 1846 quickly shifted the balance of political power from the Shah kings to the Rana prime ministers. The violent takeover assisted by members of the Pāṇḍe family, Jang Bahadur Rana assigned to the Pande family the role of *baḍāgurujyu* (chief guru) replacing the Arjyal clan, whose members retained the post of *khajanchi* (state treasurer) (Whelpton 1991: 201). Aryāl's concluding encomium communicates Śaktivallabh's status not only as a national poet but as the progenitor of a new era in Nepali culture.

> From the aforementioned rites and ceremonies, Śaktivallabh Arjyāl's humanity clearly shines through. Thus, he is viewed as Prithvi Narayan's faithful ritualist [*kāryakartā*], rājpurohit, palace paṇḍit, and the most famous Nepali poet and prose author of the period. Thus, being well-versed in cultural knowledge, possessing the pure power of a poet, and supporting the use of Nepali language—referred to as the language of the nation [*deśbhāṣā*]—he came with Prithvi Narayan Shah from Gorkha to Kathmandu, after which he was installed in the royal palace and became a wise councillor in the good graces of the king. (Aryāl 1990: 161)

More than just a poet, as Aryāl makes explicit in this passage, Śaktivallabh was instrumental in the construction of a newly unified Nepal for the Shah dynasty. The revival of the Indra festival became a key component of this project.

Śaktivallabh arrived in Kathmandu with Prithvi Narayan in 1768, but the next king, Pratāp Singh, was responsible for promoting him. Along with Bamsaraj Pande and Brajanath Paudel, Śaktivallabh was one of the brahmins who performed Pratāp Singh's coronation ceremony in 1775, after which he was appointed as *kazi* (minister), with all three serving under Svarupsimha, who was appointed *mulkazi* (chief minister) (Acharya 1978: 87; Regmi 1975: 273).[5] Listed with a number of honorific titles in the documents in which he appears—Raj Purohit, Pandit, Joshi, and others—it was under the third Shah king, Rana Bahadur, and for the extensive service that he had rendered these first Shah kings, that he received his title, "Bhaṭṭāchārya" (Aryāl 1990: 159). The ascription of this title allows us to place his *Indradhvajotsava Kathanam,* the text in which he uses this new title, during the reign of Rana Bahadur, thus between 1777, the year of Ran Bahadur's ascension to the throne, and 1806, the year of Śaktivallabh's death.

The composition of this text, whose content will be analyzed here, must be situated in the context of his larger body of work. Śaktivallabh's intellectual work follows a more explicitly military role in Prithvi Narayan's hill-based government; his ascension to the role of *purohit* reflects his transition, and more generally that of the Shah dynasty, from military conquerers to settled royal court (Regmi 1992: 337). Among his rendering of classical Sanskrit works and composition of new Nepali *nāṭya,* Śaktivallabh's most well-known work is the socio-historical *Jayaratnākaranāṭaka* (*JRN*), composed in 1792 (VS 1849) after Rana Bahadur Shah's ongoing military campaigns in western Nepal (1786–1791).[6] Regmi writes that the "*Jayaratnākaranāṭaka,* a drama in Sanskrit, written by a Court Poet of the time has some events relating to Palpa depicted as part of the main theme of royal conquest of the Nepalese ruler" (1975: 335, n2).[7] As a text explicitly concerned with matters of *rājnīti* and politics, Paudel, Vajracarya, and Nepal (2002) consider the *JRN* a Nepali application of the political principles that Kauṭilya laid down in his classical Sanskrit treatise, the *Arthaśāstra.*[8] Placing this text in a broader historical context of South Asian imperial expansion—for example, the Shah military campaigns to western and eastern Nepal, the Anglo-Nepali War of 1814–1816, and the "Indian Mutiny" of 1857—these authors consider how the *JRN* provides one means of evaluating the proper relationships between a dominant power (*vijigīṣu*) and its dependent kings (*daṇḍopanata*), a natural by-product of the imperial expansion of the time.

Influenced by more than just the military excursions of the Shah dynasty, Śaktivallabh used more expressly religious language in his writings. In an essay on the Nepalese *Svayambhū Purāṇa*, Bernhard Kölver cites the *JRN* in the emergence of what he calls a South Asian "World Picture"; he argues here that "the very diversity of topics" in Hindu and Buddhist literature "could be wedded to the directional pattern" that geographically structures Nepali cities, pilgrimage patterns, and especially the Buddhist Svayambhu *stupa* on the western rim of the Kathmandu Valley and the Sanskrit Purāṇa dedicated to it. In analyzing the chronology laid out in the *Svayambhū Purāṇa*, Kölver fixes on Śaktivallabh's reference to the four *yuga*s, a distinctly Hindu method of reckoning cosmic time, or "time as such":

> Assigning distinct properties to Yugas in itself is not all that rare, and of course preconditioned by their very names. About 200 years ago, a Nepalese poet [Śaktivallabh] e.g. wrote, "In Kṛtayuga, asceticism/mortification stands highest; in Tretā, knowledge; in Dvāpara, they say it is sacrifice; in Kaliyuga, there is only (giving) gifts." But for the [Svayambhū] Purāṇa, the point of reference is not really the Age of the World, but the holy site to be endowed with beneficial effects. If these tally with each other, so much the better: the Age of Truth (*satyayuga*) and Right (*dharma-*) are of course a most satisfactory conjunction. (Kölver 1985: 146)

Although Śaktivallabh's literary use of the *yuga* system provides a "point of reference" to "the Age of the World," Kölver quickly asserts that despite "the most unquestionable authority" that underlies the Purāṇa, such a method of reckoning time may be implicated in a "veritable clash of concepts" and that the Purāṇa reflects "a juncture of systems which in origin and intention have no connection with each other" (146). Like the *JRN*, Śaktivallabh's *Kathanam* reflects this disconnected juncture of systems: unlike his more strictly literary work written in the proto-national language of Nepali, the *Indradhvajotsava Kathanam* is written in a classical Sanskrit that is meant to undergird a politically unified Nepal, grounding it in the *rājnīti* policies of Hindu India. Written in and about Nepal, the *Kathanam* continues the clash of concepts introduced in the *JRN* by advocating the Sanskritic at the expense of the local, Buddhist, and Newar.

The *Indradhvajotsava Kathanam*

Produced at the turn of the nineteenth century, Śaktivallabh's *Indradhvajotsava Kathanam* ("the textualization of the Indra festival") is an edited work that collects and comments on the portions of a number of classical Sanskrit texts that prescribe the rites of the Indra festival. Though different in style and genre from the narrative of the *Nepālikabhūpa Vaṃśāvalī*, the purpose of the *Kathanam* is quite similar: to establish the Indra festival as a classical Hindu rather than local Newar festival that, based on the *rājnīti* texts of medieval India, supports the larger imperial project of the Shah dynasty.[9] Whereas the *NBhV* narrativizes a historical connection between the Indra festival, powerful goddesses, and the Shah dynasty, Śaktivallabh's text prescribes the intricate details of the festival, most of its attention devoted to the festival's most public object, Indra's pole—an object only introduced in the latter sections of the *NBhV*—and its installation in the center of the city. The *Kathanam* thus represents the textual foundation on which the revival of the contemporary Indra festival was based.

Despite their patronage of Hindu arts, culture, and literature, there is no evidence that Shah kings had ever celebrated the Indra festival in Gorkha, their hometown some seventy miles northwest of Kathmandu.[10] Rather, it was only with, and some time after, their successful invasion of Kathmandu in 1768 that they shifted their attention to the Indra festival as a performative strategy for shoring up their political rule. Their possession of a Hindu Sanskritic tradition and a priestly and scholarly apparatus steeped in the texts and traditions of *rājnīti* introduced Shah kings, gurus, and scribes to the techniques of reproducing a Hindu kingdom. The several-century gap in the celebration of the archaic Indra festival and the sudden Shah attention to it points to the Shah revival and strategic reconstruction of the festival rather than any sort of linear continuity. Thus, the Indra festival became a means of integrating their dynasty into a culturally Newar milieu and, more important, establishing and enforcing national unity via imperial control over local populations through its translation of a local celebration into a Hindu royal installation rite communicated via a Sanskrit-language medium.

Śaktivallabh's *Kathanam* signals its late eighteenth- or early nineteenth-century post-Malla composition with its absence of Nepali or Newar vocabulary and its writing in nonhybrid Sanskrit. Sastri describes the particulars of the *Kathanam* with the following: "III. 320. A. *Indradhvajotsava Kathanam* by *Śakti Vallabha Bhaṭṭācārya*. 9 x 5 inches. Folia, 17. Lines, 12 on a page. Ślokas 400. Date? Character, Nagari. Appearance, tolerable. Verse. Correct" (Sastri 1915: 191). Somewhat more helpful is his ensuing comment: "This is the 9th chapter of a work entitled Dāna Pravāsa. . . . The topics treated in this chapter are . . ." (Sastri 1915: 191).[11] The title of the text given in its own colophon is *Dāna Prakāśa,* not "Dāna Pravāsa" as Sastri states, a title that hints at its borrowing from (or purported incorporation into) Mitramiśra's seventeenth-century Sanskrit-language dharmaśāstric text, the *Vīramitrodaya*.[12] Mitramiśra's text, composed in the first half of the seventeenth century, has ten parts, the title of each ending with the word *prakāśa*. The *Dānaprakāśa* section remains unpublished, however, existing only in manuscript form at Deccan College in Pune. Regarding its content, Kane simply states: "It is an extensive work and contains the usual topics about gifts" (1930–1962: 1.2: 942–45). Regardless, Aryāl refers to Śaktivallabh's text as the *Indradhvajotsava Dānaprakāśa* (1990: 159), Śeṣarāja Śarmā Regmī refers to it as the "*Dānaprakāśa* (including a section on the tradition of the Indra festival)" (1992: 337), and the manuscript concludes with the following statement of its title and authorship: "Vidyālankṛta Śaktivallabha, with high poetic praise, has composed the Dānaprakāśa containing the instructions for the raising of the dear *ketu* for the Śakrapūjā. Thus, Śrī Śaktivallabha Bhaṭṭāchārya has composed in this Dānaprakāśa the telling of the Indradhvajotsava on the 12th of the bright half of Bhadra, entitled *navamaprakāśa*."

However, it seems that this text is mislabeled, miscategorized, or otherwise misconstrued, as it is the *Rājanītiprakāśa* portion of Mitramisra's text, not the unpublished *Dānaprakāśa,* that contains a long section on the Indra festival (Kane 1930–1962: 1.2: 943). Regardless, it seems that the *Vīramitrodaya* and its textualization of the Indra festival were readily available to Nepali royalty: Kane (1.2: 947) locates the source of Mitramiśra's work in Tirhut, whose brahmins were patronized by the Malla kings of the seventeenth century. Moreover, Hara Prasad Sastri, though only specifying the *Vyavahāra Kāṇḍa* section (16), notes the presence of an 1824 (VS 1876) copy of the *Vīramitrodaya* in Kathmandu's Darbar Library, thus affirming its presence in Nepal and allowing for Śaktivallabh's access to it (1905: 251–53).[13] Whereas Mitramiśra's *Rājanītiprakāśa,* also a compilation of previous sources, draws largely on the *Viṣṇudharmottara Purāṇa* and the *Devī Purāṇa,* Śaktivallabh's draws from a wider range of classical sources interspersed with the redactor's own and relatively brief commentary. In addition to these two *rājnīti* and *śākta* texts, and in order of decreasing number of citations, Śaktivallabh cites the *Bṛhat Saṃhitā* (BS), *Kālikā Purāṇa, Rājamarttaṇḍa, Brahmā Purāṇa,* and *Bhaviṣya Purāṇa.* Like the *Rājanītiprakāśa,* and due to its diligent citation of classical Sanskrit texts, the *Kathanam* eschews any reference to local and nonclassical rites, using a ritual vocabulary that allowed the Shah authors to resituate the festival in and reconnect it to its classical Indian heritage. In this callback to the Sanskritic festival, we see Śaktivallabh's innovation: reusing classical texts to resurrect a moribund and archaic festival that came to overlap with (and at least initially overshadow) the local Newar festival of the *yeṃ yāḥ punhi.*

Largely compiled from classical Indian Sanskrit sources, Śaktivallabh's seventeen-folio *Kathanam,* with its courtly aesthetic, might be more interesting for the fact of its existence in nineteenth-century Nepal rather than for its specific content, though several elements stand out as relevant to its reclamation project. Following an invocation to Ganesh, the *Kathanam* opens with a description of Indra residing in his garden in the shade of the *kalpa* tree, the wish-granting tree that serves as a multiform of two other trees, more relevant to the festival: the parijata tree, which is part of the festival's core narrative in Kathmandu, and the tree cut down to produce Indra's festival pole, with which Śaktivallabh's text is primarily concerned. A *phalaśruti* introduces the fact—though not a proper list—of the positive results of celebrating the Indra festival.[14] In the next fourteen (of seventeen) folios, Śaktivallabh details the royal benefits of performing Indra's annual festival, sequencing selections from classical Sanskrit texts according to the order in which the discrete rites dedicated to Indra's festival pole are performed: the journey to the forest to cut down the tree and its entrance into the city, installation, and final *visarjana*.

As I handled these multiple rites dedicated to the pole in chapters 2 and 3, here I detail two portions of the *Kathanam* that prove relevant to the early nineteenth-century Nepalese revival of the Indra festival. First I continue the theme from the previous chapter, the *NBhV* focus on goddesses, especially Kumari. The second section will detail the final few folios of the *Kathanam* that elide the text's earlier dependence on Sanskrit texts; its attention to the worship of an icon of Indra admits, I argue, to its knowledge of and response to similar local Newar rites. The text's attention to Kumari and icons of Indra appear to be the only acknowledgments of the culture of the author's local surroundings—and an only implicit one at that—as he reconstructs the archaic Indra festival for a new monarchy.

Śaktivallabh and the Multiple Kumari

Throughout the *Kathanam*, Śaktivallabh provides a number of brief commentaries on passages culled from Sanskrit sources.[15] Most of his commentarial energies, however, are spent on constructing the Indra mandala, the festival's central place that includes the raised pole and a number of decorations and subsidiary poles. Heavily focused on goddess worship as Nepalese kings have long been, he concludes this section with a goddess-focused statement from the *Kālikā Purāṇa* on the concept of *śrī* (feminine glory) in the king's performance of the festival: "He repairs to the temple of Indra [*surapati-gṛhagāmī*] and performs *pūjā* to Indra's pole [*śakraketoḥ*] every autumn in order to increase his *śrī*" (*KP* 87.48).[16] In leading up to this conclusion, Śaktivallabh cites the *BS* (43.40)[17] and the *Kālikā Purāṇa* (KP, 87.19b–20), detailing the worship of the multiple *kumārī* and *mātrikā*.

The *śakra-kumārī*, "Indra's girls," represent five or seven subsidiary poles, the function of whose wooden form remained somewhat mysterious to generations of commentators.[18] In a relatively bold hermeneutical move that reveals the difficulty of translating such a festival across cultural boundaries, Śaktivallabh asserts:

> Five *kumārī* of Indra are to be made for the greatest of kings.
> All of these tall *śakra-mātṛkā* are to be made of wood from

> the *sāla* tree. The *śakra-kumārikā* are to be constructed to measure as high as the base of the pole. Manu says that the twice-born makes these *kumārī* for the glorification [*śobha-artham*] of the Indradhvaja. . . . Thus, these five *śakra-kumārī* that are discussed in the *Kālikā Purāṇa*—Nandā, Upanandā, etc.—*are* the *aṣṭamātṛkā*.[19]

Incorporating the traditional Indian odd number of five or seven virginal goddesses into the more typically Nepalese enumeration of eight powerful and tantric mother goddesses reflects dominant *śākta* influences in Nepalese religion. Each Mother Goddess resides on the borders of the cities of the valley in the eight cardinal and intermediate directions. Their geographic location and protective function replicate those of the *aṣṭadigpāla,* the eight protectors of the directions, seen as far back as the late Vedic period. The Eight Mothers also represent a Nepalese form of the Indian Seven Mothers, who assist Durgā in defeating demonic evil in the *Devī Māhātmyā* and who are worshipped as a collective unit every autumn during the Dasain festival. Moreover, they represent a Sanskritized form of the Newar Ajimā, or grandmother goddesses, who, in an unnumbered and theoretically innumerable set, protect Bhairav-Āju who lives at the center of Kathmandu. Many of their shrines are visited during the *upāku* procession on the first evening of the Indra festival, as residents of Kathmandu remember their recently deceased family members. Even the mathematical confusion inherent in Śaktivallabh's statement—that seven equals eight—reflects larger patterns in goddess worship. In the city of Bhaktapur, for example, the shrine of Mother Goddess Tripurasundarī is at the center of the city, rather than on the periphery like the others, as she becomes the ninth of the city's Eight Mothers.

This statement from the *Kathanam* equating seven *kumārī* with eight *mātṛkā* signals the attention that Śaktivallabh felt obligated to give to this issue and provides a vehicle for incorporating the Indra festival into the ritual category of *śākta pūjā*.[20] Śaktivallabh refers here to the *KP*, as he frequently does, a *śākta* text that allows him to juxtapose Indra's festival to those of other goddesses that this text handles in much more detail (e.g., Tripurā, Kāmeśvarī, and Durgā). More specifically, the *KP* frequently incorporates the worship of groups of eight goddesses, different from the *saptamātṛkā* and the predominantly male *aṣṭadigpāla* of India: "In order to obtain one's desires, one should worship the [following eight] *yogini*—those who grant wishes—in their proper order: Guptakāmā, Śrīkāmā, Vindhyavāsinī, Koteśvarī, Vanasthā, Padacaṇḍikā, Dīrgheśvarī, and Bhuvaneśī [Bhuvaneśvarī]" (*KP* 64.77–79). Whereas the astronomical *Bṛhat Saṃhitā* becomes Śaktivallabh's key text for prescribing the rites of the Indra festival, the *KP* provides a classical foundation for foregrounding the centrality of goddess worship in Nepal's festival. This preponderance of goddess worship in the Indra festival is reciprocated as well. When the *KP* directs the king to worship Durgā on Śrī Pañchamī, it also directs him to worship Indra with the best offerings. Furthermore, the text asserts that the Lakṣmī-tantra is also Indra's and that the method of doing puja to Lakṣmī is applicable to Indra as well (88.21–22), in an assocation that speaks to a more general pattern of South Asian worship that arranges a group of women either devotionally around a single man (e.g., Kṛṣṇa and the *gopī*s or Bhairav and the *yoginī*s) or protectively bracketed by a pair of men (e.g., Śiva or Bhairava and Ganesh or Skanda flanking the *mātṛkā*).

In the contemporary festival, the eight short poles that surround Indra's massive pole are referred to as the *aṣṭamātṛkā*.[21] In a conflation that runs throughout this literature, the *Kathanam*'s description of the Indra puja on the festival's final day is rather unclear on the distinctions between the *kumārī* and the *mātṛkā*: "Then, there is a pūjā to the five *śakra-kumārī*. Pūjā should be offered at each of the five *daṇḍa* processually. '*AUM nandāyai namaḥ. AUM upanandāyai namaḥ. AUM jayāyai namaḥ. AUM vijayāyai namaḥ. AUM vasundharāyai namaḥ.*' Thus each of them is worshipped separately. '*AUM śakra-mātṛkābhyo namaḥ.*" The eight *mātṛkā* are worshipped collectively (ff. 17a).' "[22] From the earlier passage, we were led to believe that the five (or seven) *kumārī* were equivalent to the eight *mātṛkā*, whereas here the text glosses the word *śakra-kumārī* with *daṇḍa* (pole) but provides no such gloss of the word *mātṛkā*, thus omitting any reference to the physical description of the latter. This detailed description entails a performative distinction as well: whereas each of the named *kumārī* is worshipped separately, the group of unnamed *mātṛkā* is/are worshipped as a single unit.

Śaktivallabh follows this equation between multiple virgins and mothers with an equally simple statement that takes us deeper into the mechanics and geography of the festival. More than simply clarifying potentially confusing statements, these passages show that Arjyal's task was, again, a translation of Indian concepts into Nepalese ones.

The positing of a "single mother of Indra" in this passage reflects his understanding of the significance of the "Mothers" from the classical festival and accounts for the prominent ritual and narrative presence of Indra's mother, the Newar Ḍāgī (whose presence in the contemporary festival we encounter in this book's final chapter) further reinforces the presence of death and the veneration of the ancestors that permeates the local festival.

Among all of the classical texts that Śaktivallabh cites, his selection of these passages on the goddess most clearly cue us in to the purpose of his project. More than simply cutting and pasting from classical sources, Śaktivallabh emphasizes the veneration of the goddess and the Kumari, an authorial decision that further connects the *Kathanam* to the *NBhV*. Together, these two texts, composed in the same period and under the same royal patronage, foreground the relationship between king and Kumari. Whereas the *NBhV* focuses on narratives of the living goddess Kumari, the *Kathanam* reminds us of the mechanics, logistics, and geography of the Indra mandala that juxtaposes Indra's large pole to a set of smaller, surrounding, and supportive feminine poles and to the neighborhood poles that continue to be venerated in honor of the local ancestors. All of this goddess worship is conducted in a performative setting—the revived Indra festival—that displays and supports the Hindu king's right to rule.

Śaktivallabh's Indra Puja

The *Kathanam* is not solely concerned with goddesses. Śaktivallabh's compilation of classical sources takes up the first fourteen folios, but in the final three folios he makes a surprising move. Though written in the same scribal hand as the previous folios, this section reads something like an appendix. Absent the citations that marked the previous fourteen folios, the text changes its topic from installing the aniconic pole to the worship of relatively rare icons of Indra. Along with his attention to and translations of the wooden *kumārī* and *mātṛkā* that represent the only explicit reference to the culture of Kathmandu, this sudden shift in topic to icons of Indra represents his minimal awareness of the local Newar religious culture. On one hand, and based on his dependence on the *KP*, the structure and content of the *Kathanam* seems to reinforce the larger "plan of rehabilitation" that sought to combine the classical Hindu with the contemporary Newar festival. On the other hand, the *Kathanam*'s use of standard Hindu installation rituals negates extant Newar *pūjā-vidhi* texts and tries to reestablish the universal as the local.

Śaktivallabh concludes the main part of his text, the first fourteen folios, with a passage from the *KP* (87.35–37a) detailing the veneration of icons associated with Indra placed at the base of the pole. "The great pole is to be installed inside of a mandala. The images should be placed at the base of the pole. Indra is to be remembered, as well as the fully-worshipped images of Śacī [his wife] and Mātali [his charioteer]. Also depicted are his son Jayanta, the *vajra* [his weapon], and Airāvata [his elephant], as well as the *graha*s [planets], *dikpāla*s [protectors of the directions], and all the assemblies of the gods."[23] He continues by quoting verses 52–58 of the same chapter detailing the pole's *visarjan* (disposal), a section that concludes (with the passage regarding the king's increase in *śrī*) the main section of the *Kathanam*. The concluding three folios cite only one text, a mantra section from the *BS*, the remainder (and bulk) of the text constituted of Śaktivallabh's own commentary.

This final "appendix" reiterates the sequence of the festival's actions, beginning with the king's officials going to the forest and ending with the pole's *visarjanam* disposal into water. Compared with the preceding passage from the *KP*, the overall tone of this short section is rather devotional. Though detailing a series of pujas conducted in the vicinity of the Indra pole, its actions are directed elsewhere. A series of rituals to Ganesh, to the *navagraha*, to a *kalash* pot, and to "the wish-bearing four-armed Vishnu, whose face is bright like the moon" concludes with a recitation of the *Rig Veda*'s Purusha Sukta, a reminder of how kings in early medieval India, resembling both Vishnu and Indra, ritualized their identity with the Cosmic Man, the material and effective cause of the universe.[24] Such puja rituals "required the worshipper to attend to the bodily needs of deity placed in an enlivened image . . . [and were] homologous with the service rendered to an imperial ruler, a 'king of kings,' in his palace" (Inden 1978: 52). Expanding on the *KP*, and along with the installation of the *kumārī* and *mātṛkā*, an icon of Indra—made of gold, silver, brass, wood, or earth—is placed in the *sarvatobhadra maṇḍala* (or *dhvaja maṇḍapa*) and receives the enlivening *prāṇa pratiṣṭhā*, as the priest establishes Indra's *prāṇa* breath, *jīva* life, and senses, each with a recitation of the seed syllables *Aṃ—Hrīṃ—Kraṃ*.[25] After Indra is placed on a seat and worshipped with water, the text directs the priest to offer flowers, incense, light, sandalwood, and food, with the mantra "Indrāya namaḥ" (Honor to Indra!), a series of offerings immediately followed by an offering of the standard sixteen *upachāra*: "rice, flowers, garlands, handfuls of flowers, various fruits, etc. . . . betel nut, and mirror."[26]

Local Newar Indrapūjā Texts

The Indra installed at the base of the pole is not the only image the festival celebrates, however. Icons of Indra are raised in Jyāpu farmer neighborhoods throughout the city, thus complicating the iconic and performative referent in Śaktivallabh's text. Taking these icons and their pujas together, we can see how Śaktivallabh juxtaposes not just the multiple sections of his text but also the universal Sanskrit with the local Newar tradition, which he does in two relevant and interconnected ways: the puja places Śaktivallabh's *Kathanam* in a local Newar textual tradition of the veneration of Indra icons, while conflating the two very different types of Indra icon venerated during the festival.

Local Newar puja texts are used during the Indra festival for the similar purpose of installing an icon of Indra. These Newar texts differ from the *Kathanam* in many ways. They are two to three folios long rather than the *Kathanam*'s seventeen; they are composed in Newar script, though the language may be either Newar or Sanskrit (or both). When dated, their dates are given in the local Nepal Samvat rather than Vikram Samvat.[27] The most significant difference is the function of the text. Whereas the *Kathanam* served as a courtly text that, like the classical Indian sources it cited, was compiled as a marker of royal status, these local puja texts were composed so that priests could use them while guiding their performance of an Indra puja in a local residential neighborhood.

One of these texts, the *Indrapūjāvidhi* (E323–25) stands out because of its structural similarities to the *Kathanam*'s concluding Indrapūjā section, despite several telling discrepancies. Though the entire manuscript is written in Newar script (*rañjanā lipi*), the *Indrapūjāvidhi* is linguistically hybrid: folios 1, 2, and 6–9 are written in Newar and provide the officiating priest with a list of the materials required for the proper performance of the Indra puja. Folios 3–5, written in

Sanskrit and in a different hand than the materials list, make up the *vidhi* itself, the directions to the priest on its proper performance. For example, the *Indrapūjā* (E450/1) makes bilingual offerings in Newar and Sanskrit: the *naivedya* food that Indra is offered is hyphenated with the Newar *samay*, and the *yajñopavīta* brahmin thread offered to Indra is combined with the Newar *jajaṅkā*.

Following a brief invocation to Ganesh, the text provides the purpose for its composition: *atha indrapūjā vidhi likhyate* (Here are written the instructions for the Indra Pūjā). Texts of this type direct their puja to an anthropomorphic image of Indra that may be made of wood, stone, or clay, only referring to the Indra pole at the very end: the *Indrapūjā Paddhati* (E466/6) and the *Indrapūjā* (H323/25) read, "Having accepted this gift of Puraṃdara Śatakratu [Indra], along with all the gods and asuras, one should proceed to the *mahendra-dhvaja* [Indra's flag]."[28] The text's focus on the icon rather than the pole recalls Oldfield's distinction between the objects of Nepali and Newar worship and the relatively late revival of Nepal's Indra festival, hinting that the veneration of this icon precedes and operates independently of the attention the classical Sanskritic sources devote to the pole.

A puja to the nominally Hindu Indra, this text opens with a brief purification that concludes with a *guru namskāra* or *guru maṇḍala pūjā* (Locke 1980: 84). This opening, rather than the Ganesh- or Indra-centered introduction of the *Kathanam*, ensures that we read it as a Newar Buddhist as much as a Hindu ritual text. This attention to the guru (or *siddha*), the local priest responsible for the performance of this ritual, entails the inclusion of a series of tantric rites: a guru *namaskāra*, a *prāṇayāma* made with the hands, a *dhyāna-mudrā*, and a sixfold *nyāsa* of the heart and other body parts. The *Indrapūjā Paddhati* (E466–66, ff. 2) details the priest's *nyāsa*, as he applies *bīja* seed mantras to all parts of his body, thus purifying and sacralizing his body as he prepares himself for the puja:

> *Laḥ astrāya phaṭ* [three times]. *Laṃ* to the two thumbs *namaḥ*. *Liṃ* to the two fore-fingers *namaḥ*. *Lūṃ* to the two middle fingers *namaḥ*. *Laiṃ* to the two ring-finers *namaḥ*. *Lau* to the two little fingers *namaḥ*. *Lah* to the palm and back of the hand *namaḥ*. [*Nyāsa* to the] heart, etc. *Laṃ* to the heart *namaḥ*. *Liṃ* to the head *Svāhā* [three times]. *Luṃ* to the peak *Vauṣaṭ*. *Laiṃ* to the hair *Hūṃ*. *Oṃ Lau* to the third eye *Vaṣ aṭ*. *Laḥ astrāya phaṭ*.

The second part of the ritual is devoted to Indra, as the guru offers him a seat (*āsana*) and continues through an Indra *nāmastotra,* listing a dozen or so of his major epithets (e.g., *Oṃ Indra,* Maghavan, *Surāpati, Vajrahasta, Gajāsana*), similar to the list in the *Kathanam.* Upon recitation of these names, the priest recites several series of *bīja* mantras that progress up the register of Sanskrit vowels (*Om Laṃ Liṃ Luṃ Leṃ Loṃ Laṃ*). In several texts, this series of mantras concludes with a *kuthācāra,* a mantra that is not only unpronouncable (*LMLBRYUM*) but is also orthographically anomalous: written vertically from top to bottom, this mantra interrupts the several lines of text below it. Obviously, Śaktivallabh's more orthodox and Sanskritic *Kathanam* forgoes these non-Sanskritic mantras, and its *Aṃ—Hrīṃ—Kraṃ* marks the extent of its tantric content, the remainder replaced by two *Rig Veda* mantras: the *trātāraṃ indraṃ* passage (6.47.11) that recurs throughout the textual tradition and the Purusa Sukta (10.90).

Local Newar Indrapūjā Rituals

Seven neighborhoods currently raise an image of Indra; all of them, except the most public courtyard of Nasal Chowk just inside the royal palace, are traditionally those of the Jyāpu (farmer).[29] Van den Hoek (2004: 43) and Toffin (1992: 85) list four places where these images are installed: the four upper-city locations of Maru Tol, Nara Devi (New. Ngata Ajima), Kilagal Tol (New. Kilaghaḥ), and Indra Chowk (New. Waṅgha). Two additional images are raised in the lower-town neighborhoods near the monasteries of Musum Bahāl and Jyā Bahāl.[30] In each neighborhood, Jyāpu men retrieve their local image and perform a short puja to it before its installation on Bhādra 11, one day before the pole is installed in Darbar Square; this puja represents the only significant annual ritual attention the image will receive before it is returned to its closet or storeroom for the rest of the year.[31]

Due to its geographic and narrative centrality, Maru Tol becomes a ritually central point during the Indrajatra. Situated at a busy crossroads that connects the city's upper and lower halves near Kāṣṭhamaṇḍap—the thirteenth-century wooden structure after which Kathmandu gets its name—this image receives the most frequent ritual attention of all of the seven. Although van den Hoek implies that worship is offered to all seven icons, with baskets pulling offerings of money or *janai* thread up to Indra and *prasad* in the form of fruits and flowers returned, this worship now happens only at Maru Tol, with no priests or baskets present at the others (2004: 43). Immediately in front of the image at Maru Tol, many people offer clay lamps constituting a physical reminder of the presence of the ancestors, significant figures in the festival's foundational myth also at Maru Tol.

The small Brahmāpur neighborhood just outside of the much larger and central Indra Chowk neighborhood represents a slightly different situation. Brahmāpur is a brahmin Rājopādhyay neighborhood whose *kuldevatā* is represented by the icon of Akash Bhairav inside his temple at Indra Chowk, a neighborhood, temple, and icon extremely important for the Indra festival. The Bhairav temple is organized and managed by a Jyāpu *guthi* organization, but the Rajopadhyay—the outmarried women of the neighborhood return for this puja and the feast afterward—perform the puja to Indra.[32]

The Brahmāpur ritual represents a more complete version of what occurs in the other neighborhoods. The puja begins in the late morning or early afternoon as the elder and acting priest of the neighborhood conducted the service from a family-owned copy of the traditional ritual text, composed of long horizontally oriented sheets of paper, kept between hard wooden covers.[33] Walking the twenty-five meters down a narrow alleyway from the Bhairav temple, four Jyāpu men arrive in Brahmapur, two of them accompanying the puja inside the courtyard and during the concluding events outside with drums and cymbals: Indra's conveyance to Indra Chowk, his brief public display there (beneath either the Akash Bhairav temple or his installation platform), and his installation on a platform overlooking the Indra Chowk neighborhood.[34]

After the arrival of Indra directly from the Bhairav temple or, as is the case more recently, from the artists outside the neighborhood who decorate it, the Rajopadhyay conduct a puja that corresponds closely to the Newar ritual texts described already, those that influenced the composition of Śaktivallabh's *Kathanam*. The puja represents a form of a *prāṇ pratiṣṭhā* or *nyās pūjā*. In addition to the offering of standard items—rice, food and fruit, *sindūr* powder, and offerings of bills of small denominations—the puja consists of the *daśa karma vidhi* that constructs Indra as a mature human. As does Jan Bahāḥ Dyo (Skt. Rato [Red] Matsyendranath), the Buddhist deity enshrined in one of the city's most prominent monasteries nearby (Jana Bahāl), Indra goes through all ten rites of passage, becoming both man and woman, a dual gender evident in the makeup he receives before this puja, how he arrives dressed as a bride, and the red bangles attached to his wrists.[35] This acknowledgment of the divine feminine is made in the *Indrapūjā* ritual text that prescribes the worship of "Indra [as/ and his] shakti" (*indra yathā śakti pūjito*). In addition to the offerings of "water for bathing and rinsing, sandalwood powder, sindur, rice, flowers, incense, light, [and] food," the priest performed "*prāṇayāma* with the hands [and] six-fold *nyāsa* of the heart," thus bringing his physical body under the influence of, or vowing to protect, the deity at the center of the puja. At the conclusion of the puja, all of those present, including visiting outsiders and the four Jyāpu men in attendance, were invited to touch their heads to the image and receive *tika* blessing, after which one of the Jyāpu men picked up the image and carried it across the six-way intersection of Indra Chowk, where they climbed a ladder, lifted Indra to the top of the platform in a basket, and installed him (see figures 5.1 and 5.2).

Figure 5.1. An elder from the Brahmapur neighborhood brings the venerated icon of Indra to be installed high above the street facing the Akash Bhairav temple. Photo by author.

Figure 5.2. Icon of Indra raised in the southern Brahma Tol neighborhood. Photo by author.

Conclusion: A Narrative of Erasure

I return to the unique iconography of these icons of Indra in chapter 7, but we can already see how Śaktivallabh's *Kathanam* registers its opposition to the local, tantric, and Newar ritual texts. Though apparently aware of these rituals and texts, its puja to icons of the Hindu/Vedic Indra draws more on on the classical Sanskrit record, especially the *śākta* and tantric *Kālikā Purāṇa,* as Śaktivallabh incorporated Sanskritized versions of these rituals not for the benefit of the residents of Kathmandu's local Jyāpu neighborhoods but for the new Shah king of Nepal.[36]

The production of such a text recalls Sheldon Pollock's evaluation of the texts produced at the time of the "death of Sanskrit," when "not a single work escaped the confines of the palace" (2009:

413). Like the early medieval Indra festival texts it draws from—texts whose "aesthetic is profoundly historicist-political—and tied to the politics of [their] time" (403)—Śaktivallabh's *Kathanam* reconstructs the body of the Hindu king, the latest iteration of the quasi-Vedic Cosmic Man, by a recognizable puja ritual devoted to an icon of the similarly quasi-Vedic Indra.[37] Śaktivallabh facilitates this royal-divine homology, however, not through the devotional Jyāpu-Rajopadhyay attention to local images of Indra but through the text's *rājnīti* focus on the installation and presence of the ceremonial pole installed in the center of the capital city and the icon at its base.

Rather than simply asserting that Śaktivallabh's text reestablishes the classical status quo, I argue that he composed the *Kathanam* to function in the same way that those classical texts did: namely, as a literary-ritual device that signaled the inauguration of a new entity. Like the *Mahābhārata* that indicated the performance of a new form of dharma, the *Nāṭyashāstra* that inaugurated a new mode of ritualization, and the *Samarāṅgana Sūtrādhara* that constructed a new type of royal city, the *Kathanam* used, borrowed, selected, adapted, and adopted this festival for the Shah dynasty precisely because it provided a classical Hindu legitimation for their successful invasion, whether or not it occurred during the 1768 festival. It ascribes to the festival the classical Indian meanings of kingship and dominion, values pertinent to the Gorkhalis and representative of their larger project, facilitated by attention to the installation of Indra's central and triumphal flagstaff.

The *Kathanam*'s process of innovating around the festival of Indra was as destructive as it was constructive. Its attention to and citation of classical texts entails a universalized and Sanskritized elision of the festival's Newar local and focal areas, in what we might call a narrative of erasure. Even though Arjyal was writing specifically for the Shah dynasty that conquered the city of Kathmandu in the 1760s and that then used the Indra festival as an annual remembrance of their victory, his document, composed several decades later, excludes historical details and thus renders invisible the city of Kathmandu: the newly conquered capital city, the location where they celebrated the Indra festival, and the city where Śaktivallabh lived and worked.

Śaktivallabh ignores the festival's many celebrations of death and the ancestors—rites frequently facilitated by ritual attention to Bhairav—and the city of Kathmandu, whose borders the festival annually reestablishes in the *upāku* procession. Thus, despite the festival's intimate connection to the city of Kathmandu—its Newar name is the *yeṃ* (Kathmandu) *yāḥ* (festival)—the *Kathanam* tries to replicate the appearance of universality that occurs in the classical Indian texts, implying that the festival could be performed anywhere in the Hindu world. In ignoring the historical particularities of Kathmandu, Śaktivallabh treats the city as a multiform of the transhistorical Indian royal capital city, in the way that we have already seen in other royally produced classical Sanskrit texts. Thus Kölver's argument regarding the South Asian world picture only appears to apply to Śaktivallabh, though it in fact it completely negates it. Śaktivallabh's use of universal South Asian concepts of time, space, and now ritual reminds us of the historicity of his text by how he imports these traditionally Hindu concepts for the new Shah court.

The displacement, universalization, or erasure that Śaktivallabh's text effects delocalized the festival, wrested ritual power away from local Newars, and reconstructed the nation of Nepal as a traditional and highly Sanskritized pan–South Asian Hindu polity. Its retextualization of Indra's pole and icon led to a set of empirical and imperial structures, material sources to which subsequent generations of royalty and their scribes referred. Richard King, building on Walter Ong's work on the textualization of oral traditions, refers to the "imperialism" of such a process that "seems to work against the immediacy and particularity of the oral event and suppress[es] the fact that they [these texts] derive from a particular community with a particular agenda at a particular time in a particular cultural space" (King 1999: 63, 69). In the case of the *Kathanam,* this text worked against the local Buddhist Newar ritual event, an opposition bolstered by its citation of classical works.

Chapter Six

Sacrificing (to) Bhairav

The Resurrection of a Local Himalayan King

The early nineteenth-century Nepali literature discussed in the previous chapters worked to construct a highly Sanskritized festival of Indra. The consistent use of Hindu goddess imagery in the narratives of the *Nepālikabhūpa Vaṃśāvalī*, especially that of the living goddess Kumari whose blessings sealed the Shah military victory, constructed a lineage in which their family was made to belong in the millennium of royal dynasties in the text's genealogies. Arjyal's conscientious reference to a number of classical Sanskrit texts signaled the connections the Shah court made between their revival of the classical Indra festival and the Hindu nature of their recently won nation-state. This consistent use of Hindu rhetoric, imagery, and narrative in the texts of the early nineteenth century is only part of the larger Hinduization and Sanskritization of the Indra festival in the contemporary Nepalese tradition.

The following two chapters consider the narrative and performative features of two core figures in Kathmandu's Indra festival: Bhairav and Indra's mother, Dāgīṃ (Dagi). Connecting to the festival's collective emphasis on urban power and rivalry, innovation and archaism, and kingship and kinship, the semi-divine beings in these chapters illustrate particular ways that the Indra festival draws on a common source of South Asian narratives and performances related to the epic *Mahābhārata*. The epic is embedded in the Himalaya in myriad ways: Draupadi and her five Pandava husbands, all venerated as important village deities, pilgrimage to and die on the mountain slopes; local communities emplace scenes from the narrative in specific locales in their regions; and the narrative is performed as part of larger folk traditions. Alf Hiltebeitel argues throughout his studies of folk epic performances of the Tamil Draupadi cult in south India that the relationship between "folk Hinduism" and its Sanskritizing influences is based on filtering the Vedic tradition through performances of *bhakti* devotion, "the Mahābhārata being one of the main sources and mediums of this extension, another being the cult of the goddess" (2012: 132). Comprising elements of what Hiltebeitel calls a "free-floating Mahabharata folklore" (1991: 302), the Nepalese Indra festival, a Sanskritized folk culture similar to the South Indian cult of Draupadī, draws on these core Hindu elements—Veda, bhakti, the *Mahābhārata*, the cult of the goddess, and the presence and power of multiforms of the transgressive deity Bhairav—fusing them into a single, unique, and comprehensible whole.[1]

More than simply replicating the epic tale—much less the critical edition of the Sanskrit text—the stories and rites of Bhairav and Dagi draw on themes, scenes, and characters common to the folk epic traditions of Garhwali and Tamil India to trouble the strictly Hindu nature of Nepal's festival. The economy of practices through which this process operates, its ability "to organize all thoughts, perceptions, and actions by means of a few generative principles, which are closely interrelated and constitute a practically integrated whole," helps explain how the Indra festival has maintained a degree of relevance out of proportion to the moribund Vedic deity at its center (Bourdieu 1990: 86). Such ritual flexibility, especially amid the sociopolitical tension in modern Nepal (formalized in 1768) between local Newars and the politically dominant Hindu Shah dynasty, allows the festival to remain a contested arena for communities to reassert cultural identities.

The presence of Krishna, the Hindu deity central to the epic text and its local folk performances, looms large in these chapters and provides a lens through which we might witness this tension. His upending of the Indra festival in the classical *govardhan dhara* narrative, detailed in chapter 1, foregrounds his role as a rival in the foundational stories in these chapters: to Bhairav, whom Krishna decapitates, and to Dagi, around whom the classical story of the *parijāta haraṇa* (theft of the parijata tree) is reworked. The local version of the latter story, key for these chapters, is retold in such a way that Krishna's theft of Indra's tree in the classical story is reversed, with the Nepalese Indra now stealing a flower from that same tree from the Jyāpu farmers of Kathmandu, a crime for which he is arrested and publicly disgraced. Not a particularly prominent deity among Kathmandu's Newars, Krishna's presence in these stories speaks not simply to the presence of Hindu cultural themes in the Indra festival but also to the Hindu deity Krishna as a narrative foil signaling the presence of a dominant Hinduism against which more local and significant themes, practices, and beings—namely, the ancestors local to of Kathmandu—are recalled and celebrated. The epic *Mahābhārata* has become the primary means for framing and understanding this complex rivalry, as it simultaneously universalizes and localizes many of the diverse and dynamic facets of the classical pole-raising festival of Indra.

This chapter handles two prominent manifestations of Bhairav in Kathmandu's Indra festival: Lakhe, the quasi-demonic dancer whose home is in the southern neighborhood of Mazipāt, and the mask, temple, and narrative of Akash Bhairav in the upper-town neighborhood of Indra Chowk. In addition to being manifestations of Bhairav, both reinforce the local Newar theme of the ancestors and are directly and multiply connected to the folk epic traditions of South Asia. The regular juxtaposition of these two themes in Kathmandu's festival—the ancestors and the epic—filtered through these and other fierce forms of the protective Bhairav simultaneously reinforce the themes of kingship and rivalry in the urban confines of Kathmandu.

Indra's Elephant

It is difficult to discuss this first manifestation of Bhairav, the fierce figure of Lakhe, without first attending to Kathmandu's central city neighborhood of Kilaghaḥ Tol (Kilagal) and the central role it plays in the Indra festival. The valley's Jyāpu Kumari lives there, as does the Devi Pyakha dance troupe, consisting of Kumari, Bhairav, and Chaṇḍī; it is the destination of the royal Kumari's Nānichā Yātrā, her third and final procession on the festival's final day. It is named for the number of icons of elephants that reside there, hence the etymology of the neighborhood's name of Kilaghaḥ as *kisi ghaḥ*, the house of the elephant.[2] On a building immediately to the east of the *guthi* house sits a stone elephant whose three-foot-long body is completely covered with red powder and a red cloth; perched outside on the second floor, he faces west overlooking the main street. A streetside shrine houses a second elephant, the icon of Ganesh that marks the identity of the neighborhood and drives away all obstacles, as similar icons do in the neighborhoods of the valley's cities; his proper name, Chanchal Ganesh, "the elephant who moves wildly," is said to reinforce the wild dancing of Pulukisi, the third of the neighborhood's four elephants.

The white elephant Pulukisi is annually constructed and danced by boys of the neighborhood during the Indra festival, as he runs through the streets of the city looking for his master, who has been confined following his theft of the parijat flower (see figure 6.1).[3] Dancing at each departure of Kumari's chariot from the royal square, he and his Kilaghaḥ entourage—torch-bearers, cymbal-crashers, and general hangers-on—also raucously appear each night of the festival, interrupting one of the many nightly dances performed at Hanuman

Figure 6.1. Pulukisi runs through the streets of the city during the *upaku* funeral procession. Photo by author.

Dhoka and sending people scattering for cover. After a few minutes of wild dancing in the public square, his group traverses the narrow lanes of the old city, stopping to receive (or demand) offerings of money and drinks from local homes and businesses, and allowing people to do puja to Pulukisi.

As with most elements of the Indra festival, he is also connected to death and the ancestors. His name communicates the very material out of which his effigy is constructed. Between the decorated white cloth and white papier-mâche mask he wears on the outside and his bamboo skeleton, he wears the straw funeral mats of the dead (*pulu*). Thus, he is the "death-mat elephant" (*pulu kisi*).[4] He takes on this persona especially during the *upaku* procession for the ancestors on the night of the festival's first day. Though most people say that he is leading the city's recently deceased to their heavenly abode, his actions seem to show him repeatedly interrupting the procession.

Pulukisi's ability to lead (or obstruct) the ancestors is based on a reciprocal power with the final elephant in Kilagal, the Black Elephant. Described to me as a *rākshas* demon and a *badmāsh* miscreant, he resides in the basement of the *guthi* house, never receiving the puja of any devotees. The narrative of his confinement foreshadows those of the tantric binding of divine and demonic figures—especially of Indra—that we encounter in the next chapter. According to the logic of these tantric narratives, before the victorious white elephant can dance in the streets, his dark alter ego must be properly subdued, although as is typical in such narratives, he is not definitively killed.

Pulukisi maintains a presence in the *Mahābhārata* festival tradition. In his description of the horse sacrifice portion of the Pāṇḍava Līlā in the Garhwali epic performance, William Sax details the many frenetic activities that occur throughout the day, including the similarly wild movements of Indra's elephant. "That night, Indra's elephant appeared in the square. It had been made secretly in the jungle out of bamboo frames and woolen blankets, with large winnowing pans for ears. The men inside it danced wildly for twenty minutes or so, making it look as though the elephant itself was capering in the square before it was worshiped and then carried off by the five Pandavas" (2002: 37). Although the elephant's construction and wild movements during the festival of Indra appear virtually identical to those of this epic elephant, the Newar reading of Pulukisi is rather different from the Garhwali. In his study of Bhaktapur's Indra festival, Levy and Rajopadhyaya only hesitantly ascribe the identity of Indra's elephant to Pulukisi asserting that the elephant's "relation to Indra is now vague" and that "Pulu Kisi refers now secondarily to Indra, but more clearly to death . . . , to danger, and to threat" (1990: 461).[5] This hesitation speaks to the flexibility of applying meaning to rite, the wide net that the Indra festival casts, and the coherence of the festival around a few basic epic themes, rather than the replication of particular names and forms. Although Pulukisi is also identified as Indra's classical elephant Airavata, this festival elephant represents an additional and independent entity drawn from the pan–South Asian epic tradition and applied to the local festival themes of death and the ancestors.

Lākhe and Jhyālincha

The primary and sometimes contentious adversary of Pulukisi is the quasi-demonic Lakhe. One of the most famous and photogenic figures in the festival, Lakhe has a red mask, tie-dyed skirts, and shock of red hair. He dances with Pulukisi, appearing together at Kumari's chariot processions in the royal square, in the streets of the city, and especially at the *upaku* procession for the ancestors. The relative lack of narrativity that explains their antagonistic relationship in Kathmandu can be filled in with attention to the festival in Bhaktapur. Though the rites of Bhaktapur's Indra festival as a whole are "not integrated," representing "fragments of what may have been once . . . a coherent set" (Levy and Rajopadhyaya 1990: 462), the festival there includes slight variations of many of the same elements (and elephants!) as Kathmandu's festival, including its own Pulukisi. Instead of Kumari being pulled in her three processions, the citizens of Bhaktapur pull the temple icon of Indra's powerful consort, Indrayāṇī; instead of images of Indra being elevated in the city's neighborhoods, it is images of his son, Jayant; and instead of Kathmandu's morally ambivalent Lakhe, it is Bhaktapur's clearly demonic *mupātra* (*mupatra*) who will wreak havoc on the city's human and divine residents. Though absent from Kathmandu's festival, the *mupatra* is a key figure for understanding Lakhe's connections to the epic tradition.[6]

The central myth of Bhaktapur's festival, also slightly different from Kathmandu's in which Indra steals the parijat flower, pits the *mupatra* against Indra's family. Once, when Indra's son came to the valley and stole a *khaisi* fruit used in Newar funerary rituals, the *mupatra* discovered this and bound him to a pole. His father (Indra) sent his elephant (Pulukisi) to kill the demon. His mother, Indra's wife (Indrayāṇī), cried when she saw her son captured and asked the *mupatra* for his freedom. On the full moon day, the *mupatra* relented and Jayant returned home.[7]

On Bhādra 12, images resembling those of Kathmandu's Indra are raised throughout the city. Despite his general identification as Indra's son, Jayant, these images—each has a mask and hands affixed to a wooden cross—are also referred to as both Bhairav and Yamadyaḥ, deities associated with death and the ancestors. In addition to Indrayāṇī and Masān Bhairav (Cremation Ground Bhairav), several locally constructed elephants—Salāṃ and Chumaḥ Ganesh and Pulukisi—will search the city for Indra and Jayant and approach these images. Only the *mupatra* will meaningfully interact with them. When Indrayāṇī's procession arrives at Darbar Square, her chariot is set down. The *mupatra* then appears with his two assistants, circles the chariot three times, turns three times in place to do puja, raises his sword, and lunges toward the goddess. With these strikes, he symbolically kills the goddess, though her chariot, accompanied by Chumaḥ Ganesh, will again depart. Avoiding contact with the elephants for fear of potential violence, the *mupatra* reaches the crosses where Indra's son is bound, stops, and kills each of them also with a threefold circumambulation. A crowd of young boys follows the *mupatra*'s group and swears at them, calling them the funny-haired ones (Nep. *hās ko kapāl*) or duck-headed demons (New. *hāsakaḥca mupātra*) who have eaten the flesh of a buffalo embryo, a reference to the female buffalo whose intestines are received by Bhairav.

The *mupatra*'s symbolic and simultaneous killing of Indra, Jayant, Indrāyaṇī, and the king is matched by the similar killing of Jhyalincha, the name of two different figures in Kathmandu's Indra festival, the first of which is connected to Lakhe. Though the term *lākhe* can be used generally to refer to any quasi-demonic character, the city's most important Lakhe lives in the lower-city neighborhood of Mazipāt and dances (his primary activity) almost solely during Indrajātrā.[8] Intertwined with Lakhe's fierce character is his love of women; of the myths told of Mazipāt Lakhe, the most famous involves his relations with a low-caste Ranjitkar woman of the neighborhood. Pradhan tells of the relationship of Bhairav, of whom Lakhe is a manifestation, with young women: "There are many stories about deities sleeping with, and even impregnating, women. In these stories, which are always located in the past, the god most often named as fathering human children is Bhairava" (1986: 74). In one story, Lakhe replicates the thievery and imprisonment of Indra himself: caught for having taking a mistress from the neighborhood, Lakhe's dancing represents his annual recompense for his offense to the Mazipāt community (Toffin 2010: 111).

Located down a narrow and otherwise nondescript alleyway, the outside of Lakhe's narrow house appears as a temple: its two inward-opening front doors, a set of eyes painted on them, are flanked by two brightly painted protective lions and is topped by an elaborate wooden *torana*. A brass plaque to the right of the front doors identifies Lakhe as part of Newar heritage, names the members of the *guthi* responsible for supporting his festival activities, and identifies him as "Śānt Bhairav" (Peaceful Bhairav). A large lighted sign outside the window on the upper-most floor bears the image of Lakhe that identifies him as "Śrī Lākhe Ājuḥ" across the top and his location of "Mazipāt, Lākhenani" across the bottom.[9] Two days before Indra's pole goes up (thus on Bhadra 10), the masks of Lakhe and Jhyalincha go on display in a room on the upper floor of this domestic temple, and after a nearly four-hour private *nyās pūjā* on the next day, the rest of their regalia and accoutrements are attached and displayed and receive the veneration of people from throughout the city.[10]

Although the room contains all the objects and signs of a standard temple—bells, incense containers, *tika* powder, and flower petals to be distributed to devotees as *prasad*—it also contains a few items unique to Lakhe's presence in the festival. Dominating the back of the room is a large container whose size, shape, and material construction of unfired clay make it look something like a sarcophagus but which the priestess on duty referred to as a *mandir* (temple). It functions as both: outside of the festival—the ten days when the masks are displayed in the house and worn by dancers in the streets of the city—the box holds both masks and thus reminds visitors of the temporariness of this event. In front of the *mandir*, flanked by two brass lampstands topped by images of Sarasvati and Ganesh, is the throne on which the masks sit: Lakhe's larger solid red mask is more visible in the center with Jhyalincha's smaller mask, red but framed with white, off to the left side. Lakhe's title "Śrī Lākhe Āju" is inscribed across the back of the throne's brass covering, just above the top of his mask.

His puja, just like the space he inhabits, reflects Lakhe's unique identity. With the standard physical evidence of puja present in the form of *peḍā* sweets on the mouths of the masks and small rupee notes, flower petals, and rice grains strewn across the throne, the liquor that devotees bring him signals his nature as a fierce god. Moreover, during these pujas it is not uncommon for devotees to be overcome by his fierce, protective, and dangerous nature and exhibit symptoms of trance and possession. One woman came with several family members to do puja to the masks, her eight-year-old boy standing off to the side holding the bag of bananas that she brought as an offering. The priestess of the shrine room—dressed all in red to the polish on her finger- and toenails—led the woman, seated in front of the throne, through a complex puja, in which she offered grains of rice, oil-dipped cotton wicks, and a small bottle of whisky. Touching her head to Lakhe's mask, the final element of this puja, her actions immediately slowed down. She leaned far back in her seated position and looked toward the ceiling, returned to her previous seated position, and irregularly repeated this series of actions several times while maintaining physical contact with the priestess. The room remained silent for several minutes as she felt Lakhe's presence that we vicariously felt through her. Following the completion of her trance and puja and upon getting up slowly and beginning to leave, her son whispered to her from across the room, "kerā?" to remind her of the bananas that she had forgotten to offer.[11]

The juxtaposed masks of Lakhe and Jhyalincha on the altar signal their intimacy, but their relationship is fraught with a playful violence introduced in their origin story. Whether in the northern areas of Nepal, in Tibet, or in Assam, Lakhe spent most of his early years harassing the locals. For their own safety, the people created the boy Jhyalincha to keep Lakhe away, as he could do nothing against them as long as Jhyalincha was there, exercising his main method of protection: teasing. Beginning in Mazipāt's inner neighborhood of Lakhenani, Lakhe will chase Jhyalincha—first one boy wearing the paraphernalia of Jhyalincha and then other neighborhood boys—as they dance together throughout the duration of the Indra festival and the streets of the city (see figure 6.2).

Figure 6.2. Lakhe and Jhyalincha dance in the Mazipat neighborhood. Photo by author.

Lakhe's enduring legacy, his mythical violence, on occasion becomes quite real, however. At night, after the public festivities have ended, Lakhe and his musicians take to the streets. Leaving behind the comic violence in the royal square, Lakhe dances through the city, challenging and being challenged by each neighborhood's bold, somewhat inebriated young men. I encountered one of these local street performances, one that resulted in a knife attack on Lakhe several years before, in an alley just off the axial Chetrapati Chowk at about 10 p.m., drawn in by the distinctive three-beat rhythm that Lakhe's musicians play. As Lakhe dances, young men in imitation of Jhyalincha approached him head on, turning tail only when he moved toward them as if to attack. For the challengers, it was enough to have the courage to taunt him, to show their manhood by harassing (or teasing) him. As he approached me and came within inches of my face, my back pressed up against the houses of the narrow alley, I took the opportunity, as did several other more passive (and more sober) audience members, to touch his upturned red mask as a sign of devotional deference before he moved on to terrorize others.

Jhyalincha possesses a second festival manifestation, one that appears to be independent of Lakhe but is easily missed. Behind the famous door guardian image of Hanuman after which the entire palace area is named (Hanuman Dhoka), is an approximately one-foot-tall red wooden puppet in the full dress of a warrior gazing out of a small open palace window (see figure 6.3). Since it is only displayed during the Indra festival, most people agreed that this image represents Indra himself.[12] Anderson describes this object's unique ritual application but not its location: "A small wooden puppet is brought from the confines of Hanuman Dhoka and used as a weapon to strike similar puppets

Figure 6.3. Jhyalincha looks out of a small open palace window immediately behind the protective Hanuman. Photo by author.

placed beside the images of Indra" (1971: 137). In discussing the festival's many conflicts generally, Nepali contextualizes this obscure rite—providing the even more obscure details that Anderson omits. On the final day of the festival (*asoj kṛṣṇa* 4), "[A] wooden puppet is taken out from Hanuman Dhoka. The puppet is called *Jhyalincha*. It is struck against the two *Jhyalinchas* belonging to Indra's two idols at Indra Chowk and Maru tole, respectively" (1965: 364–65). Although Nepali tries to explain these rites as reflecting an Indo-Aryan and thus pre-Vedic feature that has survived in Nepal, local explanations obviate the need for such an anachronistic explanation.[13]

In his ethnographic description of this ritual complex, Toffin describes how, following the sacrifice of a buffalo, the three puppets are placed on a stage in the Indra Chowk (Waṃghaḥ Tol) neighborhood and anointed with its blood (2010: 112–13). Following a mock combat, the puppet of Hanuman Dhoka emerges victorious and is returned to the palace in a royal procession. Toffin offers two local interpretations of this battle. In the first, the three rival kings represent an internecine battle "between the king of Kathmandu and the Newar people of the city, here identified with the Waṃghaḥ neighborhood" (2010: 113). His second interpretation reads the battle as representing an episode from the *Mahābhārata*, as Jhyalincha's combat is located immediately in front of the Akash Bhairav temple, whose central icon represents, as we will see in the next section, the festival's most pointed connections with the local *Mahābhārata* tradition.

The confluence of so many of the festival's diverse rites and narratives in one figure positions Lakhe as a sort of microcosm of the whole Indra festival. His capture and punishment directly connect him to the festival's central narrative of Indra's capture, handled in the next chapter; his identity as Bhairav connects him to the festival's twin themes of kingship and kinship; and the multiple contentious relationships with which he is involved reinforce the festival's related themes of rivalry and warfare, the victory of good over evil and life over death, and the social fact of Kathmandu's urban tantric world as the locale for this victory. All of this exists within the overarching structure of a classical pole-raising festival recognized as the beginning of a new year. Heeding Humphreys and Laidlaw's warning against trying to "represent only consistency when in fact there may be confusion and diversity" (1994: 264), I see the relationships of Lakhe to Pulukisi and Jhyalincha as highlighting his connections to the epic tradition. The victory of the puppet Jhyalincha at festival's end becomes a victory not only over his quasi-royal claimants to the throne but also over his quasi-demonic enemy, Lakhe. This victory challenges Lakhe's otherwise powerful and welcome presence in the city and replicates the simultaneous power and victimhood of one of the Kathmandu festival's most central figures, Akash Bhairav.

Akash Bhairav

Bhairav is ubiquitous in Kathmandu's Indra festival, with particular icons serving as focal points at different times. A Shakya boy playing the role of Bhairav will accompany his sister Kumari on her three chariot processions through the city. The mask of Seto Bhairav, a pipe god (New. *hāthu dyo*), located immediately outside the palace in Hanuman Dhoka, dispenses beer as *amrita*, the nectar of immortality, to young people who brave the raucous crowds for his *prasād* blessing. A small icon in the center of the palace area serves as the final destination of the chariots of Ganesh, Bhairav, and Kumari, marking the conclusion of the festival.

Similar to Lakhe, the set of rites and narratives surrounding the icon of Akash Bhairav in Indra Chowk represents a microcosm of the whole Indra festival and an explicit connection to the South Asian epic tradition. The Newar story of the local Kirāti king Yalambar Yāluṅga revolves around his sacrificial death at the hands of Krishna and his resurrection and subsequent apotheosis as the modestly Sanskritized Akash Bhairav, who narratively returned to and is still reguarly venerated during the festival. Mimetically connecting themselves to this relatively unknown tribal king, the Newars of Kathmandu construct a self-identity that is local (to the Kathmandu Valley), Other (vis-à-vis dominant Hindu groups), and historical (genealogically connected to Yalambar).

Although Yalambar's story does not occur in the Sanskrit epic preserved in the Pune Critical Edition, it is clearly set in the framework of the *Mahābhārata* and is thus part of the larger epic folklore of the Himalayas. Rather than an omission from the text, it represents one facet of what Ehud Halperin refers to as Mahābhāratization, "a process by which a local tradition is reworked in accordance with the logic of the epic, elaborating and developing the epic in the process of doing so" (2020: 152). Newars consider Yalambar to be a son or subsequent manifestation of Elam, the first king of the local Kirāti people as named in the Newar *Gopālarāja Vaṃśāvalī*, thus placing his reign in the eleventh century (Vajrācārya and Malla 1985: 121–22). This combination of historicity, locality, and royalty imbued in the figure of Yalambar helps facilitate his adoption by Kathmandu's Newars, especially Newar Jyāpus, the "urban peasants" of the city (Gellner and Pradhan 1999: 161–62).

For the story of Yalambar-Bhairav's sacrifice—and here I use the hyphenated name, considering its occasional use by local authors (Bajracharya 2003: 20)—I draw on the narratives contained in a collection of essays ("the Renovation volume," as I refer to it) published locally in Kathmandu. This volume commemorated the 2002 renovation of the Akash Bhairav temple in the central city neighborhood of Indra Chowk (New. Waṃgha Tol), and its essays deal with an array of topics relevant to the temple: its economics, architecture, and administration, as well as its regular ritual performances. Despite the many authors contributing to this variety of themes, many of the essays focus on Bhairav's identity with Yalambar, who arrived in Kathmandu only after having traveled to Kurukshetra to be present at the Mahabharata war, when Krishna led the Pandava army into battle. The following account represents a compilation of three articles from the Renovation volume authored by Kumār Prasād Darśan (2003; "A Report on Śrī Ākāsh Bhairavnāth and Indrajātrā"), Śarad Kumār Dangol (2003; "A Short Essay on Śrī Ākāsh Bhairav"), and Nirmal Bajrāchārya (2003; "Ākāsh Bhairav on the Riverbank").

> King Yalambar traveled to the battlefield at Kurukshetra with his sixteen armies, and formed them into one camp in order just to witness the battle. Having heard of Yalambar's arrival, Krishna went personally to his camp and asked him: "On which side will you fight?" Yalambar replied: "I have only come to watch the battle," though of course he had his weapons with him. He continued, "In the end, I will fight on whichever side loses this war."[14] Krishna thought: "If this man fights on the losing side, and in the course of battle both armies annihilate each other, then he alone will remain victorious. So, this man must be removed." Using his *sudarshan chakra*, Krishna swiftly removed Yalambar's

> head from his shoulders, placing his head high up in a large tree so that the head would be able to look down upon the war, as Yalambar had requested. Krishna was still afraid of the power of Yalambar's powerful gaze, however, and he struck the severed head with an arrow, causing it to fly through the Milky Way and then to fall into the river.

From here, Yalambar's narrative leaves the classical framework completely, the locale shifting from the Indian battlefield of the *Mahābhārata* to a strictly local one—the city of Kathmandu, the neighborhood of Indra Chowk, and the Akash Bhairav temple—where Yalambar's relationship with the Jyāpu people was established.

> Yalambar's head flowed along until it reached the confluence of the city's three rivers. . . .[15] King Yalambar Yāluṅga came to a Jyāpu in a dream and said to him: "Out of love for the place of my birth, I have left but now I have returned. From now on I will be responsible for its protection (*surakṣā*), so you should establish my head in whichever place I can offer such protection to this residence of the gods." (Bajracharya 2003: 20)[16]

Having found Yalambar-Bhairav's head at Teku Doban—at the confluence of the rivers near the temple of Pachali Bhairav where Indra's pole is disposed of—the Jyāpu farmer carried the head to the place of Indra Chowk, built a small hut, and established it there in a series of actions that continues to be performed annually during the Indra festival (see figure 6.4).

Darśan continues the narrative, resuming after the arrival of Yalambar's head at Indra Chowk and its installation by the Jyāpu farmer.

> After the war, King Yalambar, arriving via the Akash Marg [Milky Way] at the meeting of Nepal's three rivers, began to become brilliant. Indra and the other deities had come to this place, according to injunction, to do puja in front of Yalambar, which means Akash Bhairav, to receive his beneficence and to request a boon, asking: "May I sit here for your festivals?" It is because of this that during the Indrajatra, Indra's platform is made and established here,

Figure 6.4. Venerating the mask of Akash Bhairav at the street-level shrine in front of his temple. Photo by author.

> and it is said that King Gunakamadeva, having come here to do puja, was visited by Sri Mahalakshmi in a dream, who ordered him to plan out the city. (Darśan 2003: 25)

Mahalakshmi's appearance in King Gundakamadeva's dream recalls Yalambar's appearance in the Jyāpu farmer's dream. These dreams establish an identification between these two men (the Jyāpu farmer and the founding king), both of whom are responsible for developing the urban space that Yalambar-Bhairav will protect. The person of Yalambar thus sits at the figurative confluence of a number of important identifications as the Newar narrative tradition metonymously identifies the neighborhood of Indra Chowk in the city of Kathmandu whose center is the head of Akash Bhairav.

These identifications draw on various ancient Newar names of the city: Yambi, Yāpṛṇga, or Yam in the distant past, and Yeṃ by Newars today (Petech 1958: 171–73; Vajracharya 1974). This "Yeṃ" provides the object of the Newar name of the Indra festival (*yeṃ yāḥ*) that celebrates the city of Kathmandu and features the Akash Bhairav temple as one of its most prominent processual nodes. Darśan translates this phrase as "the festival of Yalambar" (thus, "the *yāḥ* of *yeṃ*" [2003: 25]), but Bajracharya produces a more fluid identificatory system. After asserting that some people perform puja to Akash Bhairav as a valuable source of royal Kirati power, he focuses on the alliterative Y that runs throughout all of these terms. "According to the Jyāpu community," Bajracharya concludes, "Ākāsh Bhairav is seen as King Yalambar. . . . That Bhairav is, in fact, Yalambar has strong support: During the Indrajatra, after Bhairav is placed in his small hut, the letter 'Y' is written on his chest, according to tradition. With this letter 'Y', the person of Yalambar Yāluṅga is brought to mind" (Bajracharya 2003: 21–22). This Y thus closes the circle of identifications, as it brings together the local Newar with the pan-Indian and universal Sanskrit: the *yeṃ yāḥ* (Indrajatra) is the festival of Yalambar (Akash Bhairav), held during the month of Yaṃlā (Skt. Bhādra), celebrates the god of death (Skt. Yama), where one farmer, two kings, and one goddess founded the city of Yeṃ (Kathmandu).[17]

At this temple during the Indra festival is where Yalambar most clearly takes on the fierce appearance of Bhairav, "the epitome of the ideal of transgressive sacrality" (Erndl 1989: 247).[18] During the early hours of the festival's second day—just a few hours after the *upaku* procession around the city concludes—the four-foot-tall blue bodiless mask of Akash Bhairav is brought down from his usual residence inside the temple's second-story abode and reinstalled in a street-level shrine immediately in front of the temple. In the Renovation volume, Śrī Nārāyāṇ Maharjan, the head (*mūl thakāli*) of the Akash Bhairav *guthi* describes the *guthi*'s responsibilities: "On the night of [Bhādra] 12, Śrī Ākāśh Bhairavnāth is painted by a Citrakār, and worship [*pūjā-ājā*] is done. On this night, sixty *khalak* [*guthi* members] and their sons place Śrī Ākāśh Bhairavnāth in his *khaṭ* [small hut] accompanied by music [*bājā-gājā*]. The Tamot [Tāmrakār, brass-workers] adorn him with jewelry. At that time, a large crowd of devotees gathers in order to take darśan of Śrī Ākāśh Bhairavnāth" (2003: 41).[19] This ritual event marks many key moments in the festival narrative. The shrine establishes

Yalambar-Bhairav's severed head and the hut where the Jyāpu farmer installed it.[20] It represents the destination of Indra and the other gods who asked to attend Bhairav's festivals—it is said that for this reason an icon of Indra is placed nearby, overlooking the temple as Yalambar oversaw the battlefield at Kurukshetra. It troubles the story of King Gunakamadeva who, visited by Mahalakshmi in a dream, founded the Indra festival as he planned out the city of Kathmandu on the eight nodes of her sword. Yalambar's story replaces Gunakamadeva, splitting his roles between the Jyāpu farmer who receives the dream and the tribal king Yalambar whose unique victimhood, independently of any canonical *vamsavali*, results in his own festival founding, city protection, and royal ancestry.

Newars and Janjati

In his work on the cultural dimension of indigenous *janjāti* movements, Gérard Toffin posits the "autochthonous paradigm," the overarching structure that "conveys intense feelings among the people concerned and provides them with self-identification of overriding importance in matters of identity" (Toffin 2013: 87). His primary example is the Jyāpu Mahāguṭhi, the valley-wide organization of Jyāpu farmers who tell Yalambar's story and identify as the valley's original inhabitants. Through the ritual processions that the Mahaguthi's discrete member-groups perform in the cities of the Kathmandu Valley, Jyāpus "stress their links with most of the local, indigenous deities of the Kathmandu Valley" and thus "regularly reassert, by symbolic means, their control over the soil and over the inhabited territory" (Toffin 2013: 86). This combination of the connection to the soil of Kathmandu with feelings of being "left out and disadvantaged" in a unified Nepal allows the Newars to be categorized as *janjāti* despite, as Mark Pickett states, the extraordinarily high quality of life for most Newars in the cities of the Kathmandu Valley (Pickett 2014: 10). The consequences of the 1768–1769 victories of the Shah dynasty resulted in the secondary status of the Newars and the loss of their "economic, intellectual and political power," provoking a trauma that "is still intense among the Newars, and has induced feelings of resentment" (Toffin 2007: 18–19).

Relegated to a position of subservience vis-à-vis Hindu Parbatiya castes, local ethnic groups were compelled to conform to what Fisher calls "the reigning definition of the nation," a definition that did not immediately include the Newars (1993: 12–13).[21] These restrictions against Newar religion and culture extended to the performance of the public festivals that are common to Newar culture today. The *Muluki Ain* of 1854 codifies the ambiguous place of Newars within the "all-embracing 'national' hierarchy of castes" (Höfer 2004: 115–17). The national laws enacted under the century-long Rana regime (1846–1951) reinforced the cultural, religious, and linguistic unity of the nation begun by the Shah dynasty restricting the size of offerings made, the size of feasts, and gifts exchanged, as well as the number of people who can walk in processions (Lewis and Tuladhar 2010: 344–47). But these particular restrictions were only aimed at specifically Buddhist aspects of Newar religious culture, allowing for the Hindu and Hinduizing Shah and Rana imperial powers to use Hindu aspects of Newar culture for their own benefit. This is precisely what they did with the Indra festival, which, as we saw in the early issues of *Gorkhāpatra,* became one of the central strategies in this larger cultural process.

But the Shah dynasty did not have a monopoly on the Indra festival. I propose that Yalambar's story challenges this Hindu hegemony and offers an element of narrative resistance to this attempt at national unity. In doing so, it represents a process similar to what Fitzgerald described for the construction of the *Mahābhārata*. The Sanskrit epic was based on the "double crisis of dharma" that highlighted the "resentment and self-loathing felt by some brahmin recipients of royal largesse," with the constituent stories drawing "attention to the imbalance of power in the relationship between royal donors and their beneficiaries" (2004: 100). The story of Yalambar Yālunga represents a similar strategy deployed by the Newar, especially the *janjāti* and Jyāpu population of the Kathmandu Valley who use this story to assuage their resentment and offer a response to the singularity of the Nepali state's political vision. Constructing a series of historical, transhistorical, and linguistic associations and identifications that highlight Yalambar's (and by extension, their own) close ties to Kathmandu, they place his rule in a prehistoric time, a location outside the valley, and a tribal community that reinforces their long-standing tension with the Nepali Hindu state and its (former) king who manifested Vishnu. As a royal figure who simultaneously founded the city of Kathmandu and established the Indra festival, Yalambar replaces King Gunakamadeva, the tenth-century king who is said to have done those things. As a multiform of Bhairav, Yalambar becomes a fierce "god of justice" for Jyāpus, as Bhairav is for Harijans and others assigned a low caste, especially in Himalayan South Asia.[22] Affiliated with Newars and Jyāpus, the tribal Yalambar continues to remind us of his former tribal status by which Newar storytellers can express their resistance to what Susan Hangen calls "high-caste Hindu culture as national culture" without expressly invoking their Newar identity and thus risking censure from the dominant Hindu monarchy (2007: 17).[23] Strategizing their identity as a *janjāti* and (and via) their opposition to Hindu brahminical and royal orthodoxy through a negotiation with the same, the Newars of the Kathmandu Valley have constructed a narrative whose underlying mythology, grounded in the *Mahābhārata*, highlights features of asymmetry, inequality, and domination that look toward what Bell calls a "redemptive hegemony," "a strategic and practical orientation for acting, a framework . . . [that] creates [reality] more or less effectively . . . [and] that constitute[s] the actor's strategic understanding of the place, purpose, and trajectory of the act" (1992: 85).

Despite the ancient settings of Yalambar's story, these notions of rivalry and hierarchy point to the more recent origin of this story, as it appears to respond to two processes in the history of modern Nepal. The first is the Shah dynasty's victory over the ruling Newars of the Kathmandu Valley that ushered in an era of nation-building on the twin pillars of Hinduization and Nepalization (Burghart 1984). The second is the contemporary period, beginning with the first People's Movement in 1990 and continuing through the second such movement in 2005–2006, that saw Nepal respectively wrestle with the end of the Cold War, the rise of democracy and free-market reforms throughout the world, the inevitable end of the Hindu Nepali monarchy, and the potential end of a caste-based political hegemony. Through these historical processes, the nation of Nepal has been reconstructed, renegotiated, and reimagined. The kings of the Shah dynasty, with their growing imperial sway in the eighteenth century and their victories over the small kingdoms of the western and eastern hills and over the Newars of the Kathmandu Valley, sought to produce a unified Nepali nation that might defend itself against the growing British imperial threat to the south in India.

But Shah political unity could only be effected by promoting a cultural uniformity that could "downplay or eliminate cultural differences within its population," as it focused primarily on the Hindu religion, the Hindu monarchy, and the Nepali language as "signifiers of the national community" (Hangen 2007: 11, 12). The 1854 publication of the *Muluki Ain* (National Law Codes) is often seen as the apex of this process (Höfer 2004), as the triple signifier of religion, royalty, and language was the backbone of a centuries-long process that established cultural uniformity and national unity in Nepal. Initiated by the first Shah kings in the eighteenth century, this process was reinforced by the Rana regime in the mid-nineteenth through the mid-twentieth century and continued by Shah kings into the early twenty-first century in the dynasty's waning moments.

In the years since the first People's Movement in 1990, and even though "episodic resistance was crushed by the state" (Toffin 2013: 9), various *janjāti* have resisted this singular vision of the state and have responded to "the complex set of discriminations and inequalities resulting from this situation" (Toffin 2013: 80). Although this resistance to the state has taken a variety of forms, its more political manifestations use a relatively uniform terminology—of *samābeśi* (inclusion), *bikās* (development, progress, and/or modernization), and *nayā Nepāl* (the "New Nepal")—to counter the "monolithic" nation whose constitution "had been blamed for institutionalizing, legitimizing, and engendering patterns of exclusion and discrimination" (Malagodi 2013: 3).

Contextualizing the Severed Head

Stories similar to Yalambar's come from all over India: those of Aravāṉ and Jākh in South India, of Khātushyām in the western deserts of Rajasthan, and of Babrīk in Garhwali India. Each story tells of the participation of a local king in the Mahabharata war, his decapitation at the hands of the deceitful Krishna, and the prominent enshrinement of his head. In his reading of the Garhwali epic tradition, Sax addresses the sacrifice of Babrīk, asserting that Garhwalis sympathize and identify with him, thus affirming the value of "dignity and honor in defeat" in the face of ruthless kingdoms and "the inequities of the Kali Yuga" (Sax 2002: 102). Following Schomer's study of the north Indian *Ālhā* epic, Sax further asserts that such local readings represent "one particularly striking example of the way in which *Mahābhārata* stories and themes are incorporated into local traditions," as Garhwalis make the *Mahābhārata* their own, representing it "in rustic and homespun ways" and assisting in the construction of ethnic identity (Sax 2002: 46).

Lindsey Harlan continues this narrative connection between dignity in defeat and sacrifical decapitation and provides an opportunity to consider Yalambar-Bhairav's story as closely participating in the history of his people. Harlan relates the tales of Rajput warriors who, after being decapitated in battle fighting against their (typcially Muslim) enemies, continue to fight, headless, until they are noticed in this strange state by women, typically those of their own family lines (Harlan 2003: 77, 84).[24] After their deaths, the hero becomes the protective and dangerous deity Bheruji or Bhairav, often regarded as a manifestation of the pan-Hindu deity Shiva; a stone is raised and a shrine is constructed at the border of the village, estate, or city where he falls, signifying the ancestral relations he has with the village he now protects (Harlan 2003: 16, 138).

The intimate relationship that local communities have with their beheaded warriors can be seen in all of these examples. Garhwali audiences express sympathy for Babrīk; Tamil ritualists set up clay images of the head of Aravāṉ while men dress in the sari of the goddess Mohinī, the wife of Aravāṉ (Hiltebeitel 1988: 325); and Rajputs venerate the permanent shrines of decapitated warriors on the boundaries of the place where they live.[25] Yalambar's case is quite similar: he is decapitated at the hands of his enemies, he is converted into a Bhairav, and he is subsequently enshrined and venerated, having first been moved from the edge to the center of the city over which he presides.[26] The contrasts between the (especially Rajput) examples of heroic (self-)sacrifice and the sacrificial death of Yalambar-Bhairav are rather more telling. Whereas the Rajput warriors dutifully fight their human enemies with all of their effort, even past the point of losing their heads, the Kirāti-Newar Yalambar fails to choose a side on which to fight, does not even identify his enemies, and chooses not to fight at all—before or after his decapitation. Yalambar's passivity in the face of Krishna's aggression signals, I argue, a reluctant submission to Krishna in which he, a local and tribal Kirāti king, stood no chance in battle against the great Hindu deity of the *Bhagavad Gītā*.

Yalambar's victimization is predicated on his contrasting identity and tense relationship with Krishna, whose anomalous presence—Buddhist figures much more commonly populate local Newar narratives—directly indicates the presence of a more orthodox Hinduism. The narrative of Yalambar-Bhairav thus does not narrate simply a battle between mythical beings but also a sociopolitical conflict between communities: the killing/murder/sacrifice of Yalambar, the local Kirāti king from Nepal, becomes Bhairav, the Newar king of Kathmandu, who is then killed by Krishna, the avatar of the Hindu Brahminical Vishnu, who (until recently) incarnated as the Nepali Hindu king. These narrative replacements only superficially hide the identities of ethnic agents whose conflict resides at the heart of this mimesis. The transfiguration of the local and royal Yalambar into the pan–South Asian and divine Bhairav shows us the historical processes that continue to be at work. Seen through the lens of Rene Girard's assertion that, though "a source of violence and disorder during his sojourn among men, the hero appears as a redeemer as soon as he has been eliminated, invariably by violent means" (Girard 1977: 87), the local festival to Indra uses the pan-Hindu folk tradition of the *Mahābhārata* to draw attention to the seemingly minor figure of Yalambar and encourage the remembrance of the local Newar culture of Kathmandu, a city often said to be founded coterminously with the festival. By further addressing Yalambar-Bhairav as Āju—the familial title "Grandfather"—or as the compound "Bhairāju" (Panch 2003: 9), Newars reinforce the geographical relationship he bears with the many Ajimā, or Grandmother goddesses, who protect the city's perimeter and so make him, like Gunakamadeva before him, a royal ancestor of the city. No longer about a Hindu king or god, the continuing presence of Yalambar-Bhairav-Āju, the true king of Kathmandu, replaces memories of a cultural defeat with the stories, icons, and performances of a truly local kingship.

It is somewhat ironic that the Indra festival provides the opportunity to replicate and subsequently resolve this previous crisis between the Shah king—seen here as a manifestation of both the Vedic Indra and the Hindu Vishnu (and his avatar, Krishna)—with the local and Other Yalambar-Bhairav. Traditionally reinforcing the centrality of Hindu monarchy, the festival now, and especially after the demise of the Shah dynasty, foregrounds an alternative royalty where Yalambar-Bhairav is, as I was told several times, "our king" (New. *jigu juju,* Nep. *hāmro rājā*), thus attributing to him the royal identity typically reserved for the king of the Hindu Nepali state. The festival highlights his royalty with its clear and repeated marking out of the city's multiple geographical centers and boundaries, thus troubling the singular narrative of the festival as a commemoration of the anniversary of the Shah conquest of the Kathmandu Valley in 1768, as Oldfield asserted.

Like the Tamil Aravāṉ whose severed head is explictly likened to rice balls (*piṇḍa*) that, "representing the head are projected into full bodies for the ancestors to occupy in the afterlife" (Hiltebeitel 1995: 465), the multiple and unique festival displays of Bhairav repeatedly remind citizens of his alternative royalty and simultaneously his intimate relations with the ancestors. The mask of Seto Bhairav on the palace's outer wall, the multiple clay beer pots bearing his severed and recovered head displayed in multiple neighborhoods, and six-foot-tall wooden poles installed in local neighborhoods indicate the continued presence of the city's ancestors.

Conclusion

The narrative and performative acquisition, possession, and enshrinement of the severed head of Yalambar-Bhairav-Aju draws on similar acts told in other Hindu narratives: Shiva's beheading of Ganesh and of his father-in-law, Daksa; the self-decapitation of the goddess Chinnamastā; Bhairav's decapitation of Brahmā, for which he was required to perform penance through a pilgrimage to Benares; and Vaiṣṇo Devī's decapitation of Bhairav for the latter's sexual sins. The sacrificial mimesis operative in Yalambar's story—the head of the innocent Kirāti king is violently removed by Krishna, obtained by the Newar farmer, transferred to the center of Kathmandu, enshrined at a newly built (and annually rebuilt) shrine, and transformed into the protective Bhairav—participates in the ancient South Asian idiom of rivalry.

Like Vedic narratives that portray the sacrifice as "a cosmos which is violently broken up in order to be put back together again" and the severed head as "a treasure or secret that is the essence of the universe," Yalambar's head "can only reside in a permanently renewed contest in which the two sides exchange the head" (Heesterman 1985: 46, 47, 50; Collins 2014). As the cyclical nature of the Vedic sacrifice allowed the ritualists to rationalize the reality of death and point the way toward the sacrificer's salvation, Yalamabar's sacrificial death signals the tenuous equilibrium earned in this story.

At Kathmandu's Indra festival—an "agonistic festival," to reapply Heesterman's phrase (1985: 47)—and against the background of the epic *Mahābhārata*, Yalambar's severed head is enshrined, this equilibrium attained, and all rivalries (at least temporarily) put to an end. Despite the ancient provenance of the key elements of Yalambar's story, the historiographical weight of this story in Kathmandu can only be after the eighteenth century, following the fall of the Kathmandu Valley to the invading Shah dynasty.[27] Yalambar's story, appearing multiple times in the Renovation volume and reflecting similar regional South Asian stories that challenge Hindu and brahminical dominance, has attained additional significance, especially since the 1990s, when multiple nation-wide protests against the monarchy, the nation's decade-long civil war with the Maoist rebels, and the development of a nascent democracy contributed to an increasing awareness and strategic construction of multiple ethnic identities against the singularity of the Nepalese state. Antagonistic to the conniving Krishna, the tribal Kirati King Yalambar represents the persistence of elements of local Newar culture that had been variously supressed since the beginning of Shah rule.

Despite his more shadowy narrative, Lakhe's presence reinforces the rivalries foregrounded in that of Akash Bhairav to Krishna. Killing the royal family by his multiform of the demonic *mupatra* and vying for power in the epic battle that plays out in front of the Akash Bhairav temple, at Kathmandu's old palace, and in the streets of the city, Lakhe operates nearly independently of any classical festival narrative. Rather, his regular dancing with Pulukisi reminds the audience of the continuing presence of death and the ancestors. Together with Pulukisi he halts the progress of the ancestors during the *upaku* procession, highlighting a tension inherent in the presence of the ancestors who struggle to achieve liberation. As we will see in the final chapter, the ancestors, like Yalambar himself, must also contend with a conniving Krishna and the rivalry inherent in the *janjati* rhetoric that feeds on the violence, inequity, and death of the epic tradition.

Chapter Seven

Tantra, the *Mahābhārata*, and the Iconography of Indra

The image of Indra that sits at the base of the pole installed immediately outside Kathmandu's royal palace communicates Indra's royal authority. Seated in the *rāja-lalita-āsana* posture of royal repose, he sits atop his equally royal vehicle, the white elephant, fully ensconced at the center of the city, signaling, as van den Hoek writes, "what Indra was destined for" (2004: 42). In describing the multiple identities of South Indian poles installed at Draupadī temples, however, Alf Hiltebeitel provides the opportunity for another reading, asserting the protective power of such an image: "The post or flag-staff, once established outside a temple, has a guardian demon at its base in a position to protect it from recutting or to mark the spot of its yearly uprooting" (1991: 120–21). Considering the festival iconography of Indra, this chapter will begin with the notion that Indra is not simply the Vedic god of storms and warriors; rather, his protective nature at the base of the pole suggests that his Nepalese identity reflects the polytropic religion of the Kathmandu Valley, allowing for multiple simultaneous readings.

The ambivalence of Indra's character in his own festival—royal and protective—comes to be embodied in another one of his icons on a low table in the center of Nasal Chowk, the large courtyard immediately inside the main doors of the royal palace (see figure 7.1).[1] This equally central image, displayed in the most public area of the palace, is available to the Hindu Nepali king in a traditionally Newar domain, whose access to the image authorizes his own position

Figure 7.1. Indra sits on a low table in the center of Nasal Chowk. Photo by author.

as Indra. This central image is only one of many similar icons raised in the city, all of which are iconographically identical: a male figure seated with legs crossed and his arms fully extended to each side. It was one of these images that I described at the end of chapter 5, its puja performed by the Rajopadhyay of Kathmandu's Brahmapur neighborhood on Bhadra 11, the day before the pole's installation. Just as the small family poles dedicated to local ancestors mirror the festival's central pole, this central icon is reflected in and multiplied by a number of local neighborhood images of Indra.

The mutual distribution of Indra's power, equally harnessed by prominent but nearly opposing ritual actors, reinforces the composite nature of the Indra festival. Hardly "pitched and patched together," the festival empowers king and farmer alike, highlighting both Indra and Bhairav by performative techniques and iconographic displays relevant to each. Moreover, and to continue the theme from the previous chapter, the iconographic form and narrative foundations of these unique icons of Indra place the Indra festival in the popular South Asian *Mahābhārata* tradition. Drawing on the robust tantric tradition that underlays much of Newar religion in the Kathmandu Valley, the Indra festival places these icons against the classical narrative of the *parijata harana* that again reinforces its themes of the epic and the ancestors.

Authorizing and empowering the Jyāpu farmer caste groups that raise them, these icons—identical in size and form and raised high above each neighborhood—provide them with a power analogous to that of the king. Thus, whereas Śaktivallabh Arjyāl and the authors of the *Nepālikabhūpa Vaṃśāvalī* placed the Indra festival in the genre of *rājnīti* by translating, interpreting, and applying Hindu and Newar ritual manuals in support of the new Shah *asal Hindustān* imperium, the puja associated with these local icons of Indra belongs rather to what Gregory Grieve refers to as "prosaic tantra": a "routinized, domestic, and public system of 'dangerous' practices" (2006: 103–4). Grieve's discussion of the veneration of "stone-gods" in Bhaktapur also applies to icons and practices in Kathmandu's Indra festival. Not only is the veneration of forms of Bhairav, Kumari, and other goddesses tantric, but as I argue throughout this chapter, tantric worship of Indra also reflects the protective power attributed to him.

The Nepalese *Parijāta Haraṇa*

The local story of the *parijāta haraṇa* draws on the classical story of Krishna's theft of Indra's *parijata* flower found in several *puranas*.[2] Rooted in the classical textual tradition, this story reflects on the Sanskrit epic (especially the *Harivaṁśa*), connecting Kathmandu's Indra festival in direct thematic ways with the folk *Mahābhārata* (*MBh*) performances in both Garhwal and Tamil India. Despite variations in the narration, each version revolves around an essentially unchanging central core—shifts of power associated with the violent acquisition of another's property—that is accented with the introdution of some (semi-)divine character or urban location.[3] The telling of the *parijāta haraṇa* that I provide here incorporates details from different versions that I have heard and read, as I foreground those details that lead into my conclusion regarding the continuities of Kathmandu's Indra festival with local *Mahābhārata* performances throughout India.

Indra's mother, Dagi, residing with her son in heaven, began to perform a Basundharā *bartā* (Skt. *vrata*, vow). To properly carry out her vow, she required a flower from the parijat tree, which does not grow in the realm of the gods.[4] To help her, Indra traveled down from heaven to the Kathmandu Valley riding on his elephant, Airavāta. He descended at Kilagal Tol and wandered around the city for a bit. Arriving at Maru Tol, the city's central neighborhood, he chanced upon a Jyāpu gardener. Keeping his identity and the purpose of his visit hidden, Indra requested a single parijat flower, which the gardener freely gave to him. Other citizens of the area, however, not recognizing this "outsider" with one of the garden's prized flowers, seized the "thief," bound him with strong ropes, and put him in a cage high above the ground to humiliate him.[5] While Indra sat arrested and bound, Airavāta continued wandering around Kilagal Tol, increasingly distressed about the disappearance of his master. For four days, Indra's elephant wandered and worried, and his mother, without contact from her son, came down to Earth in the guise of the demonic white-faced Dagi (Skt. Ḍākinī), accompanied by spies in the form of Bhairavs to find out what had become of him. Finding Indra bound and humiliated for the entire valley to see, her Bhairavs engaged in combat with Indra's Jyāpu captors, liberating him and raising a banner (*dhvaja*) or pole (*yaḥsi/liṅgo*) as a symbol of their victory. In return for her son's freedom, Indra's mother promised to furnish the valley with the fog and dew necessary for productive agriculture and to take those captors of Indra who were killed in battle to heaven with her when she left. At the request of the captors, she promised to take all of Kathmandu's residents who had died in the previous year to heaven with her, too.

The continuities of this story with Indra's classical, even Vedic, identity are fairly evident, as he reprises his role as a divine thief. Examples of Indra's thievery abound: in *Rig Veda* 4.26–27, he and the eagle steal *soma* from heaven; he steals the the horse traveling the country as part of King Prithu's *aśvamedha* horse sacrifice at *Bhāgavata Purāṇa* (*BhP*) 4.19.2 and the horse intended for King Sagara's horse sacrifice at *Rāmāyaṇa* 1.39.7; at *Aitareya Brāhmaṇa* 7.14 (and *Rāmāyaṇa* 1.60.6) he steals the child Rohita, the son of King Hariścandra and the king's intended offering to Varuṇa; and at *Śatapatha Brāhmaṇa* 2.1.2.16, he steals a brick from the altar that the *asura*s had established for their *agnyādhāna*, causing it to collapse. Thus, one of the traditional identities of Indra—the thief—is given a place of primacy in the Nepalese festival and is even made to tally with or instantiate a more generic Newar *khundyaḥ* (thief-god).

On the other hand, this story inverts the classical South Asian *parijāta haraṇa* story in several significant ways. The Nepalese story relocates the flower and its tree, reidentifies the woman who desires the flower, and, most important, inverts Indra's role from victim to thief. Blending the essential components of the classical story with Indra's Vedic identity as thief, however, its reversal remains incomplete, thus doing little to exonerate Indra. Instead of victoriously placating his wife/mother by returning with the parijat in hand like the chivalric and heroic Krishna—a character well known for his thieving ways (as a child in the *BhP*) and for using martial deception (as the Pandava adviser in the *MBh*)—the victimized Indra of Nepal is portrayed as a little boy unable to complete a simple errand for his mother without being overtaken by a group of local farmers. Despite the variations and inversions seen in the local story, the theme of Indra's theft and punishment points to the larger Hinduization, Sanskritization, and Mahābhāratization process we see in Kathmandu's festival.

Cucumbers

The theme of theft, a key element of the Indra festival's telling of the *parijāta haraṇa*, provides one simple and introductory connection to the epic folklore that Alf Hiltebeitel proposes and I argue underlies the contemporary Indra festival. In his account of the celebration of the Indra festival in the Kathmandu Valley village of Pyangaon, Gérard Toffin explains that although the festival is otherwise very similar to that in Kathmandu (1984: 90), the foundational story there has "Indra Maharaj [descend] to the Valley of Kathmandu not for taking the parijat flower, but the cucumber *tusi*" (1978: 121). Indra, the main deity of Pyangaon's festival, is symbolized by a crown displayed in the village and is named *tusi khuima dyaḥ*, the divine thief of cucumbers. On the first night of the festival there, village boys replicate Indra's theft by going into the gardens of the village and stealing cucumbers; on the fourth day, they put these cucumbers in front of the local protective deity Chetrapāl, after which they are taken as *prasād* by the gathered crowd (1978: 113, 118).[6] Hiltebeitel also notes connections made between cucumbers and the related themes of fertility, sexuality, and protection. When Krishna calls on Hanuman to rouse Aravāṉ, Hanuman is told, incorrectly, that Aravāṉ is in the cucumber fields; once found elsewhere, he tells his mother, "The Pāṇḍavas are calling me" and moves to the battlefield at Kurukṣetra (Hiltebeitel 2018: 176).

Baumata and Ḍāgīṃ

Just as the *parijāta haraṇa* narrative and the figures of Pulukisi and Lakhe bear relationships to local performances of the *Mahābhārata,* so does one of the festival's most explicit celebrations of death. Two days after the *upaku,* on Bhādra 14 (the "Indrajātrā" day), Newars walk a pair of simultaneous and related processions directed to the ancestors. In the second one, Manandhars (New. Sāḥmi) carry the Baumata, a long bamboo structure covered in oil lamps, through the streets of the old city, precisely following the route taken by Kumari earlier in the day.[7] The meaning of the Newar term *baumata* is disputed: while *mata* clearly means "light" (Skt. *dīpa,* Nep. *diyā*), the initial part of this compound (*bau*) is unclear. Pradhan explains *bau* in terms of the Sanskrit *bali* as "both an offering to and the representation of evil spirits" (1986: 367–68).[8] His statement in that same section that *bau* also represents "offerings of piṇḍas to preta, crow and dog at sraddhas" explicitly includes the role of such offerings in rites to the ancestors. A different local explanation of the term *baumata* is that it is an Apabhramsa variant of the Newar *bīmata,* a reference to this object's "snakiness" (*bī*): the object is a *sarpa,* and the Baumata festival is a "*sarpa ko jātrā*" (snake festival), one local man told me as he connected this rite—in the larger festival's focus on rains, fertility, and agriculture—with the Vedic Indra's defeat of the serpent Vṛtra and the release of the rains. Many local people asserted the similarly serpentine nature of Indra's pole, whose fashioning in the forest resulted in its resemblance to the head (and body) of a snake.

Reinforcing Levy's positing of the performance of antistructural rituals during this "problematic" period of the year, Baumata onlookers hurl obscenities at the Manandhars as they process the streets of the city, a nullifying response that equally points to the life, generation, and procreative possibilities of those being remembered.[9] Those being remembered are those for whom the Sahmi *guthi* members and *bau-*

mata light the way: representatives of the recently deceased—typical recipients of the offering *bau*—who are led by Indra's mother, Dagi, who ritually reprises her role from the *local parijāta haraṇa* story.

The processions of Dagi and Baumata partially replicate the *upaku* that was walked on the first day. The Jyāpu man who plays the white-masked Dagi is accompanied by a long train of followers; each is a mourner who, wearing all white as a sign of a recent death in the family, might have had already walked the *upaku* two days ago. Instead of the long procession of the *upaku,* however, those of Baumata and Dagi follow the route that was taken by Kumari just two hours before. Dagi and her entourage depart first, setting out for the city's upper part (*thone*), during which time the Manandhars finish their preparation of Baumata. Upon her return to Kasthamandap in Maru Tol, the city's midpoint, and before leaving for the city's lower section (*kvane*), the Sahmi immediately take up Baumata and set out for the *thone,* following Dagi's route at a half *jātrā* (and thus a half-city) behind (see figure 7.2).

Figure 7.2. Indra's mother, Dagi, leads a procession of mourners late at night. Photo by author.

These two *jātrās* display several relevant contradictions. Despite following Kumari's route and traveling through the city's halves in an auspicious clockwise fashion, they reverse the order of Kumari's two processions. Whereas Kumari traveled to the southern part of the city on Bhadra 14 and to the north on Bhadra 15, Dagi and Baumata travel to the north before traveling south. Thus, whereas Kumari and her entourage establish the proper circumambulatory direction, these two processions, carried out between Kumari's two processions, temporarily challenge the city's auspiciousness, using the same space to affirm the loss and sorrow annually experienced in and by the city. This ritual challenge reinforces the logic of the insults and obscenities hurled at the Sahmi. Although it is often said that Baumata, whose participants are explictly not mourners but Sahmi *guṭhīyars,* lights the way for Dagi and her train of white-clad mourners, the Baumata structure clearly follows the mourners. One local scholar affirmed this reversal by telling me that "the Manandhars go on the way and carry that light in order to search for them and find them [the ancestors]."[10]

Henry Oldfield's 1880 account of Nepal copies Kirkpatrick's 1811 account virtually word for word when it comes to his accounting of Dagi's procession (1974: 314). Interesting here is that both authors actually account for Dagi, a relatively minor figure who only appears once during the festival. Both refer to Dagi's procession from Kathmandu to Dahachowk (Kirkpatrick's "Deh-choak" and Oldfield's "Deo Chowk") but not within the city, and both connect this procession to the Balkumari temple in Thimi, a goddess, temple, and town that play virtually no role in the contemporary festival. Whether these passages represent a relic of the past or the authors simply misunderstood their sources, their references require a bit of a geographical corrective. The town of Thimi lies east of Kathmandu on the road to Bhaktapur, whereas Daha Chowk ("the place of the lake") lies ten kilometers west of Kathmandu and continues to serve as the destination of Dagi's procession, though its pilgrims still are, as Oldfield notes, "few in number."[11]

The *parijāta haraṇa* narrative ends in (at least) two different ways, neither of which ends well for the mourners who trail behind Dagi. The first ends with what we might call Dagi's "sin of omission." "But when she arrived at Indra Daha with her son and her required *parijat* flower in tow, the queue of the spirits of the deceased that was also following her broke and the spirits fell into the lake. With the spirits left helpless in the lake, Indra's mother returned with her son up to heaven, leaving the crowd of deceased to remain on earth and to be mourned by their descendants." In the second, however, Dagi commits, though is not found guilty of, a "sin of commission."

> But when she arrived at the lake with the trail of recently deceased following her, Dagi required that each of the deceased first bathe in Indra Daha before arising to heaven; while they were bathing, she enveloped herself and her son in a cloud preventing the crowd from seeing her and following her up to heaven. Having thus deceived the crowd of ancestors, Indra's mother stole away with her son up to heaven, leaving the crowd of deceased to remain on earth and to be mourned by their ancestors.[12]

Thus the ancestors who are multiply regarded during the festival, whose processions are coeval with the city of Kathmandu (in the *upaku* procession) and the royal Kumari (in Dagi's urban procession), and whose myths permeate the Indra festival and the antistructural and "problematic" period of the *cāturmāsa,* are summarily discarded at the end of Bhadra. The following day, the first day of the dark half of the month of Asoj, sees the rehabilitation of these same ancestors with the beginning of the sixteen-day *sohra śrāddha.* One *guthi* member from the southern neighborhood of Musum Bahāl, where one of the seven images of Indras is raised, explained to me: "Since Indra died on the full-moon day [of Bhādra], a *śrāddha* is performed on the following day. On the first day of Asoj, a *homa* is performed, and *samay baji* [festival food] is distributed." Thus it seems to be at this moment, between the full moon day of Bhādra and the first day of Asoj, that the classical and contemporary festivals come together, reflecting the defeat of death and chaos and issuing in a new year of life and royally sponsored civic order.

The penultimate moment of Dagi's deception that sets up this victorious moment connects to contemporary epic performances and to an event that Hiltebeitel describes as one that sees "epic mythology tied to the locally performed ritual cycle" (1988: 436). The Tamil epic performance ends with Draupadī's walk over burning coals. Despite this event's absence from the epic text, an absence of which local performers are well aware, performers make connections between the procession and the text that "reveal a series of fragmented but important contextual keys" to both the procession and the text (437). The ritual of the firewalk is connected by different storytellers largely to three different textual events, though they are thematically related. For some, the event is tied to Draupadī's serial marriages to the five Pandava brothers, after each, in order to maintain her virginity, she "bathed in turn in the very hot loving fire which gave birth to her" (438). For others, her purificatory bath followed her near-abduction by Kicaka, thus serving as an *agni parīkṣā* fire test like that performed by Sita after her return from Lanka to Ayodhya, to prove her chastity to Ram.[13] Due partly to the inconsistency of narrators in relating the ritual to these two stories, Hiltebeitel favors a third textual context: an expiatory postwar firewalk that clears the remaining land of all impurities and reminders of the horrific war that just ended. In a more orthodox but rare local variant of this story, Draupadī and her five husbands construct and then cross a firepit to perform *prāyaścitta* for the sins they have committed.

Several of the Draupadī cult professionals Hiltebeitel consulted provided a fourth and very different story, one of "considerable ingenuity" that I quote in full (without bracketed Tamil terms).

> After the war is over, Dharma is desolate. He laments his responsibility for the deaths of Karṇa, who should have been king, of Bhīṣma, and others. Having come to Hāstinapura to be coronated, he has no will to rule, despite Kṛṣṇa's entreaties that he prepare to do so. Around him he sees the womenfolk weeping, wailing, having lost their husbands in battle. "Why should I rule and be happy while others are weeping," he asks Kṛṣṇa.
>
> At this impasse, Kṛṣṇa decides to do a trick. He calls Draupadī and reminds her of her birth from fire. He tells her to create another sacrificial fire and walk through it. "Ordinarily people won't walk through fire, but knowing that you were born in fire, if you say they will get back their children, husbands, etc., they will follow you, believing that by doing so they will get their loved ones back, that those whom they lost in battle will come back to life. When this is done, Dharma's coronation can then proceed."

> This Pāñcāli then enters the fire and comes out, because of her powers. But the others who follow do not come out, as they are ordinary men, women, and children. They all die in the fire. Only Pāñcāli-Śakti comes out. So now there are no more voices of wailing or weeping, nothing to deter Dharma from becoming king. This is another aspect of Kṛṣṇa's trick. The scene is now calm, auspicious. Dharma has no disturbances. And the ones who died did rejoin their loved ones, but in heaven. Their bodies, flesh and blood, were destroyed by the fire, but their souls were released. So people walk on fire now. (Hiltebeitel 1988: 440–41)[14]

Elements of this story are familiar from the epic text. Just as before King Dharma Yudhiṣṭhira's *rājasūya* in the epic's second book, before his entrance into Hāstinapura in the twelfth, and before his *aśvamedha* in the fourteenth, he hesitates before taking a further imperial stride. Just as in those three passages, the perennial trickster Krishna appears with encouragement and a ritual solution that is grounded in the familiar trickery he uses throughout the epic text. Different from the resolutions of those previous moments of Dharma's doubt, however, this ritual will be performed not by the king himself but by his *śakti*-bearing wife, Draupadī.

Despite the absence of fire in the Nepalese narrative, it should be clear that this narrative bears a striking resemblance to that underlying the procession to Indra Daha by Dagi and her trail of mourners. In the stories and rituals of each, we see the centrality of a goddess paired with a male relation, who together concoct a scheme so deceptive and vile as to be nearly incomprehensible. Although the textual basis for King Dharma's original doubt serves to contextualize this deception—how could he rule in the presence of so much despair?—Krishna's goal of eliminating all of these weeping widows from the city seems extreme, if not illogical, resulting in yet another Pyrrhic victory for the Pandavas who now rule over a desolate kingdom. Both narratives and their accompanying rituals reinforce the fundamental gulf that exists between life and death and the ultimate separation of the living and the dead, although each offers a different solution. Whereas Draupadī's followers can rejoin their ancestors only in heaven after death, the Nepalese pilgrims learn that in the absence of a physical reunion with their ancestors in heaven or on Earth, their connection can be maintained only ritually, with the regular performance of the *śrāddha* beginning on the immediately following day, the epic's new year's day when the classical Indra festival was celebrated.

Multiple Readings of Indra

Indra and his mother, Dagi, are related not only by blood but also by their shared iconography (Ahmed 2003). Wearing a simple white mask, garlands of multiple types of flowers, and a full dress of *tās*—the same red-and-gold fabric that protects the royal sword and is worn by the Kumari—she is flanked by two men who hold onto and lead her by her arms, which are fully extended at her sides. Distributed in neighborhoods through the city, all seven images of Indra are similarly positioned: seated in a cross-legged position, he faces forward, his arms also fully extended at his sides. Placed on Kumari's processional routes, these images contribute to the relationship of Indra and his festival with the prevailing classical theme of royalty. Also, and somewhat contradictorily, these images are nearly universally said to represent Indra at the moment of his arrest for stealing the *parijat* flower for his mother's puja. Moreover, these festival images all face west, signaling the festival's focus on death and the ancestors. The remainder of this chapter attends to five different readings of these images—brahminical, Vedic, epic, tantric, and folk. Drawing on the twin themes of the epic and the ancestors and on the narrative of the *parijata harana*, each icon, seen virtually nowhere else in the South Asian world, points to the kaleidoscopic nature of Kathmandu's Indra festival that collapses these various modes of narrative and performance into a single simple image.

The Brahminical Indra

The narrative of Indra's theft played out in several ways during the puja to the Indra icon in the Brahmapur neighborhood. The first highlighted the precarious and hierarchial nature of the multi-*jati* relationships that can appear in South Asian societies, especially during festivals when individual *jati* perform traditional tasks. Reprising their often supportive role in festivals, two Jyāpu men were present to musically accompany the puja conducted by Rajopadhyay brahmins. One musician routinely took cigarette breaks, seemingly as an act of resistance, such that the Rajopadhyay twice had to interrupt with a harsh directive of "Bājā!" (Music!). The tension displayed reflects their hierarchical relationship and is reinforced by the narrative of Indra's theft, as it is the Jyāpu who arrested Indra for stealing their flowers and tried to humiliate him through his public display.[15] The Rajopadhyay, on the other hand, uniquely conduct the puja in Brahmapur; identifying themselves with Indra and identifying Indra as a brahmin like them appears to have produced a sort of resentment among the Jyāpus, who otherwise maintain this icon in the nearby temple of Akash Bhairav over which they preside.

The narrative of Indra's theft played out a second time and more explicitly toward the end of the puja. Before the Jyāpu men again played music and carried Indra back to Indra Chowk for his installation above the street, many of the neighborhood's female attendees made a unique offering not found in any of the ritual texts. Requesting the *janāī* threads wrapped around their husbands' wrists, the Rajopadhyay women placed them on Indra's outstretched wrists, with the attending priest concluding the puja by doing the same. For some of the participants, the stated purpose behind this gifting of the *janāī* (janai) was either to protect Indra during his return to heaven or, more commonly, to participate in binding the arrested flower-thief.[16] This simple action, performed by brahmin families, reflects older pan–South Asian narratives, especially that of the festival of *rakshā bandhan*, commonly attributed to the *Bhaviṣya Purāṇa* and celebrated throughout the subcontinent today. One day, when a nervous Indra was heading off to battle the serpent-demon Vṛtra, his wife, Śachī, at the request of Bṛhaspati, the brahmin priest of the gods, tied around Indra's wrist a thread (*rakhi*) that she had imbued with powerful mantras. Thus, these Rajopadhyay women, rather than serving as assistants to the citizen's police force of Jyāpu farmers, reperform the role of Indra's *śakti*, his powerful and ritually required wife, protecting him in his perpetual battle against demons and thus ensuring the annual rains.

Giving the janai thus contributes to the chronology of the Indra festival. A twenty-six-day span that begins with the full-moon day of *janāī pūrṇimā*, this period ends on Bhādra 11, the day before the raising of Indra's pole, when the thread is re-placed on Indra's outstretched arms. As the festival of *janāī pūrṇimā* requires a brahmin for its focal event, relinquishing the janai by the residents of Brahmapur explicitly recalls this earlier ritual, via the display of a suddenly threadbare wrist, interposing a clearly brahminical element into an otherwise Jyāpu-focused rite. Moreover, through this largely private ritual, the Rajopadhyay caste displays and reasserts its brahmin status—vis-à-vis the Jyāpu farmer-musicians who mistakenly apprehended Indra—through their communal performance of the role of the divine guru.[17]

The Vedic Indra

In a review of Levy's *Mesocosm*, Michael Witzel (1997), picking up on Kuiper's (1977) theory of the Vedic origins of the Indra festival, of Indra's identity with the *skambha* (*axis mundi*) in two hymns from the *Atharva Veda*, and of its manifestation in the festival's tall wooden pole, asserts that these icons represent the Vedic Indra at the moment of his creation of the world. "The Vedic Indra festival, Indradhvaja, was characterized by the raising of a pole symbolizing Indra, the demiurge, who, as soon as he was born, raised heaven with his outstretched arms. . . . Indra, the Hindu Atlas, is also a symbol of royalty, from ṛgvedic times. The king in the Vedic inauguration ceremony (*abhiṣeka*) has to stand up, firmly, just like Indra" (*RV* 10.173) (1997: 520). Witzel recalls two potential antecedents for what he refers to as this "strange form of Indra": the Vedic myth of Indra separating Earth from heaven, and the king's *abhiṣeka* rite, part of the larger *rājasūya*, in which the king stands up firmly. Also from the Vedic *rājasūya*, in a preparatory rite before the *abhiṣeka* and after the recitation of the story of Indra's slaying of the *asura* Namuci, the king mounts a chariot (*gartam*) and raises his arms (*udgṛhṇāti*). Here, the text draws particular attention to the king's two arms, which are likened to Varuṇa and Mitra, to Aditi and Diti, and to a pair of Indras (*Śatapatha Brāhmaṇa* [*ŚB*] 5.4.2.14–16). The intense focus on the king's arms in the *ŚB* passage and on those in the unique iconography of the Nepalese Indra draw our attention to these most royal of all body parts; the Puruṣa-sūkta hymn of the *Rig Veda* (10.90.12b), quoted several times in Śaktivallabh's Indra puja, also associates the arms with the *rājanya* warrior class (*bāhū rājanyaḥ kṛtaḥ*). Heesterman explains the possible cosmological significance of this posture of the king being "the sun, about to rise, or he is Indra raising his bolt to crush Vṛtra; he raises the cosmic pillar, which is mounted by Mitra and Varuṇa or Indra and Sūrya at daybreak" (1957: 102).

Despite the positional flaw in these examples—the vertical motions depicted when Indra raises heaven or his thunderbolt and when the king stands up, rather than the horizontally oriented and seated posture depicted in Indra's Nepalese images—and despite my consistent line of argumentation against the Vedic origins of the Indra festival, the similarities in these images belie a formal economy available to the ritualists and artists in all of these eras. In an article on the *yūpārohaṇa* (ascension of the *yūpa* pole) rite of the *vājapeya*, Francesco Brighenti draws on examples of the ritual embrace and ascension of Vedic poles that also seem to contribute to a postural habitus that might have influenced the form of Indra's contemporary images. He explains how the ritualist (with his wife) climbs the pole, touches a wheat cake placed at the top, and "spreads his arms like the wings of a bird" (*ŚB* 2.1.9–20) (Brighenti 2012: 109). Using the same language as the royal *abhiṣeka* text above ("Having finished [the climb], he raises his arms" [*āntaṃ gatvā bāhū udgṛhṇāti*]), this domestic text (*Baudhāyana Śrautasūtra* 11.11.80.6) provides "a means to apotheosis, which conforms with the main purpose of the *vājapeya* as a ritual of status elevation" (109).[18] This ritual means of connecting the domestic ritualist to the king and thus to the divine Indra provides a mechanism for similar power sharing between king, priest, and farmer seen in the Indra puja but also troubles Indra's strict identity as king.

The Epic Indra

Just like the domestic Vedic ritualist who extending his arms (*udgṛhṇāti*) shares in the identity of the initiated and conquering king, the inverse also becomes true: the placement of multiple Indras—one inside the palace and the others by Jyāpus—renders problematic the identity of Indra with the king of Nepal. Thus the stark bivalence of these images suggests the king's identification with the king of the gods and with the king of thieves, and the central image in the palace tells us something that the local images do not: that this icon of Indra—and by extension all of his icons in the city—have a certain power that is available to be harnessed.

Indra's essentially bivalent identity—as "king and clown," to borrow David Shulman's phrase—is evident throughout the myths, rituals, and iconography in this festival and more generally throughout his biographies. Shulman writes that this bivalent pan–South Asian royal clown "who is held responsible for the society's proper order may be seen to undermine this order, to unravel the fabric even as it is being woven, to open up his kingdom to indeterminate forces of transformation and flux" (1985: 215). The resultant bivalence, largely a product of the social uses of this image, serves as an example of the type of "ritual practice" that, as Bourdieu suggests, "performs an uncertain abstraction which brings the same symbol into different relationships by apprehending it through different aspects, or which brings different aspects of the same referent into the same relationship of opposition" (1990: 87). The two major aspects of Indra—king and clown—arise from the different relationships he bears to the citizens of Kathmandu, namely, to the Jyāpu farmers and to the Rajopadhyay brahmins.

Indra's clownish aspect is defined by the event of his arrest, facilitated by his descent from heaven and incognito travels in Kathmandu. Comparing Indra's tale with similar narratives, especially that of the Pandava brothers in the *Virāṭa Parvan,* Indra's travels belie something darker: an exile. As a forced departure to a foreign land when "the king is brought into contact with an area of experience perhaps ultimately *more* 'real' than any prescribed role," the condition of exile has "a transcendent aspect crucially important for the king" (Shulman 1985: 218). It is in the forest where—mythically and ritually—the king obtains the spiritual authority that undergirds his urban power through contact with forest-dwelling brahmins and defeating the forest's demonic denizens. In his descent from heaven to the garden, Indra leaves behind his royal responsibilities and persona and, like the Pandava brothers living the life of their absurd alter egos, establishes his clownish persona. Like the exile of the Pandavas, Indra's exile, annually repeated by the citizens of Kathmandu, is similarly purifying. Cultural identities are asserted, urban boundaries are multiply reaffirmed, and the recently deceased are remembered and celebrated.

Yet this annual celebration is not complete without the display of these images, physical memories of Indra's sole—and humiliating—descent to Earth. Concluding his section on Indra's classical downfall, Shulman, referring to the mirroring cast of characters whom these authors held up to the clownish Indra, provides an analysis that applies just as well to the festival images of Indra as to the alter egos of the Pandava brothers: "'Disguised' as a shadowy caricature of his former self, the exiled king finds mirrored fragments of himself littered around the ominous landscape of his trials. . . . [T]he eery images of his lost self will haunt his memory as a living presence until they assume external form again, in his next exilic phase" (1985: 228).

The icons of Indra displayed in Kathmandu depict kingship, kinship, and fertility, all through the narrative of Indra's thievery. Bound and displayed on a platform high above the streets of the city, Indra is no longer an independent ruling king, but is a royal captive held in place by those who seek his power. These icons bring us back full circle to the final image we have of the Chedi king Vasu in *MBh* 1.57, the first performer of Indra's festival and another royal captive foreshadowing Indra's captivity. In *MBh* 1.57.13–14, Indra provides Vasu with the gift of a "sky-going chariot" as one of several strategies to convince him not to renounce the world but to remain king of Chedi. In verse 13, Indra depicts the sense of motion that defines the wheeled (and here, flying) chariot, telling Vasu

> In the heavens is a great crystalline, divinely pleasurable sky-going chariot (*ākāśagaṃ vimānaṃ*).
>
> It will approach you (*upapatsyate*), and it will be given to you by me.

In verse 14, Indra changes course by depicting its subsequent stability, twice using forms of the verbal root √*sthā* (to stand):

> Among all mortals, you are the only one who will stand (*sthitaḥ*) atop this grand *vimāna*.
>
> You will become established (*chariṣyasi uparistho*) in the heavens, as if you were a god.

Indra seems to be alluding to icons of the gods carried in and processed through the streets of the city in grand public festivals, such as with Kumari's chariot processions in Kathmandu's Indra festival. But the end of the epic narrative shows Vasu not moving through space on a swiftly moving chariot (*vimāna*) but remaining motionless in the sky on a static platform (*prāsāda*): "The king is seated (*vasantaṃ*) on the crystal platform in the sky; *gandharva*s and *apsarase*s approached (*upatasthur*) the Great-souled king [to pay homage]. His name was [now] known as Rājā Uparicara" (1.57.31).[19] Though the object remains the same (still *sphāṭika* and still residing in the *ākāśa*), and though he is being worshipped in the sky by divine beings who themselves are in motion, the changes in language from *vimāna* to *prāsāda* and from verbs of motion (√*gam*) to verbs connoting stability (√*vas* and √*sthā*) signal a change in Vasu's situation.[20] Though having earlier performed the Indra festival joyfully (*hāsyarūpeṇa*, 1.57.21), Vasu's final condition stuck motionless in space—having accepted Indra's gifts, acquiesced to Indra's royal demands, and given up his desire to lay down his weapons, perform acts of *tapas*, and take up residence in an *āśrama*—strikes me as rather pathetic and similarly eerie to Indra's own.

Suspended in midair, the liminal Vasu resembles other figures from epic literature: Jaratkaru's descendants who hang like bats in a cave (1.41), the serpent Takṣaka suspended in midair at the *sarpasattra* (1.52–53), and Triśaṅku in the *Rāmayāṇa* whom Indra curses when he tries to become like a god and enter heaven in his physical body (1.59). These characters remain physically suspended, and they keep their readers in suspense as to how their incomplete story might end. Confined by Indra, Vasu performs the Indra festival and becomes a proper brahminical king. His confinement, however, draws him into another category of person; not only a *brāhmaṇya rājā*, Vasu resembles the powerful and quasi-demonic tantric figures we will see in the following section.

As Indra confines Vasu to do his administrative bidding, so do Jyāpu farmers ensure the continuity of Indra's blessings at the end of the monsoon season in preparation for the rice harvest by venerating and harnessing his power. Guarding the royal Indra icon at the base of the pole and installing his ambivalent and eerie icons throughout the city, Kathmandu's Jyāpus participate in the city's prosaic tantra by operating coagentively with the city's most powerful people (the Nepalese king), communities (Rajopadhyay brahmins), and deities (Yalambar-Bhairav-Aju), extending their power over nature, ancestors, and the city.

The Tantric Indra

In *Sketches from Nepal*, Oldfield notes the relationship of these images with the ancestors: "Figures of Indra, with outstretched arms, are erected all about the city, and are invoked as especially sacred to the memory of deceased ancestors. Other deities also, as Bisna Rup, Bhairav, &c., but chiefly those of Indra, are often placed in little temporarily-raised shrines or 'machams'" (1974: 314). Oldfield's association of Indra's images with those of other deities is important in evaluating the role of Indra in his own festival. In his studies of the Indra festival in the nearby village of Pyangaon, Toffin asserted that the festival's two aniconic poles—one male and the other female—are not explicitly identified with Indra (1978; 1992: 82–83). G. S. Nepali suggests a similar ambiguity regarding the identity of Indra's pole: "The *linga* is, therefore, typically a symbol connected with Bhairava and Bhairavi. But how it came to be associated with the festival of Indra is hard to explain" (1965: 359). Similar images raised in Bhaktapur, just twelve kilometers down the road, are also identified as Bhairav, Yama, or Indra's son, Jayant. Stitched together from elements of local Newar culture and a revived Hindu festival, the images of Indra in Kathmandu—all of which face west in the universal direction of death and indicate the story of his mother's procession to the lake of Indra—draw on the themes of death, the ancestors, and the tantric protection of urban space.

In her study of the texts and practices dedicated to the Newar goddess Svasthānī, Jessica Vantine Birkenholtz describes how certain visual cues "mark the first of an increasing number of Tantric elements that permeated Svasthānī's iconography in the nineteenth century" (2018: 66). Accompanied by the protective Bhairav just as frequently as by her husband, Shiva, and traditionally portrayed aniconically—as a *yantra* depicting a *darpaṇa* mirror on which an eight-petaled lotus provides the names of her accompanying Aṣṭamātṛkā—the goddess is brought into the "expanding influence of Tantrism in the Nepal Valley" (66).[21] The basic concepts of Tantra have been in place in South Asia for centuries, with their influences, basic to Hindu and Buddhist ritual and iconography in Nepal, expanding well beyond the roles, images, and identities of any particular deity and becoming included in the Indra festival, whose classical performance contained few (if any) of such elements.

Central to Tantra is a quest for power that David Gordon White describes as "an effort to gain access to and appropriate the energy or enlightened consciousness of the absolute godhead that courses through the universe" as part of the "body of beliefs and practices which . . . seeks to ritually appropriate and channel that energy, within the human microcosm, in creative and emancipatory ways" (2000: 8, 9). One ritually appropriates the "divine energy of the godhead that creates and maintains that universe" through two main "strategies of embodiment" (9)—possession and binding, both of which are relevant to these local images of Indra and intimately relate the practitioner to the divine in somewhat ambivalent ways. Much of the language of possession is based on the Sanskrit verbal root √*viś*—*āveśa, praveśa,* or *samāveśa*—and implies an event in which a divine being enters a human being, a concept Frederick Smith further translates as "interpenetration" (2006: 372). Examples of possession—those that are seen more as a gift rather than requiring exorcism, to use Kathleen Erndl's distinction (1993: 106)—appear throughout some of the more private and Tantrically tinged rituals and festivals of the Nepal Valley, including in the Indra festival. Most notable are devotees who exhibit signs of possession at the sight of the masked deities they worshipfully approach, and the masked dancers who are, like Dagi, escorted by two human guardians who attach themselves to the dancers' outstretched arms.[22]

This particular gesture of possession is related to the strategy of binding, the second technique for ritually appropriating the "divine energy of the godhead." A nearly inverse strategy to possession in which a divine being enters a human vehicle, the act of binding entails an expert human practitioner exercising external agency over the deity. White writes on the ways that practitioners use such vernacular Tantric ritual technologies to venerate Bhairav in cases where a person is "'sealed [in]' or 'nailed [down]' [by a demon]" (2010: 209). The inverse case, in which Bhairav is restrained, shows the two related functions of ritual binding together. First, it can be used to confine destructive demons to a single, immobile, and harmless location, using paraphernalia—often iron nails and wooden pegs—to prevent them from mercilessly unleashing the afflictions they are known for: disease, madness, and misfortune. White provides an account of a unique Rajasthani form of Bhairav, who is found by the side of stepwells and "is represented as a standing human figure, with his head turned sideways and his body encircled by chains. . . . There are those who say that his image represents that of a human criminal who, bound in chains and thrown into the well, is now worshiped as its divine guardian, Zanzīr Bherum-jī ['Chain Bhairav']" (n.d. 22–23). Second, binding practices can be used to put others under one's control, utilizing their powers for one's own benefit. White refers to the binding techniques mentioned in the *Kathāsaritsāgara* as "the special prerogative of Yoginīs, who use mantra-enchanted threads to ensnare their human prey"; he also provides the example of Siddhanāth, an incarnation of Kāl Bhairav at the Maharashtrian Gosain cult center of Sonarī, who goes to the underworld and hangs a garland on Yogeśvarī, thus bringing this powerful goddess under his control and forcing her to obey his commands (20).

These related and ambivalent functions of binding, confinement, and tantric control permeate Himalayan ritual and narrative. The goddess Taleju was harnessed for the benefit of Newar Malla kings, and guardian *lokapāla*s and malevolent *krodha* deities are summoned and welcomed with proper mantras and *mudra*s to protect the inner mandala of the Buddhist deity Karuṇāmaya (Locke 1980: 89–90; Bledsoe 2000: 196). Sax offers an extended example from his study of the Pāṇḍav Līlā, the Garhwali performance of the *Mahābhārata*. In this story, Krishna confronts the demonic preincarnation of Arjuna's son Abhimanyu, closing him inside a drawer and locking the box. Threatened with his life, Krishna "dug a hole, buried the box, and covered it with mud and rocks," later digging up the box, grinding the demon's bones to powder, putting the powder back in the box, and ordering that nobody look at it. Krishna specifically orders the woman of the house, his sister Subhadrā, not to open the box; her curiosity gets the better of her, she disobeys, and thus revives the formerly pulverized and confined demon. The demon's life-breath returns and enters Subhadrā, thus issuing forth Abhimanyu's reincarnation (Sax 2002: 103–4).

In many Nepalese cases, it is goddesses who are bound. In the forests to the northeast of Bhaktapur, the Nava Durgā (the Nine Durgās) would catch people who walked by, sacrifice them, and drink their blood.[23] One day, Sunanda Āchāju, a tantric priest passed through the forest and was caught by them, but before he could be sacrificed, he insisted that he be able to worship them. Having bought himself some time, he chanted a mantra that bound the goddesses, making them unable to move; he shrunk them, put them in his basket, and took them home. At the tantric's home, the Nava Durgā were hidden in a locked room where he worshipped them with tantric *bidyā*, offered them sacrifices, and made them dance. This powerfully symbiotic relationship would last, the goddesses stipulated, only as long as they were not found out. One day, the priest's wife opened the door and saw the goddesses dancing, at which point the relationship was immediately severed. En route to resuming their sacrificial labors in the forest, the tantric priest convinced them to remain at the center of the city at a temple that remains their home today. Nutandhar Sharma tells the similar stories of Gayaḥbājyā, the tantric guru and hero from Patan, the central theme of whose stories is the quest for immortality through his "siddhi-tantric powers" (1999: 253). In one story, Gayaḥbājyā helps his students catch and imprison the Aṣṭamātṛ kā by placing a *tāraṇ* (invisible wall) around them; having done so, Gayaḥbājyā was able to bring them from their home on Phulchokī Mountain to the monastery of Piṃbahāl in Patan where, until his death, they danced in a nearby courtyard (1999: 244).[24]

In these Himalayan cases, we see powerful and ambivalent deities who are tantrically bound for the power they possess, deities whose bondage prefigures, highlights, and empowers a more sympathetic or heroic character. Levy's statement regarding the ensuing phase of the mythic career of the Nava Durgā describes this ideal harnessing: "Through the wife's meddling an essential transformation takes place, however—the powerful amoral gods move from the private personal realm of the Tantric Brahman to the public space of the city for the use and good of the city as a whole" (Levy and Rajopadhyaya 1990: 506). Local communities in Bhaktapur use this public space of the city during the Dasain festival as they invite, host, and thus harness the power of the low Gāthā-caste Nava Durgā dancers/goddesses. These dangerous divinities, in their serial appearances throughout the area,

> have a special position in the maintenance of order in Bhaktapur, where Tantra . . . has been captured and put to use by the social order as the legend of the origin of the Nine Durgās attests, rather than representing attempts by renouncers, magicians, and peripheral social groups to escape from that order. . . . [T]he dangerous deities are responsible for the *protection* of the traditional ritual and

> moral life, although they are beyond morality themselves. They are ambivalently made use of when that moral order is being threatened. (574; emphasis in original)

Whether applied toward ensuring particular benefits or simply toward the "ambivalent" assurance of protection, binding deities represents a standard ritual technology in the "prosaic tantra" of the religion of the Kathmandu Valley (Grieve 2006: 103–14).

More than a possession event, the similarity in the posture of Indra and his mother reinforces the urban tantra that underlies much of Newar religion in Kathmandu. Indra's mother's name, Dagi, directly connects her with powerful and often Buddhist *ḍākinī*, such as the mother of Macchendranath, the Buddhist deity at the center of Patan's most important annual festival. "Herself a *ḍākinī* (witch)," N. J. Allen writes, she is (in)directly related to the deity's "shady" company, which Allen identifies as the spirits of the dead: *bhūt-pret*, *yakṣa*, and *yoginī* (1986: 89).[25] Similarly, in referring to the veneration of the goddess Pūtanā specifically, and to the classes of *yoginī* and *ḍākinī* to which Dagi more generally belongs, White states: "One calls her and her dangerous host down upon oneself, and through ritual manipulation, compels them to do one's bidding" (2000: 19). Indra's arms signal this tantric manipulating, compelling, and bidding through not only their extension but also their binding. Like Dagi's arms bound by her two male guardians during her late night procession, Indra's are similarly bound by the janai threads applied to his arms during his local pujas. Attached by the Rajopadhyay and Jyāpu residents of the Brahmapur neighborhood, these janai are said to protect him during his return to heaven, to bind the arrested flower-thief in place, or as G. S. Nepali writes, to signify "that he is in chains" (1965: 360).[26]

Indra's unique iconography participates in many of these valences of tantric binding and possession, with Kathmandu's images combining the valences of all of them.[27] Moreover, binding Indra in threads or chains recalls a key moment in the *parijāta haraṇa* narrative of the *Harivaṁśa*, the appendix to the *Mahābhārata*. Steeped in the same themes of politics, rivalry, and kingship, later "manuscript developments [of the *Harivaṁśa*] echo the larger Indian tradition, which assigns to the adventure of the Pārijāta tree a significance shared by no other episode of Kṛṣṇa's adult life" (Austin 2013: 250). This story highlights, as Christopher Austin argues, two themes "fundamental to the understanding of Kṛṣṇa's adult identity," and also, I argue, fundamental to the Indra festival: "vigorous conflict over the tree and the role of the auspicious feminine" (2013: 250). The conclusion of this passage focuses these two themes through a narrative of binding, as part of Satyabhāmā's performance of the Puṇyaka rite, whose narrative elements draw Kathmandu's festival within the ambit of the epic tradition.

> Satyabhāmā places a garland on Kṛṣṇa's neck and ties him to the Pārijāta tree (II. 1522–23). In so doing she hands Kṛṣṇa over into Nārada's possession along with many precious substances. Nārada then unties Kṛṣṇa and clowns about, making Kṛṣṇa follow him around and respect every command (II. 1530–35), and finally removes the flowers from Kṛṣṇa's neck and demands the ritually appropriate (*vihita*) *niṣkraya* or fee by which Kṛṣṇa is to be ransomed from captivity: a Kapilā cow, together with her calf, and a black antelope skin packed full with sesame and gold. (Austin 2013: 257)

Satyabhāmā ransoming Krishna from bondage is one that, Austin argues, hearkens back to Vedic ritual forms, that represents a gesture that is "all-important, fundamental to the Puṇyaka ritual carried out by Satyabhāmā, and that speaks in the most elemental way to the identity and ideal character of the married women." Like Aditi, Indrāṇī, Ṛddhi, and Rohiṇī before her, Satyabhāmā "desires to enact physically the loss and binding of her husband, to rehearse, intervene in, and cancel out his death . . . [via] the Puṇyaka rite [that] portrays the husband bound and given over into the possession of a third party, with the act of binding taking place at a tree" (Austin 2013: 259, 260).

The connections of this story with that of Kathmandu's Indra festival should be fairly clear. A semi-divine female (Satyabhāmā / Dagi) requires (a portion of) the *parijat* tree for performing a puja (Puṇyaka / Tij); the divine male she sends to acquire the *parijat* (Krishna / Indra) is apprehended and bound to a tree (Parijāt / Indra pole) by a third party (Nārada / Jyāpus). The female frees him by offering a fertile ransom (a cow / fog and dew). Austin concludes that the *parijāta haraṇa* narrative establishes the identity of Krishna as a "prosperous man of the world [who] established domestic felicity and auspiciousness only by fighting for women who, as forms of wealth themselves, are appropriately tied to fabulous treasure-objects of ever-renewed fecundity" (2013: 265). Although operating in a different narrative universe, Indra, connected to the domestic felicity of Dagi, as well as to the numerous other goddesses implicated in the Indra festival narrative—especially Kumari and Mahālakṣmī—reinforces the renewed fecundity at the heart of Jyāpu farmer interests and the fruition of Dagi's promise to send the fog and dew required for their crops.

Though the procession of Dagi's human form more actively displays possession and binding, the inverted and adapted *parijāta haraṇa* narratives and the Jyāpu images that depict this story place Indra in the realm of the valley's prosaic tantra.[28] As Indra's binding draws on the imagery of Vedic royal figures, it also closely resembles those of Zanzir Bherum-jī, the demonic Abhimanyu, and the maternal Aṣṭamātṛkā, Nava Durgā, and his own quasi-demonic mother, Dagi. More than simply a subdued thief, Indra is bound, displayed, and guarded, his power "captured and put to use by the social order."

The Folk Indra

The local and most common explanation of these Indra icons, that he is being punished, arrested, and humiliated for having stolen the *parijat* flower, reflects the tantric strategy of harnessing the power of Indra—the Vedic god who freed the waters from the clutches of his enemies—for the forthcoming harvest.[29] But the presence and identity of these icons has long vexed scholars: Witzel calls them "strange"; Shulman refers to such multiple clownish royal images as eerie; and Nepali finds it "hard to explain" how Indra might be distinct from Bhairav. Part of the difficulty in identifying these images is based in how art historian Gautamvajra Vajracharya, like many Newars, sees the development and Sanskritization of the local Indra festival. In an interview after a lecture in Kathmandu, he said, "At that time, Indrajātrā had nothing to do with Indra or Bhairava. The tradition was based among the ancient nature-worshipping Newar farmers. It was only later that, within the culture of the valley, the god of rain became associated with Indra and the sky with Bhairav. On the basis of all of this, it turns out that Indrajatra was not originally Indrajatra" (Giri 2019).[30] In his work on the nature imagery in Newar art, Vajracharya uses this local history to explain the anthropomorphic iconography of Indra as the end result of simple, rural, and aniconic cross-like structures that Newars worshipped "either as a deity or as a deceased ancestor" that are still installed for the Indra festival especially in Bhaktapur. These aniconic forms, Vajracharya concludes, "are the originals of the unusual Newar iconography of the god" that later developed into the anthropomorphic forms found throughout Kathmandu (2016: 156).[31]

Vajracharya is no doubt correct about these cross-shaped structures, although his assertion still prompts the question of the development of the aniconic and rural into the anthropomorphic and tantric, as the latter acquires and adapts the classical *parijāta haraṇa* narrative with its own epic and tantric overtones. He states that this distinctive style of anthropomorphic Indra "icon, with its hands vertical at both sides, is not found anywhere except Kathmandu. Not so in India" (Giri 2019).[32] There is one deity, however, whose icons are depicted in this same cruciform posture, a deity we spent a good amount of time with in chapter 6, who might help us flesh out the complex figure of the Nepalese Indra. He is the protective and eventually headless warrior Aravāṉ from the Tamil cult of Draupadī, whose story is identical to that of the Kirati-Newar Yalambar-Bhairav-Aju, celebrated at the center of Kathmandu's Indra festival.[33]

Aravāṉ, multiforms of whom are also known as Kūttāṇṭavar, is one of the most significant figures in the Draupadī cult within Tamil performances of the Mahābhārata. Though he shares much of his extensive narrative with Yalambar—especially his close relationship with goddesses and his assassination by Krishna at the Mahābhārata war—he shares his iconography with the Nepalese Indra. Hiltebeitel spends a significant amount of space illustrating the gradual construction and destruction of these images within the celebration of the deity's annual pre-war marriage to Pommiyammaṉ (2011: 359–75), offering a few clues as to why he takes this particular form. "As to the cruciform body," Hiltebeitel writes, "the only local exegesis I heard was that the outstretched arms signify that 'he is a mighty warrior going to war. It is the pose of a warrior,' " and "the outspread hands make Kūttāṇṭavar look like a dancer, one who is doing *kūttu* (dance)" (2011: 336–37). Because this marriage represents the latest layer of his narrative—added to the ninth-century core of his self-sacrifice to Kālī and to the "(probably) fourteenth century version of Villiputtūr Āḻvār that adds his request to be allowed to watch the war for some time with his severed head" (276–77)—and because this marriage represents no part of Bhairav-Aju's story in Kathmandu's Indra festival, we might easily presume that the anthropomorphic form given to the Nepalese deity who would become Indra occurred after the fourteenth century. Given the aniconic forms that Indra retains throughout his festival tradition—in Sunkothi, where they are multiple "thief gods"; in Bhaktapur, where they represent various gods of the dead; in Pyangaon, where male and female pine-wood poles "are not explicitly identified with Indra"; among the Rathva tribe of Gujarat, who install nine branches cut from two different trees; and in Kathmandu, where local families continue to raise wooden posts for their ancestors and for a variety of gods and goddesses—we should see Indra's iconography and his relationship to the classical *parijāta haraṇa* narrative as of a much later time. Given the absence of such identifying features even in the works of Śaktivallabh and the *NBhV*, we might even push this Sanskritizing effort all the way into the nineteenth century. Only later, however, did the goddess-centered "free-floating *Mahābhārata* folklore" come to be a dominant lens through which people see the flexible and composite material culture of Kathmandu's Indra festival.

The connections among these iconographic forms of Indra and the meanings that they have acquired are complex and wide-ranging. Even though the precise development and vectors of this process are difficult to map out, we can see how these images and narratives reflect a series of dialogic processes—between Newar and Hindu, local and universal, *rājnīti* and tantra—that acknowledges the festival's long and complex history, beginning with the ancestral and nature-related functions of the simple aniconic form. Indra's local identity as a thief came to explain "the unusual Newar iconography of the god" in a way that fills in narrative gaps while playing with his other identities as king, bringer of rain, and even an epic form of Bhairav. Indra's extended arms, ambiguously playing on his royalty and thievery, help define the festival's opposing (and related) valences. Though Indra's kingship is "obvious," his theft of the cucumber and *khaisi* fruit throughout the rural valley recalls his further associations with fertility and the ancestors, while his theft of the *parijāt*, occurring only in Kathmandu, reflects the higher degree of dialogue between Newar and Hindu/Sanskrit in the wake of the 1768 Shah victory. This socio-political tension foregrounds the presence of the devious Krishna who, though scrubbed from the inverted Newar story, serves as a Hinduized foil to Bhairav and Dagi, local Newar figures whose settings in the Mahābhārata epic personify the caste- and ethnicity-based tensions that have troubled the place of the Newars ever since.

Conclusion

Violence, Politics, Danger, and Ritual Change

In April 2006, the three-week-long series of marches, protests, strikes, curfews, and shootings that became known as Nepal's second *Janāndolan* (people's movement), following the first movement against King Birendra in 1990, brought an end to the Shah royal dynasty. King Gyanendra twice capitulated on national television, the first time allowing for the resumption of Parliament and for the selection of a prime minister (April 21), and the second time for the resumption of the Constituent Assembly and its power to redraft the constitution (April 24). Gyanendra's actions almost immediately resulted in the conclusion of the Maoist-led People's War, the eleven-year-long civil war that had killed some 11,000 people. The legislative and popular processes after these actions led to the ceremonial demotion of Gyanendra and the official conclusion of Nepal's monarchy, transforming the country into a secular republic that no longer enshrined the concept of the Hindu kingdom.

This conclusion takes up the question that naturally arises: What becomes of the Indra festival, whose Nepalese origins lie in its revival by the Shah dynasty for the popular and tantrically powerful support it provided? One response should be evident given the festival's intense focus on kingship and kinship: the Indra festival will maintain its place in the Newar festival calendar because it represents one of many regular ritual acts of veneration toward the ancestors. Operating fairly independently of the king, the ancestors continue to reside in Kathmandu and remain one of the festival's focal points. Treating the Indra festival as a unified and archetypal aspect of Nepalese culture allows us to bypass previous theories that highlight the difficult relationships among the festival's multiple constituent parts: that it is "in reality two distinct festivals" (Oldfield 1974: 313); that "the worship of Indra . . . is again so mixed up with the *jātrās* of Kumārī and Bhairav" (Regmi 1966: 615); and that festival elements were "progressively combined" (Toffin 2006: 54).

The archetypal perspective allows us to better understand the survival of Kathmandu's Indra festival into the distant future in the absence of a Hindu monarchy. I use the term *survival* here because during my research in Kathmandu in the early 2000s, a common local attitude was that the lack of interest in festival culture by young people, a lack of governmental support of the traditional Newar *guthi* structure, and King Gyanendra's inauspicious ascent to the throne in June 2001, the festival would certainly come to an end within the next decade or so. What I observed in the latter part of my research is that the Indra festival has become a continuing part of Kathmandu's vibrant festival culture, and Newars are using this renewed interest, vitality, and centrality as a means for asserting their identity vis-à-vis the central (and formerly Hindu) Nepali government.[1] This contemporary material provides a significant avenue for future research into Kathmandu's Indra festival, into other Newar festivals in the valley, and into the changing religious culture of the valley as a whole.

Having maintained a sense of continuity through its history, the Indra festival has drawn on Vedic, classical, and local sources to construct narrative, performative, and artistic elements that fit its local cultures. Troubling any notion of its ultimate origins, I have attempted to show how the festival has always contained the seeds of political change, often via conflict and challenge. All of these continuous, contiguous, and coterminous powers provide a flexibility that will allow for the festival's indefinite survival. Accounting for the contemporary festival's twin emphasis on kingship and kinship, I respond to the issue of the festival's kingless future by considering an example of a different royal ritual whose dynamics—including the related pair of archaism and innovation—seem strikingly similar to those of the Indra festival and can illustrate the mechanics of Kathmandu's festival.

Maurice Bloch's (1986) historical ethnography of the circumcision ritual of the Merina people of Madagascar presents a ritual analogy to Kathmandu's Indra festival. Based on Western accounts from the early nineteenth century, transcribed Merina speeches, and his fieldwork in the 1970s, Bloch's history of this rite shows how King Andrianampoinimerina parlayed a family-based circumcision rite into a grand royal ritual with statewide implications. The king's method of co-opting these family rites—rites that ultimately link a newly circumcised boy into a lineage of (male) ancestry rather than one simply of (female) biology—required the king's manipulation of physical objects (silver chains and a spear) whose cultural links to "holiness and purity of royalty" run deep (Bloch 1986: 126). Referring to the altered ritual of the opening of a gourd by the king, his representative, or a spear that was said to have come from the king's palace, Bloch writes: "This innovation was of the utmost importance in that it meant that without changing the symbolic form of the ritual the monarch had suddenly gained a central role in it. Not only was the circumcision ceremony being 'orchestrated' calendrically by the state; it had also become for every Merina, in part at least, a royal ritual, because, even though most of it took place in individual circumcision houses, one element took place centrally" (126).

This alteration of the ritual mirrors that of Kathmandu's Indra festival, whose very first textual appearance in the *Mahābhārata* represents an archaism and whose contemporary revival, filtered through the Sanskrit textual tradition that highlights the proper astrological time to perform royal rites and the centrality of the goddess, similarly draws on a local and ancestral festival whose shift from a simple domestic rite to a central and complex state ritual is still evident. Drawing on the numerous pole-raising festivals celebrated in South Asia, Kathmandu's Indra festival highlights the mutual presence of kingship and kinship through the presence of analogous ancestral poles raised in local neighborhoods. The presence of these poles renders invalid a strict reading of Oldfield's assertion that the raising of Indra's central pole records "the exact hour when the city fell into the power of the Gorkhas" (1974: 320). Similarly, the *Nepālikabhūpa Vaṃśāvalī*'s assertion that Prithvinarayana Shah obtained the right to rule from Kumari's blessing during the Full Moon Festival (Nep. *pūrṇimākā jātrā*) acknowledges the Newar festival of literally the same name (New. *yeṁ yāḥ punhi*).

Also negotiating the presence of the city's ancestors, Shaktivallabh's *Kathanam* similarly attempts to Hinduize and universalize the festival with a focused attention on the Vedic pole of a Hindu Indra in a South Asian capital city. Attempting to erase the Newar culture of the festival in service of the Shah kinship, the *Kathanam* passively acknowledges the festival's revival by succumbing to the local festival's gravity and conflating the many local Jyāpu icons of Indra with the classical icon at the base of the pole. Replicating how the ancestor poles become peripheral to the central Hindu pole, these many local Indra icons become peripheral, centripetally arranged around Indra's central icon. Unable to fully replace the ancestors, the Nepali Hindu king could only try to merge with them, the similarity and simultaneity of their aniconic forms belying their supposed difference.

In the conclusion to his ethnography, Bloch theorizes on the surprising stability of the circumcision rite throughout serious changes in Merina sociopolitics. His conclusion revolves around the notion that ritual, which constructs and carries ideology, is sufficiently separated from the political so that even significant changes in the political life of the state do not necessarily result in changes in the performance of religious ritual. For the Merina, ideology consists of the fundamental notions that the blessings accrued from the ritual are obtained by all citizens, and these blessings provide a recipient the opportunity to become an ancestor, despite the terrestrial social hierarchies signaled by the ritual. To properly earn and accept these blessings, one must belong to and identify with a transcendental force, mediated by a terrestrial authority that legitimates and demands "the violent conquest of inferiors by superiors who are closer to the transcendental ancestors" (Bloch 1986: 189). The promise that ritual participants will become the powerful transcendental ancestors is more powerful than an identification with any particular mediator, thus the continuing relevance of the ritual in changing political circumstances: "The substitution of the king for the elders . . . [was] a change only in who precisely was the agent of mystical reproduction and violence, not a change in that fundamental notion itself" (190). As the royal ritual simultaneously affirms the power of the ancestors and the power of the state, rejecting the terrestrial mediator of power (the king)—as happened in Nepal in 2006—might also imply the rejection of the ancestors.

The application of this double rejection to Kathmandu's Indra festival is productive but problematic. On the one hand, shifting political situations in contemporary Kathmandu have borne out Bloch's observation regarding the inextricable relationship between king and ancestors. Despite eliminating the king from the Indra festival, the many performances in which he previously participated remain, with only the names and faces changing.[2] The palace remains the origin point from which the royal sword emerges, an object that signals the presence of the king as it travels on the pole's procession from the forest and on Kumari's processions around the city. The king's ritual presence at the pole's installation is marked with the appearance of his representative white horse, and regardless of political party, Nepal's president or prime minister distributes gold coins to the crowd immediately before Kumari's first procession and exchanges blessings with her on the festival's final day. Thus, despite the nation's current secular identity as the Federal Democratic Republic of Nepal, the Indra festival has retained its focus on royal figures, actions, and locales.

On the other hand, shifts in Nepal's politics have resulted in new facets and emphases that bear no relationship to royalty. These new activities, completely absent from the classical textual record, raise the issue that I addressed with the Ban Yatra, inquiring to what extent its themes of sexuality and violence, permeating the liminal space between forest and city, might have been a more significant part of the entire festival but were purposefully avoided by court scribes, priests, and gurus whose focus was squarely on the palace. By ignoring these themes, the royal court attempted to disregard the ways that such antistructural activities worked to deconstruct the state showing that the state has been brought into existence and thus that it can be questioned and resisted.

In an area that warrants significantly more research, signaled by its absence from the current literature, is the participation of local Newar youth in the *jatra* culture of the Kathmandu Valley. Youth participation is one of the most interesting dynamic shifts in the past few decades. Against the backdrop of the end of the People's War, the increasing consumption of Nepal's heritage by global tourists, "the awareness of Nepal's position in the global order, i.e. geographically, economically, politically and socially marginalised on the periphery" (Snellinger 2013: 81), and the reconstruction of the city, valley, and country after the devastating 2015 earthquakes, young Newar men and women are becoming more interested in and are actively participating in preserving and restoring tangible and intangible heritage, including the successful 2022 rebuilding of Kasthamandap, the centuries-old building from which Kathmandu derives its name.[3] During the Indra festival, young Manandhar men and women from the Thahiti Manandhar Guthi play flutes at the events surrounding the movements of the pole; young

Manandhar men perform masculinity following their installation of the pole, exercising their control over the area, by flexing and posing for photos afterward. Young Newars are involved in social media, creating websites promoting the festival, recording and uploading photographs and films to popular social media platforms, creating new renderings of the festival's background stories, and participating in art and photo contests during each year's festival.

Although these activities might not be described as explicitly political, politics is never far below the surface of the Indra festival. The festival has long provided the setting for local populations to publicize grievances against the state government and assert local identities against the unified Nepalese state, mainly in performing socially conscious street plays.[4] Rajendra Pradhan describes at some length the secular-themed street plays performed by lower-caste groups in their neighborhoods during the festival. Pradhan writes: "Some of the plays, for example, caricature traders, landlords, politicians, civil servants and others who trouble the less fortunate. Some plays depict scenes of greedy traders cheating simple farmers; other plays depict doctors mistreating poor patients; and there are plays in which politicians and civil servants are portrayed seeking bribes" (1986: 400). For Pradhan, these plays question and even threaten the social order in the same way the masked dances, frequently performed during the festival and depicting the conflict between gods and demons, threaten the cosmic order.

Whether on the stage or in the streets, Nepalese theater represents a powerful social medium. Sunil Pokharel's contemporary Aarohan Theatre Company is one of the most well-known Nepalese theater troupes that recognizes conflict as "the essence of theatre" (Mottin 2018: 66). In the wake of King Gyanendra's suspension of the constitution rights of free speech and assembly on February 1, 2005, theater allowed artists to "build a deliberative forum, one where citizens were able to remake their own republic from the ashes of civil war, despite regular rebel blockades of the city, and in the shadow of a newly imposed dictatorship" (West 2005: 50). Many people told me that such performances had died out and were no longer a part of the Indra festival, having been performed only until the successful 1990 people's movement, whose resulting democratic reforms were said to have rendered such performances unnecessary.[5] Perhaps this explains Pradhan's focus on them in 1986 and my ignorance of them in more recent times. On the fifth day of the 2006 Indrajatra performance—that is, during the festival immediately following King Gyanendra restoring the Constituent Assembly—the online newspaper *ekantipur* ran a single photo on its front page of a performance near the royal palace, with the caption: "A street play organized by the Social Work Institute about the plight of Dalits being performed at Basantapur's Durbar Square, Friday."[6]

Acknowledging, continuing, and transforming this tradition, Alok Tuladhar's local cultural organization ImPACT! Productions has organized the Newa Film Festival since 2012. Its mission is: "Coinciding with the ancient and highly colorful Yenyaa (Indrajatra) festival of Kathmandu, this event is the modern manifestation of the now extinct Daboo Pyakhan tradition. Daboo Pyakhan, which has been completely and irrevocably replaced by cinema and television over the past few decades, was the age-old tradition of putting up street dramas for the public at particular neighborhoods of Kathmandu during the week-long Yenyaa festival. The Newa Film Festival strives to revive the Daboo Pyakhan, but in digital format."[7] This film festival, set in the heart of old Kathmandu near the monastery of Jana Bahal, channels the dissent and conflict at the heart of the festival's street plays into a format that is simultaneously traditional and modern, with the medium of Newar-language film as the engine for celebrating local ethnic identity.

The dissent that is part and parcel of the Indra festival has led to a number of additional and not unrelated conflicts. King Gyanendra's 2006 appearance at the Indrajatra was boycotted by all cabinet members, as most diplomats made an effort to avoid the dubious photo op with the king. That year's festival was attended by tight security, with dozens of activists from the Maoist-affiliated Newaḥ Mukti Morcha (NMM, Newar Liberation Federation) protesting throughout the area. The group's president, identified simply as Shrestha, said: "We, the NMM, announced to protest the attendance of the Shah king to protest king Prithvi Narayan Shah's takeover by tricking the local Newar residents. We should culturally, socially, and morally boycott the king." This same year, the royal motorcade was required to change its route to avoid thousands of Maoist activists affiliated with the All Nepal Trade Union Federation (Revolutionary), attending their national convention in Ratna Park, the usual staging grounds for political protests.[8]

But it was the 2008 festival that was especially protested by local Newar groups. Following its popular election, the atheist Maoist party, led by Prime Minister Pushpa Kamal Dahal (a.k.a. Prachand) and Baburam Bhattarai, the minister for Finance, advocated decreasing state funding for the Indra festival (from the offices of Guthi Samsthan, the Department of Archaeology, and the Kaushitoshakhana) and completely eliminating funding animal sacrifices for the Dasain festival.[9] The Nepali government was accused of attempting to extinguish Newar traditions, attacking arts and culture, and harming the valley's vibrant tourist industry. As the NMM protested the king's final Indrajatra in 2006, several groups strongly protested Prime Minister Dahal's first one in 2008. As part of these protests, groups stopped vehicular movement at central locations in the old city, torched revenue collection booths, burned tires, and vandalized several government vehicles. An agreement between the government and some interested parties was rejected, and the protests continued for four days. On the final day of the Indra festival, during the *nanichā yāḥ* procession of Kumari in Kilagal Tol, a member of Lakhe's contingent put his sword into the ground as protest and the movement of Kumari's chariot ground to a halt. In the wake of these protests and in an unprecedented move, President Ram Baran Yadav, scheduled to receive Kumari's blessing, canceled his visit.

An eventual resolution created more Newar autonomy over the festival, specifically through the Indra Jātrā Vyavasthāpana Samiti, a committee that has brought together twelve different festival committees. But more than that, the conflict galvanized the Newar community, reinforcing the festival's tendency to spur innovation. The final day of the 2008 festival has come to be seen, as historian Kashinath Tamot told me, "the day when Newars became united." Thus, rather than marking "the exact hour when the city fell into the power of the Gorkhas," the "Indra Jatra has become," as Tamot concluded, "the symbol of Newar civilization."[10]

Chapters 6 and 7 of this book elaborate on this new symbolic centrality of the Indra festival. Focusing on the festival's two ritual figures of Bhairav-Āju and Indra's mother, Dagi, these chapters connect the festival to the larger Himalayan tradition of the epic *Mahābhārata*. Though not completely eschewing the connections to the Sanskrit textual tradition, these two figures further the festival's intimate relationship to the ancestors. Embodying two of its core narratives in public performances that allow city residents to mourn the recently deceased (through Dagi) and the city's first king (as Yalambar), the local festival erases the overtly Hindu and Sanskritic focus on Indra's pole that had relatively recently been made the centerpoint of the Shah revival, while retaining the multivalent Indra whose tantric power is regularly harnessed for domesticity, fertility, and power.

The commemorative Renovation Volume that is an encomium to Bhairav and his temple similarly ignores the physical centrality of Indra's pole that mimetically represents and indicates the Hindu Nepali king. Drawing on the cultural connections between the Sanskritized fierce god Bhairav, the tribal king Yalambar, and the Newar grandfather Āju encircled by the many female Ajimā, the narrative of the local king's sacrifice at the hands of the overtly Hindu Krishna at the site of Kurukshetra indicates a shift in realpolitik. This retrospective strategy on the part of Newars to exemplify dissent and catalyze citizenship counters the eighteenth-century usurpation of local kingship by the Shah dynasty and the ensuing textualization of that victory in the *NBhV* and Shaktivallabh's *Kathanam*. The Renovation Volume—especially the Nepali *Bhairav Stuti* with which it opens—localizes Bhairav in ways that Shah texts never did: "Appearing so glorious, the Lord is the king in Indra Chowk. Pacifying all disease and illness, the Lord protects us all" (1).

> *jhalmal pārī indrachowk mā | nāth prabhu ko rāj bhaeko ||*
> *rog vyādhi sab śānta garīkana | rakṣā garne sab ko ||*

In the conclusion to his introductory essay, Baldev Juju further connects Bhairav-Ājudyaḥ to the nation as a whole: "Thus, Ājudyaḥ as the protector of the country (*deś*) is a deity of great power. We should pray that his beneficent image will always circulate among the Nepali people" (2003: 15). Just as Krishna lifting Mount Govardhan overturned the celebration of Indra's festival in Braj, so does the contemporary focus on Bhairav mitigate the Indra-centric festival in the epic, *puranas*, and related *rājnīti* literature of the Sanskrit tradition. His outstretched arms identifying him alternately as a shaman, a king, a dancer, a thief, and a tantric victim, the Vedic Indra retains his power over the annual rains, while the contemporary festival transforms him into a domestic form of Bhairav who maintains an intimate relationship with the well-being of the city's residents and ancestors.

Notes

Notes to the Introduction

1. Anne Mocko (2016) details the loss of Gyanendra's official presence in Nepal's festivals, which she refers to as "rituals of reinforcement," during this period.

2. This use of a distinctively Newar name for a Hindu festival celebrated throughout the South Asian subcontinent and more commonly known by a Sanskrit term applies to other festivals as well. For the two most prominent examples, Newars refer to the Dasain / Dassera / Durga Pūjā festival as Mohani and Tihār / Diwāli as Svānti. This distinction is not simply linguistic but points to more significant differences in the chronology and content of these local celebrations, often with attention directed to local ancestors. The distinctive features of the *yeṃ yāḥ* (*punhi*) will be clarified throughout this book.

3. Two monographs on the Indra festival have been published, both of which I am heavily indebted to. Gérard Toffin's 2010 French-language, *La fête-spectacle: Théâtre et rite au Népal,* analyzes Nepal's Indra festival as theatre. And Kulchandra Koirala's 1985 Nepali-language *The Indra Festival: a Research Essay into its Cultural Tradition,* published by the Nepali government's office of culture (Guthi Samsthan), provides a wealth of detail into the performance and history of the Nepalese festival, with nearly half of the book devoted to descriptions of a number of similar pole-raising festivals celebrated throughout Nepal.

4. On the momentariness of Indra and the ambiguity of Indra in his own festival, Kuiper writes: "The obvious conclusion is that Indra, at the moment when he 'propped up' the sky, must have been identical with the tree. On the other hand, there are sufficient indications to show that in general Indra has nothing to do with the cosmic tree and the world center. His identity with the pillar at the moment of creation, when he himself literally was the world axis, must accordingly have had a momentary character" (1975: 110).

5. Installed in a north-facing section of the palace, this Bhairav is hidden behind a heavy wooden screen that renders it virtually invisible until it is removed during the Indra festival. The most accessible of the nine sections of this screen, the bottom center one, is also removed during the festival of Dasain, and as of approximately 2017, this same section is removed beginning with the full-moon day prior to Indrajatra, coinciding with *janāī pūrṇimā*.

6. Like Bhairav, her temple is also difficult of access, open only to Nepalis and only once every year during the subsequent Dasain festival (Durgā Pūjā) in honor of the goddess.

7. He immediately quotes Toffin (1992: 75) who refers to the "dialectic between state centralization and local ethnic assertion [as] one of the most interesting and pervasive aspects of the modern Indra jātrā" (van den Hoek 2004: 46).

8. G. S. Nepali's analysis falls into this category as well: "Indra Jatra is however not one festival, but appears to consist of two different festivals—one in honour of Indra and the other in honour of Bhairava and Kumari, which are inter-mixed" (1965: 359). For Nepali, the inter-mixing of these festivals is "hard to explain" and "quite strange" (359).

9. Toffin offers a similar critique in his review of van den Hoek's book (2015: 433). Van den Hoek's application of the sacrificial paradigm to the living virginal goddess Kumari is especially telling: her blessing of the king marks the latter's preparation "not for an immediate sacrifice, but for what is considered the king's long-time duty: the sacrifice of war—which may involve, though, his (sacrificial) death" (2004: 52).

10. Jan Gonda states in his measured assertion regarding the festival's textual record that "It would therefore be vain to attempt explaining the variants exclusively or chiefly as chronological differences and tracing a single historical development of this socio-religious phenomenon from prehistoric times up to the present day," but he also acknowledges that "all accounts of this ceremony emphasize . . . *vaijayanta-* . . . the king's victoriousness and invincibility" (1967: 415, 416).

11. Palihawadana refers to the militant and "distinct political overtones [of] the Indra cult" in the *Rig Veda* (2017: 75).

12. In an unpublished and unavailable conference paper from 1996, "The Festival of Indra in Kathmandu: An Archaic Survival or an 18th Century Construction?," van den Hoek appears to address this point. Toffin also briefly addresses some of these historical issues in a short essay (2013: 228) and earlier asserted, "The rituals have been clearly reshaped by the new ruling dynasty and the Parbatiya elite" (1992: 77).

13. Toffin's emphasis on the theatricality of the contemporary Newar performance does not preclude him from alluding to "l'hindouisme classique" (2010: 81), offering brief references to its classical, textual, and sacrificial heritage.

14. Birkenholtz refers to a similar process of "Puranicization" (2018: 133–36). Burghart (1984: 120) and Inden (1978: 46) emphasize also the more specifically Vaiṣṇava processes that mark the political rhetoric behind royal initiation rituals in Nepal.

15. Johann Jakob Meyer's 1937 *Trilogie Altindischer Machte und Fest der Vegetation* (the "trilogy" handles the festivals of Kāma, Bali, and Indra) treats Indra as fundamentally a god of the sun and vegetation and deals with the festival texts serially and independently.

16. Toffin, however, describes countering efforts by modern Tharu activists in Nepal to reconstruct a more strictly Theravada Buddhist culture by building Theravada temples, reading Pali texts, and tracing their history back to the historical Buddha (Toffin 2013: 86).

17. Performances of the Indra festival seem to respond to Buddhist regimes, whereas in modern India, texts and performances of the epic *Rāmāyaṇa* tend to respond to Muslim religious Others.

18. The Nepalese Gai Jātrā festival before and the Tihār festival after the Indra festival both devote significant attention to the presence of local ancestors.

19. Pradhan asserts that the "Indra Jātrā begins on the eleventh of the bright half of Bhadra" (385), only to state later that it "officially begins with the pole-raising ceremony in front of the palace on the twelfth day" of Bhadra (1986: 391).

20. Vajracharya asserts that until the time of Pratap Singh (1775–77), during whose rule the festival became more Sanskritized, the pole was raised on the previous day (Bhādra 11), the same day that the icons of Indra, detailed in chapter 7 of this book, continue to be raised throughout the city (1976: 170). Vajracharya cites as evidence for this classical chronology *BS* 43.29 when the king begins his overnight vigil (on Bhādra 11 [*jāgaraṃ ekādaśyāṃ*]), rather than 43.38, which describes the pole's installation (on Bhādra 12 [*dvādaśyāṃ utthāpyo*]).

21. *BS* 43.67 and *VDhP* 2.155.25 refer to the four-day duration of the pole's installation; the next day, the day of the *visarjana* and the festival's final day, is clearly referred to with *pañcame*, "on the fifth [day of the festival]."

22. This extended eighteen-day duration of the festival matches the similar duration of the Tamil performances of the *Mahābhārata* (and the duration of the Mahābhārata war itself), a festival that also "overspills that frame at the end," in a larger comparison I return to later (Hiltebeitel 2011: 290).

23. In a footnote, Todd Lewis notes that the "Indra Pillar" referred to in a story of the Buddhist Pañcarakṣā dharaṇi text "is still erected each year for the five-day festival in Nepal" (Lewis, Tuladhar, and Tuladhar 2000: 198).

24. M. C. Regmi provides the following as the mission of Guthi Samsthan, established in 1964: "To perform religious functions and ceremonies according to the deed of gift or endowment, or according to tradition, or arrange for their

performance, in such a way that religious acts are not violated; to utilize the movable and immovable property of Guthis, or the income accruing therefrom, for existing or new religious, cultural, social, or philanthropic institutions or activities, and to curtail unnecessary expenditure from *Guthi* income, check leakages, and finalize new schedules of staffs and expenditure according to need in order to manage *Guthis* in a more systematic way" (2002: 293).

25. The document lists Kumari's three processions separately and in sequence—to the lower, upper, and middle parts of the city—although they are not proper *sāit* and so their times are not listed. For the Nānichā Yātrā, Kumari's third procession on the festival's final day, this schedule simply reads *sohi din rātī* (nighttime of this day).

26. Other lists, such as that provided in Pant (1995), name the festival's fifth and final *sāit* as the disposal (*visarjan*) that immediately follows the lowering (*pātana*).

Notes to Chapter 1

1. Witzel (1997: 520) and Kuiper (1975: 110–11). Irwin (1975: 641) and Gonda (1967: 417) also place Indra's festival pole in the same category of the Vedic *yūpa,* as a type of axis mundi.

2. In his article on the *Indrotsavavidhi,* a Sanskrit manuscript from Orissa influenced by the sixth-century *Bṛhat Saṃhitā,* Tripathi acknowledges the absence of information on the Indra festival in Vedic texts, asserting that its village roots support its identity as "a festival for simple peasants and animal raisers . . . the festival was celebrated without priests and, only because of its popularity and its religio-magical significance did it spread to the ruling class" (1977: 1009). Jan Gonda writes that the Indra festival "is no doubt a very ancient religious festival which is possibly genetically related to the European maypole and Midsummer Day . . . festivities of which it is the Indian counterpart" (1967: 413).

3. Hiltebeitel also frequently uses the words "reworks" and "recreates" to communicate examples of this sort of translation of Vedic referents into the epic's post-Vedic context.

4. Lidova specifically critiques Kuiper for his regular assertions of the Vedic provenance of the Indra festival (2004: 98–100).

5. Van den Hoek refers to "the similarities between textual traditions (including the ādiparvan of the Mahābhārata and the Atharvaveda) and Indra yātrā" (2004: 39). Toffin says that "The link between Indra's feast and the king is also perfectly clear in these old texts" (1992: 80). Though Pradhan accounts for how "variations in detail reflect the sectarian influences on the texts," he spends only one pararaph on the entire textual tradition (1986: 393).

6. A longer version of this argument can be found in Baltutis (2011).

7. The prediction of this assassination takes place at the house of Yādavī, Krishna's father's sister, who resides in the city of Chedi (*chedipuram*, 2.40.14). As part of the preliminaries of Yudhiṣṭhira's horse sacrifice, Arjuna returns to conquer the Chedi city of Śuktimati (14.84.2).

8. The epic contains many similar parallel dialogues between begging Brāhmaṇs and beneficent kings, including the emaciated Brāhmaṇ Tanu, one of many personal manifestations of dharma in the epic (Fitzgerald 2004: 102); the "ambivalent Yudhisthira" who must be cajoled into performing his royal dharma following his depression at experiencing the pyrrhic victory in the great war (130); Pṛthu, who "provides, in embryonic form, the basic model of Brahmanic polity and partially describes the epic's synthesis of old and new dharma in the king" (2004: 131), and Krishna, who provides "sophisticated arguments" to Arjuna in the *Bhagavad Gītā* (140).

9. Romila Thapar argues that Ashoka's subjects "would not have found . . . alien" these heterodox dharma campaigns and that Ashoka's "conversion" to Buddhism represented a mode of religious affiliation that must be seen as "multiple, characterized by the presence of a variety of heterodox and orthodox sects" (2012: 18, 25).

10. McGovern's (2019) study of the mutually constructed categories and identities of "the snake and the mongoose"—the "Hindu" *brāhmaṇa* and "Buddhist" *śramaṇa*—represents a relevant part of this argument. Hiltebeitel argues that the purpose of the epic's "non-Buddhist and non-Jain" uses of the term *ahiṃsā* is "to revitalize an ideal Kṣatriya who will fight to reestablish an ārya dharma" (2001: 202–4). Daud Ali asserts "the articulatory relation between courtly and monastic technologies" (1998: 181).

11. Vasu's intimate relationship with Indra—he is "my dear one" (*mama priyaḥ*) (1.57.7) and dear to Indra (*indra-prītyā*) (1.57.27)—closely resembles Ashoka's desired intimacy with gods and kings in his self-styled moniker, *devānāṃp[r]iya*.

12. Olivelle elsewhere asserts that the brahmanical focus on the concept of dharma is largely a response to its Buddhist adoption generally and to Ashoka's reforms specifically, after which "no one could ignore the term" (2009: 42; 2015: 171).

13. Thapar correctly notes that the inscriptions on Ashoka's pillars bear no direct relationship to the Indra festival (2013: 300).

14. Van Buitenen's translation (1973: 131) is problematic as he interprets the words *praveśam* (used twice) and *ucchrayo* (used once) as describing the raising of the pole. Thus, in his translation, the raising of the pole is referred to three times: by Vasu at the end of the year, by the best of kings generally, and then by kings on the following day. Roy's translation is smoother here.

By translating verse 20 as, "After erecting the pole they decked it with [ornaments]," he eliminates one of the pole's "three" raisings (1970: 136).

15. *Nāṭyaśāstra* 1.54 refers to the festival as a *dhvajotsava* (and a *mahendra-vijayotsava* in the following verse) and 1.59 refers to the object of the *dhvaja; Bṛhat Saṃhitā* 43 is entitled *indra-dhvaja-sampad*, "the glory of Indra's flag," twice referring to the object as the *dhvaja* (43.7, 43.51).

16. Inden names similar rituals—the *mahādāna, tulāpuruṣa,* and *hiraṇyagarbha*—as ritual components in later *rājnīti* texts, "donative ceremonies [that] were of immense significance because they were used by regional Hindu kings to establish (or renew) their universal, imperial sovereignty" (1978: 55). Geslani names these same rituals as formative in the development of the field of *jyotiṣa* and its constituent *śānti* rituals (2018: 167). Vajracharja describes the similarly donative *tuladāna* performed by the Nepalese king Pratāp Malla in 1664 for his dying son; though performed for health and longevity, the large expense of the *tuladāna* ensured that it came to be performed only by wealthy kings (2003).

17. *Sadā* can also translate as "always," providing a playful contradiction to the periodicity of Indra's worship in South Asia and to the festival's origin story presented here.

18. If this is the case, the *Garga Saṃhitā* would be the best candidate for the earliest text, as it precedes Varahamihira's *Bṛhat Saṃhitā,* which mentions Vasu's story by name, by nearly a century.

19. This new year's festival is celebrated on the first day of Chaitra (Bühnemann 1988: 125).

20. Ann Gold describes the celebration of Indar Puja in the village of Ghatiyali; although no pole is raised in this festival, Indar maintains his Vedic associations with rain and fertility and the festival's classical chronology, celebrated on the twelfth day of the bright half of the month, despite Gold's assertion that this date was selected "by happenstance" (1988: 53–58).

21. Equally curious might be Indra's absence from the *jarjara* itself, an object inhabited by other deities: Brahmā, Śankara, Vishnu, Skanda, and the serpents Śheṣa, Vāsuki, and Takshaka. Kuiper again attributes this absence to Indra's "character of a seasonal god" (2004: 252), and foregrounding the stage's *sūtradhāra* director: "He is the "god of the universe and while holding the world tree upright *in his hand* he represents the cosmic centre" (256).

22. In this opening chapter, the authors juxtapose—in their text and with the physical objects on the stage—four synonomous and identical objects that represent Indra's weapon, all of which are in the possession of the actor's presiding deity, Indra: *vidyut, vajra, dhvaja,* and *jarjara.*

23. "tad yad yajñe stūyate yacchasyate yat pracaryate, sā prajāpateḥ senā sā | 'tha yad vīṇāyāṃ gīyate yan nṛtyate yad vṛthācaryate sā mṛtyoḥ senā sā."

24. Kuiper asserts that the distribution of scores of deities placed around the *nāṭyaveśman* "shows that the theatre was considered a replica of the cosmos" (1977: 147). Included among these are the *nāṭyakumārī* and *nāṭyamātṛkā*, groups of female divinities (girls and mothers, respectively, but also different types of wooden poles) seen in attendance at the raising of Indra's pole in the *Bṛhat Saṃhitā* and in the contemporary Nepalese festival.

25. "pāṭhyaṃ nāṭyaṃ tathā gāṇaṃ citraṃ vāditrameva ca | vedamantrārthavacanaiḥ samaṃ hyetad bhaviṣyati."

26. Lidova argues similarly, asserting that the Indra festival stood "at the cradle of sweeping historical and religious reforms . . . , which gradually took shape round the *pūjā* cult eventually to become known under the conventional name of Hinduism" (2004: 100).

27. In his essay on urban images in Sanskrit and Tamil literature, Ramanujan observes a further identity, especially in the case of the *Rāmāyaṇa*, of the synecdoche of king (Rāma) and city (Ayodhyā) (1970: 232).

28. In their study of the relationship of Varāhamihira to his predecessor, Garga, Geslani and colleagues write of similar innovations in the *śānti* (appeasement) ritual that "combines techniques of bali, homa, and dhūpa . . . characterized as a transitional stage between Vedic and later Hindu (Purāṇic and Tantric) forms" (2017: 172).

29. The *VDhP* stipulates the king's overnight fast (*rātrau jāgaraṇaṃ*) (2.155.15–16).

30. The Śaṃnodevī mantra is found at *Rig Veda* 10.9.4 and reads: "śaṃ no devīr abhiṣṭaya āpo bhavantu pītaye | śaṃ yorabhi sravantu naḥ." Jamison and Brereton assert that the full hymn is meant to revivify the patron of the sacrifice and translate it: "O Waters, today I have followed (you). We have united with your sap. Full of milk, o Agni, come here. Merge me with luster" (2014: 1380).

31. "atha rājñām indramahotsavasyopacāra-kalpaṃ vyākhyāsyāmaḥ (1.1) | prauṣṭhapade śuklapakṣe (1.2) | saṃbhṛteṣu saṃbhāreṣu brahmā rājā cabhau snātav-ahata-vasanau surabi-sujātānulepanau karmaṇyau vratavantāv-upavasataḥ (1.3) | śvo bhūte śaṃnodevyāḥ pādair ardharcābhyām ṛcā ṣaṭkṛtvodakaṃ pari vācam ācānto (1.4) | barhir upakalpayitvā rājānam anvālabhya juhuyāt (1.5) . . . śvaḥ-ṣvo 'sya rāṣṭraṃ jyāyo bhavaty eko 'syāṃ pṛthivyāṃ rājā bhavati na purā jarasaḥ pramīyate ya evaṃ veda yaś cai 'vaṃvidvān indramaheṇa carati iti brāhmaṇam (3.9) | itī 'ndramahotsavaḥ samāptaḥ" (Bolling and von Negelein 1909: 120–21).

32. Geslani argues that relative to Garga's earlier text, Varāhamihira's contribution to the textuality of the Indra festival "should not be seen in terms of invention, but rather integration. . . . Rather, he sharpened a nascent ritual logic of exchange, added relative specificity to the ritual's mantric liturgy, and

implemented a structural overlay that harmonized the Indradhvaja with the yātrā cycle" (2018: 94).

33. Inden also refers to the king as a "replica of Viṣṇu, the Cosmic Man of the VDhP" (1978: 71).

34. A second *praveśa* occurs at 19.62 when the pole is brought into the temple.

35. See Doniger (2016) for the intimate connections between these two texts and their collective focus on the *nāgarika,* the city resident.

36. The mandala that Arjyāl describes in *Kathanam* from nineteenth-century Nepal is a *sarvatobhadra maṇḍala,* reflecting the "universality" of the structure that we see in *VDhP*.

37. These versions can be found at *Bhāgavata Purāṇa* 10.24–27, *Viṣṇu Purāṇa* 5.10–13, and *Harivaṁśa* 15–19. Translations in this section are mine, unless otherwise noted.

38. In these passages, Nanda evokes the name of Indra's Vedic predecessor, the rain-giving Parjanya. *Rig Veda* 8.6.1 establishes the separate identities of these deities by comparing Indra's power to that of Parjanya's prolific rainfalls.

39. On the battlefield at Kurukṣetra, Krishna tells Arjuna that each person must behave according to their own individual nature (*svasyāḥ prakriter*), concluding with a similar question, "What good will restraint [against your nature] do?" (*nigrahaḥ kim kariṣyati* [*Bhagavad Gītā* 3.33]). Following his inevitable defeat, Indra returns to the language of the three *guṇa*s, placating Krishna with (among other conciliatory paeans) the following verse, reinforcing their fundamental and unmediated opposition: "Your very form is pure *sattva* and peace; it is composed of *tapas* [energy] and without *rajas* and *tamas*. The mix of *guṇa*s that is bound up in ignorance is not found [in you]" (*BhP* 10.27.4).

40. The *Harivaṁśa* reads: "Let the auspicious cows be worshipped, let the festival to the mountain [*giri-yajña*] begin. Let Indra be worshipped by the thirty [deities], but let the mountain be worshipped by us" (16.44). Tripathi (1977) asserts a similar replacement of Indra by Krishna and the performance of their festivals in Puri's Jagannāth Mandir.

41. Āḻvār poet Nammāḻvār describes Indra's rains as being "the downpour of heaven's evils" (Nammalvar and Ramanujan 2005: 13).

42. The narrator Śuka uses language that alludes to the materials of the Indra festival by describing Indra's torrents of rain as being "thick as pillars" (*sthūṇā-sthūlā varṣa-dhārā*) (*BhP* 10.25.10) and the duped villagers as being led to destruction like beasts to the sacrificial post (*stambhaṃ*) (*BhP* 10.25.6). The epic story of the burning of the Khāṇḍava Forest—another story of a deluge sent by Indra and thwarted by Krishna (and Arjuna)—similarly describes Indra's rainshowers as *akṣamātrā,* "thick as a chariot's axle" (*MBh* 1.217.19.)

43. Jonathan Geen asserts as much for the Jain tellings of this story, that the heroic act of lifting the *koṭiśilā* mountain "is purely a political affair,

in which the *vāsudeva* becomes the officially recognized *ardhacakrin* of the southern half of Bharatavarṣa" (2015: 120).

44. Regarding the underlying history of the appendix to the *MBh*, Brodbeck speculates that "some aspects of the *Harivamsha*'s world of story are no doubt based on it, but it is hard to know exactly which ones or to what degree, and perhaps the text does not expect us to know" (2019: xviii).

45. Fred Smith also discusses the ways in which "the images of the Vedas were transmitted and transformed in the . . . *Bhāgavata Purāṇa*" (1994: 97).

46. Vaudeville (1989), Srinivasan (2005), and Hawley (1991) show how the Sanskritization of the original folk Govardhana story might have provided a fitting vocabulary and setting for the ascription of the archaic Indra festival as the backdrop for Krishna's new festival.

47. This conclusion draws heavily on Vaudeville (1989: 106–7). Considering similar passages in the devotional poetry of Sūrdās, Hawley writes: "When the people of Braj see evidences of Indra's anger in the sky, they turn for protection to the child who has kindled his wrath by proposing to his father, the village chief, that they all deflect their worshipful attention toward the mountain itself, the symbolic center of their world, rather than squandering it on Indra and his company of distant, unpredictable gods" (2015: 90).

Notes to Chapter 2

1. *Bṛhat Saṃhitā* (*BS*) 43.12, *Devī Purāṇa* (*DP*) 12.3, *Kālikā Purāṇa* (*KP*) 87.4–5. Geslani asserts that while the oscillation between forest and city is present in Garga's earlier text, it is first made explicit in Varāhamihira's *Bṛhat Samhita* (2019: 87).

2. "vana praveśa vidhinā śakra-yaṣṭiṃ tato nṛpaḥ" (*VDhP* 2.155.5a).

3. See http://kathmandupost.ekantipur.com/printedition/news/2017-09-23/marching-to-the-tune-of-history.html.

4. During the Indrajātrā, the mask of Akash Bhairav installed in the neighborhood of Indra Chowk, is temporarily covered with *tās* while it is being prepared, and Kumari wears a garment made of this same material during her processions and at other appearances. Vergati also notes the presence of the sword at the beginning of Biskaḥ Jātrā (2002: 179).

5. Punyaratna Vajracharya includes in the royal coterie the *toli* and the *nāike* of the government priests; the *mahānāike*, the primary *gūṭhī* member; the *sarkār-dvāra*; and the royal *purohit* (1980: 60).

6. The texts allow five types of trees: Arjuna, Ajakarṇa, Priyaka, Dhava, and Udumbara. The *pariśiṣṭa*s of the Atharva Veda, in describing the construction of a wooden staff, pole, or seat, also list the disqualified trees and certain conditions that will disqualify otherwise appropriate trees. In its description of the construction of the *araṇi*, such qualifying trees are referred

to as *yajñavṛkṣa* ("trees fit for sacrifice" [*AVPari* 22.7.2]). The *Bhaviṣya Purāṇa*'s account of the Indra festival (2.2.8.82–96) details these trees and the dangers resulting from a variety of inauspicious events.

7. In describing the construction of a Himalayan deity's *palkhi* (palanquin) from the wood of a tree taken from the forest, Berti refers to a similar practice: "On a chosen day, the *gur* [human medium] will incarnate the deity and, blindfolded with a bandage on his eyes, will run and touch a tree, showing it to be the selected one" (2004: 90).

8. *KP* 87.16b–17 provides the height of the pole as anywhere between twenty-two and fifty-two *hasta,* in a passage that resembles its earlier description of the construction of the goddess's throne: "The wise man should paint the wood, etc. [of the *āsana*] white. The wooden *āsana* should be twenty-four fingers long, sixteen *aṅgula* wide and four or six *aṅgula* high. It should not be higher than this" (68.25–26).

9. The *Bṛhat Saṃhitā* and *Kālikā Purāṇa* both use the phrase *dhvajārthaṃ devarājasya* to indicate this transformation (BS 43.17–18; KP 12.13). "*Śaktivallabh*: āchāryaḥ sāyaṃsaṃdhyā vandanādi-kṛta nityakriyo vṛkṣamūlaṃ gatvā | pūjāsāmagrīṃ saṃpādya. pūrvamukho daṅmukho vā bhutvā dīpaṃ prajvālya. kuśa-tila-yava-jalān-pādāya saṃkalpayet | AUM adhetyādi deśakālān saṃkīrtya Bhādra śuklā amuk-tithau. amukagotra-utpannasya amukavarmaṇo narapateḥ purarāṣṭra-janapada-grāmāṇāṃ preta-kuśmāṇḍa-piśāca-bhūtapūtanā-yoginī-gaṇa-śākinī-vīra-vetāla-rākṣasa-janito-padravaśamana-sakala vyādhi-vināśaṇa divya bhauma antarikṣotyāta-śānti pūrvaka. yāniha vṛkṣe bhūtāni tebhyaḥ svasti namo stuvaḥ || upahāraṃ gṛhite mantriyatāṃ vāsaparyayaḥ."

10. "vakra-tuṇḍa-mahākāya-sūrya-koṭi-samaprabhā."

11. "svacakra-vṛddhi-paracakrāgamā 'bhāvau hi kānaṃ tu bhogottarā apsaro-gaṇa-veṇu-vīṇādi-saṅgīta-śobhita-vimānārohaṇendraloka prāpti kāmanayā krīyamāṇendra-dhvajotsava karmāṅga-bhūta dhvajadaṇḍa-grahaṇa nimityarthaṃ dīpakalaśaṃ gaṇéśa-pūjanapūrvaka pūjana-mahaṃ kariṣye."

12. Tripathi (1977: 1003) notes a similar situation in the introductory *Vanayāga* section of the *Indrotsavavidhi* text from Keonjhar in Orissa, as does Jain (1984: 61) in the preparations for the festival of Bābo Ind among the Rathvas of Gujarat.

13. Another man told me that the second was for the kharga rather than for Indra.

14. The texts say that the tree is to be cleanly cut so that it lands on the ground with its tip pointing to the east or to the north (*purvodak*) (*BS* 43.19); the axe used is to make a sweet sound (*snigdha ghana*) and—with an apparent pun on one of the names used for the pole in the *Nāṭyaśāstra,* the *jarjara* ("that which destroys [the asuras]," 1.70)—not a dull noise (*jarjara shabda*).

15. Guthi Samsthan supports five separate *guthi* that operate during the Indra festival, and all five are responsible for activities related to the Indra pole, the royal Kumārī, or Bhairav, and thus only for those rites that directly

involve the presence or power of the king. These *guthi* manage approximately eighteen acres of land (141 *ropanī*) (Hari Joshi, Guthi Samsthan, personal communication, September 27, 2005).

16. According to Guthi Samsthan, these men performed this work for the accumulation of dharma, though this is difficult to ascertain.

17. Before 2005, much of this work in the forest was done by the army, though it was done "in the name of the Manandhars" (Triratna Manandhar, personal communication, September 17, 2005).

18. Toffin (1992: 75–76) and Anderson (1971: 129) provide similarly scant descriptions of these rites.

19. The military truck bearing the Mātṛkā poles does not proceed straight to Kathmandu, but sporadically drives ahead of the pole-pullers, allowing them to catch up periodically, thus keeping all of the poles together.

20. The only portion of the route that has changed recently is the part leading from Salagarhi to Bhaktapur. The route that once led from the forest through several farmers' fields along the Dorakhu and Chunādevī Rivers changed when the farmers began to complain that the government had co-opted too much of their land. The route was changed and now proceeds down the gravel road leading from Nālāchāp and Tāthalī toward Bhaktapur.

21. The constitution of Nepal (2015) expresses its commitment to embracing "multi-caste, multi-lingual, multi-cultural and diverse geographical specificities."

22. Scott Schnell, working on the energetic *matsuri* festivals of Japan, similarly asserts: "In fact, for many Japanese, the first impression that comes to mind upon hearing the word 'matsuri' is 'chaos'" (1999: 19).

23. This list of potential problems closely mirrors a list in a *Rig Veda* hymn to the chariot of Indra (3.53.17–20).

24. This traffic jam represents an example of what urban theorist Rem Koolhaas refers to as "Jam-space, the totally negotiable, usually illegal and hugely productive space of the traffic jam, [which] is not something to fix, solve, or even rationalize. Jam-space cannot be controlled or short-circuited, only bypassed" (2000: 685).

25. It is possible that they were also punning on *ghāro*, a seldom-used word for pole.

26. I have heard that citizens also used to hurl obscenities at the pole during its funeral-like *visarjan* disposal on its last day as it was pulled toward Teku, the cremation grounds on the Bagmati River at the city's southern edge.

Notes to Chapter 3

1. "Yo Sib liṅg ho. Dhokera jānus. Indar Jātra ko deuṭā ho. Nāgan hundaina."

2. In a Newar story of the protective goddess Mahāmantrānusariṇī, the Buddha commands his disciple Ānanda to recite the *rakṣā* text at the base of the Indra pole, as a result of which "the misfortunes in the country were all eradicated" (Lewis, Tuladhar, and Tuladhar 2000: 153).

3. Nīlakaṇṭha, in his seventeenth-century commentary on the *Mahābhārata,* also focuses on the pole's entrance as the festival's archetypal element: "Nowadays one can still see the 'entrance' of the pole in Mahārāṣṭra and other countries at the end of the year [*saṃvatsarānte yaṣṭipraveśo 'dyāpi mahārāṣṭrādiṣu dṛśyate*]" (in Kuiper 1977: 133).

4. *Kālikā Purāṇa* 87.16a adds: "On the bright eighth of Bhādrapad, the flag is led up to an altar" (*śuklāṣṭamyāṃ bhādrapade ketum vedīm praveśayet*).

5. While a phallic reading of the pole seems simple—it is often referred to as Indra's (or Shiva's) *liṅgo* in Nepali language—this reading becomes somewhat problematic as the Sanskrit word here, *yaṣṭi,* is a feminine noun.

6. Noting their "remarkable" lack of an extra-valley origin story, Gellner asserts that by "not claiming to come from outside, the Maharjans may be seen as the true locals" (Gellner and Pradhan 1999: 160).

7. The sign read in full: "Dhālāsikva Mānandhar Sanāḥ Gū Khalaḥ. Dhālāsikva, Asan Tyoḥ, Yeṃ, V.S 2001 [established 1944]." These men wore matching vests bearing the same identification. Toffin describes the function of a *sanāḥ guthi* as "a charitable institution which assumes the responsibility of assisting the family of the deceased, both psychologically and financially, at the time of a death" (1999: 252).

8. On the final day of the *rājyābhiṣeka,* the king is ritually bathed with clay brought from different places in the kingdom. By bathing his neck with clay from the place where Indra's pole is installed, the suggestion is that the king "should be physically as strong as the well-established pole" (Chaulgain 2019: 206, 207).

9. The Tamil *Mahotsavavidhi* prescribes a similar installation of a flag-pole that "marks the beginning and end of the festival period" (Davis 2009: 30).

10. These texts detail the desired shape, sound, and appearance of their ritual fire at the construction of the *śāntigṛha*: *BS* 43.31–37; *AVPari* 21.7.1–6; *AVPari* 24).

11. "asmākaṃ vīrā uttarā bhavantu." This passage in the *BS* echoes *AVPari* 19.6 that also draws from the original *trātāraṃ indraṃ* passage.

12. During Tihār/Svānti in November and the three-day spring Pahāṃ Cāhre festival, similar (smaller) poles are raised at the shrines of the goddesses Bhadrakali and Kankesvari and at the Akash Bhairav temple in Indra Chowk (Pradhan 1986: 347). Hiltebeitel (1991: 79) affirms flag-hoisting and flag-lowering as the chronological boundaries of the festivals of Draupadī and "for numerous other Tamil goddesses."

13. Feldhaus (2003: 55) describes the decoration of the pole in Maharashtra: "They tie to the top a clump of long fibers of the ambada plant that have been stripped like jute to form a white, hair-like plume, and they decorate the pole with colorful cloth and silver ornaments." Toffin says in Pyangaon: "To their extremity, the young people arrange two small parasols, *chatta*" (1978: 112).

14. Lidke notes that people of the Changu Narayan neighborhood also mark this day: "The twelfth day of the bright half of the month [of Bhādra] is Indra-jatra, one of Nepal's longest and biggest festivals, marking the end of the monsoon season. During this time special homage is paid to Indra, the god of rain. At Changu Narayan a special pole ceremony is performed. Devotees come to dance around the pole and offer yoghurt and beaten rice to Vishnu" (1996: 173). Sax (2002: 36) describes similar festivities at the pole-raising at the *pāṇḍava līlā* in Garhwal.

15. Pradhan writes that the police raised the pole, while "the leader [*nayo*] of the Manandhars is present to witness this ceremony" (1986: 391).

16. Gutschow and Kolver describe the use of similar instruments for Biskaḥ Jātrā in Bhaktapur: "At a little pond near Yahsikhel, people soak the forked boughs which are used as temporary props in the erection of the *linga*" (1975: 32).

17. Vajracharya notes that at the Indrapur temple, "It used to be that during Indrajātrā, an image (*mūrti*) of Indra was placed in the upper story of this temple, but these days this tradition is no longer practiced" (1976: 76).

18. See http://kathmandupost.ekantipur.com/news/2016-09-14/2-hurt-during-indra-jatra-lingo-hoisting.html.

19. In his work among the Nepalese Kulunge Rai, Martino Nicoletti narrates the story of a couple whose baby was killed during the construction of their new house. While the central pillar was being installed, the baby fell into the hole and was immediately killed: "From that moment on, however, the pole stayed firmly fixed in the ground. . . . To avoid this incumbent peril [of the pole falling on future children], they therefore decided to celebrate a rite. Thus it was that, for the first time, the chicken sacrifice was officiated. The same one, that still today, we Kulunge Rai celebrate whenever a young married couple goes to live in a new dwelling" (Nicoletti and Gaggini 2004: 41–42).

20. Emmrich observed that the dangers at the Rato Macchendranāth chariot festival in Patan—namely, the precarious chariot tipping over, as it did in 2004—are "said to be ominous for the coming year" (2007: 138). He also observed, as did Parish, a number of reasons asserted for the 2004 crash, with fault attributed to a variety of agents by parties who intended "to make claims and push for negotiations" (144). Also for the Patan festival, Emmrich

attributes "danger and its aversion [as] one of the main powers that drive the whole effort" (2014: 281).

21. "Feeling distraught at the sight, he fell weeping to the ground like Indra's pole might fall while being raised" (sa tu dṛṣṭvā rudandīnaḥ papāta dharaṇītale | utthāpayamānaḥ śakrasya yantradhvaja iva cyūtaḥ, *Rāmāyaṇa* 2.71.9). The monkey king Vālin's a-dharmic death at the hands of Rāma is described similarly: "he fell like the *dhvaja* of the king of gods when its ropes are released" (apatat devarājasya mukti-raśmir iva dhvajaḥ) (*Rāmạyaṇa* 4.17.2c) (also at 4.16.27).

22. Toffin (1978: 112) describes the simpler musical accompaniment of the pole raising in Pyangaon: "During the worship and decoration of the poles, two musicians of the *kusle* caste (or *jugi*) come from the neighboring village; some play some music on the tamborine *dholak,* others on the oboe *mohali.*"

23. I am using the terms "iconic" and "aniconic" in their traditional, though somewhat flawed, art historical sense, despite Susan Huntington's critique (2015).

24. Bernier (1979: 89) describes the theological function of these metal temple flags as the vehicle that a deity uses to descend to Earth to help their devotees.

25. Koirala lists the signs on the *patākā*: *Indra-pratimā* (Indra image); *śrivāsa-lāñchan* (the sign that sits on Vishnu's heart); *kamala; chatra* (royal parasol); *pūrṇa kalaś; śvet cāmar; matsya; gajur* (*chuṭṭai*)*; śaṅkha; sugā; cakra; vajra; aṣṭa-koṇa yantra; khaṛgā; ghaṇṭā; cār-veda; moṭīmālā; pūrṇaghaṭa; kamala* (2003: 103–4).

26. For the Indra festival in Gujarat (Jain 1984: 61), the Rathvas cut and install nine branches in a row: eight from the *kaḷam* tree and one from the *kaḍo* tree, the latter placed at the extreme north. As with the ambiguous identities of these objects given by the priest on duty in Kathmandu, Jain reports that the identities of the nine branches "varied from village to village" (62).

27. Indra is also associated with the veneration of the ancestors, as Vajracharya shows in an inscription dating to 1463 (2016: 139).

28. Levy and Rajopadhyaya refer to the new-moon day of the following month of Asoj as Dhalaṃ Salāṃ and counts the sixteen-day period of *sorha śrāddha* from that day, thus extending to the ensuing full moon of Asoj (1990: 462).

29. Members of these families, especially children, had walked through the heart of the city during the Gai Jātrā/Sapāru festival, as the spirits of the deceased hold on to the tail of the cow Vaitāraṇī and are led to "cross over" (the translation of her name) the mythical river of the same name.

30. Regarding *samay bajī,* Per Lowdin asserts that in the village of "Sunakothi it is above all associated with Inyapunhi, the full moon during Indra yatra, when every household in the village brings a basket with [*samay*] *baji* outdoors and distributes it to the children" (1998: 106). *Samay bajī* is the prototypical Newar festival food (or "sacramental food"; Gellner 1992: 302–4)

and consists of six main parts, from bottom to top: *syā bajī* (puffed rice), *bajī* (beaten rice), *musyā* (soybean with ginger), *bhutī* (black-eyed pea), *ālū* (potato), and *māsu* (buffalo meat).

31. Although van den Hoek mentions a number of neighborhoods where similar poles—"so inconspicuous that they are hardly noticed by the general public"—are raised, he doesn't relate them to Indra's central pole (2004: 43). G. S. Nepali refers to these icons as "Bhairavas and Bhairavis or Bhagwatis" (1965: 360). In one local version of the origin story of the Indrajātrā, citizens raise poles such as these in remembrance of the victory that protective Bhairavs won for the city's ancestors.

32. The nineteenth-century Nepalese *Kathanam* asserts that the tree from which the Indra pole comes receives its *prāṇ pratiṣṭhā* during the Gaṇesh Pūjā in the forest (ff. 12a).

33. "When [the pole] is decorated, installed, brought into town, bathed, adorned with garlands, and finally given its *visarjana*, the king should recite numerous auspicious mantras in front of the pole" ("prapūraṇe ca ucchrayaṇe praveśe snāne tathā mālyavidhay visarge | paṭhet imān nṛpatiḥ sa upavāso mantrāṃ śubhān puruhūnīya ketoḥ") (ff 13b). "Having recited, 'This destruction is for the prosperity and the saving of all the worlds,' the adorned *ketu* is given its *visarjana* in the water. . . . At daybreak, they bathe in the water, perform the necessary rites, and go home, after which a feast is eaten with relatives and attendants" ("bhavāya sarvalokānāṃ tarāya vināśakaḥ || iti paṭ hitvā sālaṅkāraṃ ketuṃ jale visarjjayet || tataḥ prabhāte jale snātvā | nityakriyā vibhāvya | gṛham gatvā | vaṃdhujanaiḥ sānucaraiḥ sahabhojanaṃ kuryāt || tat ācāryādayo api svasvagṛham gacheya") (ff. 17b).

34. "antapāde bharaṇyāṃ tu niśi śakraṃ visarjayet || supteṣu sarvalokeṣu yathā rājā na paśyati | ṣaṇmāsān mṛtyum āpnoti rājā dṛṣṭā visarjanaṃ."

35. The royal kharga is also present at this festival, exchanged once every twelve years with the king of Nepal. The nearby confluence of the Bāgmatī and Vishnumatī Rivers will be significant for the festival narrative of Akash Bhairav in chapter 6.

Notes to Chapter 4

1. The Sanskrit motto at the top of its front page is only the first and most public clue: *sarve bhavantu sukhinaḥ sarve santu nirāmayāḥ | sarve bhadrāṇi paśyantu mā kascid duḥkha bhāgjanaḥ* (may all become happy, may all be free from illness. May all see what is auspicious, may no one suffer in any way).

2. This section draws on the following four issues: Āśvin 12 *gate* VS 1983 (CE 1926), 26 (24); Bhadra 21 *gate* VS 1984 (CE 1927), 27 (22); Āśvin 5 *gate* VS 1988 (CE 1931), 31 (24); Bhadra 21 *gate* VS 1989 (CE 1932), 32 (21).

3. The newspaper accounts improbably have the military accompany the procession to Indra Daha—the lake of Indra west of the valley—on the evening of the third day, following the processions of Kumārī, Ḍāgī, and Baumata.

4. The 1927 article has them circumambulate the *deś*, "the land."

5. One exception to this general exclusion of specifically Newar rites is a mention in the 1926 article of one of the festival's more exotic rites: giving a buffalo for sacrifice at the royal palace to one member (presumably Bhairav) of the Sawa Bhaku troupe from the neighborhood of Hal Chowk in the northwest part of the valley.

6. This relationship focused on Varanasi, India, the source of "the stronghold of Hindu values" and "the root of this version of proto-nationalism" (Gaenzle and Sharma 2002: 9, 29). Relatedly, these Shah texts focused on their own lineage rather than on the place of the Kathmandu Valley (Lecomte-Tilouine 2011: 195).

7. Hausner (2007) discusses the ways the Pashupatinath Temple, like these texts, reinforced the Hindu identity of the state of Nepal.

8. The inscription of the Licchavi king Manadeva from CE 480 (NS 402) refers to the "installation of the sun-god Lord Indra" (*saṃsthāpito tra bhagavān indro nāma divākaraḥ*), though its relationship to the Indra festival is difficult to determine (Gnoli 1956: 10). Regmi asserts that a CE 1441 inscription from Bhaktapur represents the earliest reference to the Nepalese Indra festival (1966: 614).

9. Vajracharya offers a number of other early Newar references to the festival with additional names, known from Malla-era inscriptions and *ṭhyāsaphu*: the *endakiri svāṅā* of CE 1681 (ŚS 802) (1976: 170, n2; 175, n1); the *indrajātrā* of 1683 (ŚS 804) (172, n4); the *indrajātrā* of 1684 (VS 1741) (172); the *ekila svāṅā* of 1720 (ŚS 841), the *indrayātrā* of 1724 (ŚS 845) [*iti indrayātrākṛtyaṃ* || *matāṃtare ekādaśyāṃ dhvajasthāpanaṃ* |] (170, n2).

10. The page numbers in this section refer to the translation of the *NBhV*. I refer to this text by the *WV* only when having direct recourse to Daniel Wright's 1877 publication (Wright 2000).

11. Rishikesh Shaha describes them as "literary rather than historical compositions" (2001: 6). Brinkhaus (1991) describes how a number of *vaṃśāvalī* promoted King Jayasthitimalla, attributing to him a number of political actions (e.g., introducing the caste system into Nepal) for which he could not have been responsible. Malla describes the "deliberate falsification of social-political history by the later Mallas" that occurs in versions of the much earlier *Gopālarāja Vaṃśāvalī* (1985: 78). Regarding the related Nepalese genre of the *māhātmya*, Malla suggests that they were later transplanted into traditional Hindu *purāṇa* "as pious fraud, adapting and assembling from several of them" (1992: 145).

12. Describing a cultural analogue, Ehud Halperin argues that in the Himalayan Kullu Valley, "kings navigated between Brāhmaṇic ideology and

indigenous religion in their quest for legitimacy and power, and did so by striking sacrificial alliances with the indigenous goddess Haḍimbā" (2019: 202).

13. Geslani questions the supposed Vaiṣṇava nature even of the *VDhP*, the text that underlies much of the royal ritual tradition of Shah Nepal (2018: 177).

14. Bledsoe refers to the "cosmopolitical order" of the Newar Malla kings whose use of tantric rituals dedicated to Taleju "was actively extended at every turn to include divine as well as human beings in a single conceptual frame" (2000: 196).

15. Here and elsewhere, I use the term "Kumari" rather than "Kaumari," except when citing the original Nepali. The Nepali of the *NBhV* "establishes" Kumārī through its repetition of her name followed by a form of the transitive verb *garnu* ("to do") "*putrī lāī kaumārīdevī bhāvanā garī kaumārī sthāpanā garī kaumārī kā pūjā garyā rīt calāyā*" (53).

16. Following inscriptional evidence, Koirala asserts that Jaya Prakash Malla also placed the city-wide processions of the three living divinities in the Indrajatra (1985: 72).

17. The Shah dynasty further reinforced its connection to Kumari in 1969 by sponsoring the refurbishing of the chariots of Kumari, Bhairav, and Ganesh, inscribing on its brass railing the names of the king and queen, Sri 5 Maharajadhiraja Mahendra Bir Bikram Shah Dev and Sri 5 High Queen Ratna Rajya Lakshmi Devi Shah.

18. "indrajātrā kumārīgaṇa sahit sthāpanā garī [kumārījātrā bhani] jātrā banāyā" (*NBhV* 52).

The text has Gunakamadeva establish a few other festivals as well, including the clearly Buddhist "Matayāta and Sringabhērī" and additional festivals that "were established before the foundation of Kāntipura [Kathmandu]" (59).

19. Gutschow (1982: 120) and van den Hoek (2004: 5) all give slightly different names to these eight points than do Juju and Shrestha (1999: 38–39). The latter list the Sanskrit *mātṛkā* as Brahmāyaṇī, Māheśvarī, Kaumārī, Vaiṣ ṇavī, Bārāhī, Indrāyaṇī, Cāmuṇḍā, and Mahālakṣmī, connecting them to their respective Ajimā of Pāsikva, Lumari, Phibva, Nai, Kaṅga, Luti, Thavahi, and Candralakhu.

20. It is presumably this image of Viśvarūp Mahālakṣmī that the *NBhV* refers to in its section on King Pratap Malla who, in the 1650s, "made a metal image of Viśhvarūpa and arranged for it to be displayed outside during the Indrajātrā for public viewing" (106).

21. Devi Pyakha's approximately eight members come from the central-city neighborhood of Kilagal Tol and consist of Bhairav, Kumārī, Daitya, and a number of ghostly *bhut-pret* assistants. Mahakali Pyakha's larger group from Bhaktapur, dancing nightly at Hanuman Dhoka, revolves around Mahakali, Bhairav, and Chaṇḍī and includes additional *bhut-pret* assistants.

Sava Bhaku from Halchowk on the city's northwest fringes consists of Bhairav, Kumārī, and Chaṇḍī.

22. Michael Allen's (1984) study of Kumari is the most thorough. See also Shakya and Berry (2005) and Tree (2015).

23. Regarding Kumārī's Buddhist identity, Todd Lewis writes, "Before this procession begins with the king's appearance outside the royal palace, the Pañcaraksa dharanis must be read" (Lewis, Tuladhar, and Tuladhar 2000: 160).

24. Witzel (1997: 529–30) improbably connects the appearance of these divinities to the three characters of the *Rig Veda* Vṛṣākapi hymn (10.84).

25. I have often watched children play on these chariots, their parents taking photos of them approximating the divinity of the children who will ride on them during the festival. Never have I seen a child dare to sit in the chariots' thrones reserved for the living deities.

26. Aside from Kumari, from among these festival figures only Lakhe is mentioned in the *NBhV* (172).

27. Outside of Kathmandu and outside of the Indra festival, the city's center (*dathu*) remains a relatively vague designation that is neither fixed nor debated. Holle, Toffin, and Rimal (1993: 45) assert: "Only the Maharjan of Maru state that they belong to *Dathu*." The Maru *tol* area is also important as it contains roughly one-third of all of the city's residential *bahāḥ* monasteries (Gutschow 1982: 115).

28. Other people have told me in passing that this rite was added by Gunakamadeva (tenth century) or Prithivi Narayan Shah (eighteenth century), as it was their concubine who missed the earlier procession. Vajracharya notes that the *ṭhyāsaphu* of CE 1684 celebrates the Indrajatra until Asvin 3, thus ending on the day before *nānichā yāḥ* (1976: 172).

29. Kumari's chariot stays here for nearly twenty minutes to witness Daitya's defeat. Van den Hoek's (2004: 79) statement that *nānichā yāḥ* probably has more to do with Kumārī's passing of the four Indra icons of the upper town than with "the trivial origin accorded to it in the story" of the king's concubine, seems more correct.

30. Also present at Kilagal is a second, nonroyal Jyāpu Kumari (or Kilagal Kumari); although she had been present during some of the festivities, she is not to come into physical or visual contact with the Rāj Kumari as she makes her way through the neighborhood (Allen 1984: 70–71). Despite this particular avoidance—similar to the restriction on the erstwhile king of Nepal visiting the massive reclining Vishnu in the northern neighborhood of Buḍhanīlakaṇṭh that is said to be identical to the king—the presence of Devi Pyakha during Kumari's procession and thus of multiple Kumaris has the opposite effect: many people told me that Kumari (the divinized girl in the chariot) purposefully stops in Kilagal to watch Kumari (the dancing goddess) defeat her demonic enemy.

31. This translation is a reworking of those from Wright (2000: 198) and the *NBhV* (97) with recourse to the Nepali text (83).

32. Wright's footnote here reads: "The troops and most of the people were drunk, as is the custom at the Indra-jātrā festival" (2000: 231, n2).

33. This translation is a reworking of those from Wright (2000: 231–32) and the *NBhV* 118 with recourse to the Nepali text (100–101). Shreshtha is one of the few authors who hints at the mythology of this entire event, preceding his account with "According to one story" (2014: 200).

34. The *Nepālarājaparamparā* names many kings who built, venerated, and ritualized at Pashupati (Riccardi 1986).

35. On this day, a Vajracharya priest performs an elaborate *homa*—an Indra Pūjā—in front of the golden mask of Akash Bhairav inside the royal square at Hanuman Dhoka. In this puja, the priest employed thirty-two small brass dishes containing such earthy items as seeds, beans, and legumes, which were thrown into the fire at the end of the ritual. In addition to chanting mantras, the priest held a *vajra* and *ghaṇṭa* in his hands, ringing the latter throughout the ceremony and using *mudras* with both hands. This ritual concludes with the sacrifices of chicken, goat, and buffalo.

36. Gellner attributes this absence of opposition to the decades of war that brought deprivation and suffering to the Newar people (1999: 10).

37. See also Shaha (1990: 35); Regmi (1975: 80); Gellner (1999: 10); Slusser (1982: 76).

38. For these same reasons, including the large crowds, the Indra Jatra of 1950 was the original proposed setting for the launch of a rebel attack against the Rana regime (Rana 2017: 337).

39. Acharya refers to the setting of the invasion as "the Indrajatra and Kumarijatra festivals" (1973: 55).

40. Hamilton's 1819 study, *An Account of the Kingdom of Nepal* (1971), does not mention the Indrajatra at all.

41. His assertion that the festival (performed in Bhādrapad, not the previous month of Śrāvaṇ) is a "holy progress" across the Kathmandu Valley from Dahachowk to Thimi (in their current spellings) and involving the Bālkumārī, though not wholly incorrect, hardly represents a key component of the festival. The Balkumari of Thimi has no part in Kathmandu's festival, as she typically appears only in festivals in Bhaktapur (Kirkpatrick's "Bhatgong") district, such as during the April 14 new year's festival, Biskaḥ Jātrā, celebrated when the city's "many Deotas" are worshiped.

42. Wright's translation of the phrase *prativarṣa liṅga ḍhāli jātrā garāyā* with the archetypal "the Linga-dhāli-jātrā (known now as the Indra-jātrā)" contributes to the culture and reception of the festival as a Sanskritic and Hindu one. The translation offered in the *NBhV* rectifies this by translating this phrase more literally, offering more of a description than a definition: "an

annual festival in which the pole is installed and then pulled down," footnoted with a reference to "the annual festival of Indrajātrā" (Wright 2000: 134, n5).

43. This passage draws on the translations of both Wright (2000: 260) and the *NBhV* (134).

44. Many local scholars asserted that this was the case (personal communication, Bal Dev Juju, August 26, 2005; Kashinath Tamot, September 12, 2018; and Mahesh Raj Pant, October 1, 2018); also Pant 1995: 36. In Hasrat's only other reference to the Indra festival, he names Pratap Singh as the king who, during his short reign, "established the Indra-Yātrā" (1970: 93). Vajracharya refers to the role of Pratap Singh in an unpublished manuscript of the *Bhāṣā Vāṃśāvalī* that notes the same, further emphasizing the pole's annual journey from Nawakot (1976: 170, n3).

Notes to Chapter 5

1. Astrologers from the line of Daivajña Śiromaṇi Lakṣmīpati Pāṇḍe established the Indra festival's *sāit* structure in 1843.

2. Regmi (1975: 273) and Aryāl (1990: 161) corroborate Śaktivallabh's connection to Prithvi Narayan.

3. Similarly, in his short study of the Arjyāl family, Sūrya Bikram Jñavāli, quoting several small Sanskrit texts (including the *Arjyāl Vaṃśāvalī*) traces the name "Arjyāl" back through Islamic India to the village of Āryā, where several members of the early lineage lived; there, they became known as "Āryālaya" or "Ārjyāl" (1983: 11).

4. For this reason, the Arjyāl family is listed among the Six Clans (Nep. *cha thar*) in the eleventh of Ram Shah's edicts (Riccardi 1977: 49). Specific priestly offices are given to particular members of the Arjyāl clan (*hotu* and *āchārya*) in the nineteenth (57), and additional royal offices (*dharmādhikar*, the highest criminal judge; *sardār*, high military official; and *bhānsyā*, the royal cook) in the twenty-second (60).

5. He arrived from Kaski along with his brother, Radhavallabh Arjyal, who became *rājpurohit* of the Shah dynasty after Śhaktivallabh's death, an office he held until his own death in 1812 (VS 1869) (Vajrācārya 1980: 575). Radhavallabh's literary output was relatively insignificant compared to his more famous brother (Acharya 1975b: 144–45), but his donative inscription on the southern interior door of the Pashupati temple that includes the phrase *bhrātā (paṇḍit) Śaktivallabh dharādevasya yukto* reminds worshipers of his connections to his esteemed elder brother (Vajrācārya 1980: 573).

6. Among Śaktivallabh's other well-known works, virtually none of which have been translated into English, are a 1770 rendering of the Virāṭ

aparvan chapter of the *Mahābhārata* (Hutt 1991: 173), *Sudhātaraṅgiṇitantram* (Sastri 1905: 266–67), *Lalitamādhav* (Regmī 1992: 337), and the Nepali drama *Hāsyakauṭuka* or *Hāsyakadamba* (Acharya 1975a: 235, 1975b: 145). Gautam identifies the latter, written in 1792, as the oldest Nepali-language play (1965: 31).

7. Pant notes Śaktivallabh's poetic license in the latter's imitation (*anukaraṇa*) of a north Indian *subhāṣita*: originally extolling the virtue of the pre-Mughal king Sher Shah, Śaktivallabh uses this poem to praise his own benefactor, Rana Bahadur Shah (1985: 65).

8. Noting the coincidence that the *JRN* was written in the same year that Kirkpatrick arrived in Nepal, Vajrācārya notes that Kirkpatrick's 1811 *Account* contains more information on Nepal's traditions than does the *JRN* (1969: 95, 102).

9. The name of this text as written on the document's official National Archives title page is *Indradhvajotsava Pūjā*. Sastri (1915) names it the *Indradhvajotsava Kathanam* (191) and, in his preface, the *Indradhvajotsava Varṇanaṃ* ("description"; xxxiii).

10. Dinesh Raj Pant (1985: 494–500) provides a lengthy list of the many rock-cut inscriptions (*śilāpatra* or *śilālekh*), manuscripts (*abhilekh*), and pillar inscriptions (*stambhalekh*) produced under the reigns of the first Shah kings, beginning with Chatra Shah in 1609. These early kings also copied and composed Sanskrit texts and commentaries, including those of the *Viṣṇusahasranāmastotra* (CE 1610), Kalidasa's *Meghadūta* (CE 1621), the *Kāśikhaṇḍa* (CE 1635), and the *Hitopadeśa* (CE 1655).

11. The thirty-two topics in the *Kathanam* are listed on a separate folio at the end of the document, in a sort of table of contents with each topic connected to the folio number wherein it appears (nos. 1–17). This final page also contains the seal of Prime Minister Chandra Shamsher Rāṇa with an accession date of 1913 (VS 1970); Sastri, compiling his index in 1915, presumably had access to this additional page and based his own table of contents on it.

12. In my possession are copies of two versions of this text from Nepal's National Archives. The first (3-320, 17 ff.), numbered as the ninth (*navama*) and undated, is referred to in Sastri (1915); the other (5-1520, 14 ff.), numbered as the seventeenth (*saptadaśa*), provides its date of writing (rather than its composition) as VS 1931 (CE 1874), and its scribe as the brahmin Indravilāśa Sarman. They are adjacent documents in Nepal's National Archives system (reel nos. A1150-9 and A1150-10).

13. Other texts related to the Indra festival were available to the Shah kings. Sastri lists two Newar copies of the *Viṣṇu Dharma* (with a reference in the colophon to the *dharmottara* [Purāṇa]) (1905: 29–30), and Aryāl states that at the command of King Prithvipati Shah, Viśveśvara Arjyāl produced a commentary on the *Bṛhat Saṃhitā* of Varāhamihira in 1677 (VS 1734) (1990: 27).

14. "Śrī Gaṇeśāya Namaḥ. This regards the raising of the Śakra-pole. I praise him who is praised first among the eight protectors of the directions; he of the lotus-compound(?); the lord who was born of Puloma; the one who possesses a good sound in the garden; he who carries the *vajra;* wears the set-pearl, the crown and the *kuṇḍala;* who is together with the Gandharvas; who indulges his pleasure in dancing and sporting with the apsarases. He is the one named Vāsava. The festival of Indra is on the 12th day of the bright half of Bhadra. These, it is said, are the fruits of the Indradhvaja festival."

15. For two relatively minor examples, he clarifies *sānuyātaḥ* (*sa anuyātaḥ,* "with sons") from the *Brahma Purāṇa* with *saputra* [ff. 2b]), and *dine dine* ("every day") with *vacanāt dvādaśīm ārabhya yāvad avasthānaṃ pratyahaṃ sampūjyaḥ* ("It is to be worshiped every day from the commencement of the speech on the twelfth [of Bhādrapad], following its installation" [ff. 2b]).

16. "surapati gṛhagāmīḥ hi arccanam śakraketoḥ pratiśaradam anekaiḥ pūjayet śrī vivṛddhyai."

17. This text is regularly referred to in the *Kathanam* as the *Varāha Saṃhitā.*

18. Bhaṭṭotpāla's tenth-century commentary on the *Bṛhat Saṃhitā* is quite confused, leaving it unclear as to whether he saw the *kumārī* and *mātṛkā* as two sets of discrete objects.

19. "kumāryyaḥ pañca-karttavyāḥ śakrasya nṛpa sattamaḥ | sālamayās tu tāḥ sarvā aparā śakra-mātṛkāḥ | ketoḥ pāda-pramāṇena kāryyā śakra-kumārikāḥ || manuḥ | indradhvajasya śobhārthaḥ kumāryyāḥ kārayet dvijaḥ | atra kālikā purāṇa nanda-upanandādi pañca-śakra-kumāryyā aṣṭamātṛkāḥ" (*Kathanam* 1150-10, ff. 6b–7a).

20. Kane (1930–1962: 2.2: 826): "five or seven wooden figures (called the *śakra-kumārī*) are also to be placed near [the pole]."

21. Similarly, the tantric deity Khaḍgarāvaṇa, "the Lord of Ghosts," is "visualized as sitting on the central pericarp of a shining white lotus [with his] eight female attendants . . . seated on each petal oriented toward the cardinal and intermediate directions of the compass" (Slouber 2016: 156).

22. "tataḥ pañca-śakra-kumārikā pūjā | pañcadaṇḍeṣu tathā krameṇa pūjayet | OM upanandāyai namaḥ | OM jayāyai namaḥ | OM vijayāyai namaḥ | OM vasuṃdharāyai namaḥ | iti pratyekam pūjayet | śakra-mātṛkābhyo namaḥ | iti aṣṭaumātṛkā samudāyena pūjayet." Missing from this list of *kumārī,* however, is *śakra-janitrī,* the pole whose name Bhaṭṭotpāla glosses with *indra-mātā,* "the mother of Indra."

23. "tam utthāpya mahāketum pūjitaṃ maṇḍalāntare || pratimā tām nayet mūlaṃ ketoḥ śakraṃ vicintyayet || yajet taṃ pūrvavat tatra śacīṃ mātaliṃ eva ca || jayantaṃ taṃ tanayaṃ tasya vajraṃ airāvataṃ tathā || grahāṃ cāpi atha dikpālān sarvāśca gaṇadevaṭāḥ."

24. Locke describes the Newar *kalash pūjā* as "a ritualization of the *sadhana,* the yogic evocation of a deity" (1980: 95).

25. Śaktivallabh cites the *trātaraṃ indraṃ* passage (*Rig Veda* 6.47.11), a version of which occurs also in the sixth-century *Bṛhat Saṃhitā,* throughout the *puja.*

26. "Firmly establishing this worshipped image of Indra at the base of the poles, meditating again first on Śakra, worship should be made with the appropriate *upachāra*" (tatas tāṃ pūjita śakrapratimāṃ dhvajamūlesu dṛḍhaṃ kṛtvā saṃsthāpya punaḥ śakraṃ pūrvavat dhyātvā yathā militopachāraiḥ pūjayet.)

27. For reference, the year 2020 of the Gregorian calendar is 2077 in Vikram Samvat and 1140 in Nepal Samvat.

28. "sarddhaṃ surāsuragaṇaiḥ puraṃdara śatakrato || upahāraṃ gṛhitvā imaṃ mahendra dhvaja gamyatāṃ."

29. In this same palace courtyard, the masked dance troupe Sava Bhaku, mentioned in the *Gorkhāpatra* article, used to sacrifice a buffalo on the festival's third day. The sacrifice was a particularly gruesome one, in which a buffalo was fed large amounts of alcohol before being turned loose; three members of Sava Bhaku, armed with knives, would repeatedly slice the buffalo until it bled to death. Van den Hoek (2004: 147, n8) reported, "The custom was revived after more than forty years in 1993, but now in a stadium and sponsored by a Kilagal youth-club." The palace is still the site of the mass sacrifice of buffalo and goats on the Black Night of *Kālrātri,* the seventh night of *Dasain.*

30. In the past, presumably, many more images of Indra were raised, possibly one in each of the thirty-two Jyāpu neighborhoods. Toffin refers to one periodically raised in the neighborhood of Thahiti, raised by the king (New. *juju*) of the upper city and descendant of the former Newar Malla kings. The *guthi* at Banghemuda stopped installing theirs due to an internal dispute; the lower-city neighborhood of Jaisi Deval was often mentioned as displaying an Indra, though it currently does not. Stella Kramrisch's *Art of Nepal* (1964) includes similar images of Indra on display at Asia House in New York that at one time presumably were raised in local neighborhoods. An Indra image now permanently resides at Kva Bahāḥ (Skt. *Hiraṇyavarṇa Mahāvihāra*) in Patan, upstairs in the Amitābha Sukhāvati Bhavan, amid actively worshipped images of the Buddhist Amitābha and Tārā. This image used to sit in the royal square of Mangal Bazaar south of the Bahal until it was moved to its present location, reportedly for its own security. Newars visit and venerate this image at the beginning of pujas to the *aṣṭa-digpāla* (Eight Protectors of the Directions), Indra always sitting in the east and invoked first.

31. The Indra of Musum Bahāl was stolen some fifty years ago and had to be remade. Here, there is no *guthi* proper; rather, three brothers do the majority of the work, with the eldest serving as the *thakali* (the headman of a *guthi*) along with anyone else who wants to assist (Tulsi Narayan Maharjan, personal communication, August 27, 2006).

32. Van den Hoek (2004: 43) briefly mentions this anomaly: "The display of these Indras is a purely Jyāpu (Farmer) affair, with the exception of a small puja which is given to the Indra of Indrachowk (Vamgah) by a Newar (Rajopadhyaya) Brahmin at his house."

33. Other such texts are often kept inside a protective wooden box. By 2018, the elder of Brahmapur had died and his nephew was conducting the puja; though the text was no longer present—it is currently lost among his uncle's personal belongings—the nephew continues to perform the ritual in virtually the same way, as if the text were still there. While I do not have a copy of this particular text, I incorporate manuscript copies of other ritual *paddhati* texts prescribed for use on Bhādra 11: *Indrapūjā* (H323/25), *Indradhvajotsava Nirṇaya* (B324/12), *Indrapūjā Paddhati* (E466-66), and *Indrapūjā* (E450/1), which gives its date as NS 901 (CE 1781).

34. One played the *dhime*, the drum particular to the Jyāpu, and the other struck the thick metal *kepui* cymbal with a wooden hammer. The drum beats sped up when the musicians entered the neighborhood and again when they left it, a musical signal of the deity's presence.

35. The *daśa-karma vidhi* represent the equivalent of the Sanskritic eighteen *saṃskāras* (Locke 1980: 208–16). Only the *Kathanam* asserts that the tree from which the Indra pole comes receives, during the Gaṇesh Pūjā in the forest, its *prāṇ pratiṣṭhā* (ff. 12a).

36. This analysis again refers to Lecomte-Tilouine's assertion that "By contrast, the chronicles of Gorkha take the geographical context [of the Kathmandu Valley] into account only when it relates to the Shah dynasty and its conquests" (2011: 195).

37. By "quasi-Vedic," I am reinforcing the theme of the non-Vedic ("Vedish") nature of the festival and, now by extension, the deity at its center.

Notes to Chapter 6

1. Sax (2002: 50) mentions that one Garhwali village has a strong tradition that the Pāṇḍav Līlā should last eighteen days, the same length as the Mahābhārata War. Another tentative epic connection that some have made with Newar festivals is the identification of the five Dhyāni Buddhas of Buddha Jayanti and the five Dīpaṅkara Buddhas of Pañchadān with the five Pāṇḍava brothers, though Andrea Wollein questions the validity and usefulness of the "multiple [Hindu] identification" of these fairly strictly Buddhist figures (2019: 126–30).

2. Though the masks of Sava Bhaku, consisting also of these same three members, stay year-round at their *guthi* house on the northwestern

edge of the valley at Hal Chowk, they reside in a private home in Kilagal during the Indrajātrā.

3. The name Aravāṉ is connected to the epic warrior Irāvat, the son of Arjuna and the serpent woman, Nāgī, whose name (the snake/elephant) immediately clues us in to Aravāṉ's connection to elephants (Hiltebeitel 2011: 210–13). His derivative name, Airāvat, is the name of Indra's elephant who dances in Kathmandu's Indra festival as Pulukisi and in the Garhwali epic performance.

4. During the Dasain festival, an image of Bhairav is painted on a *pulu*, daubed with the blood from an animal sacrifice, and attached to the exterior of his main temple in the central Taumaḍhī Square in Bhaktapur.

5. Witzel substantiates Levy's connection between elephants and death with a Vedic reference to the elephant-shaped remnant of the solar deity Mārtāṇḍa, the father (or uncle) of Indra and Yama (1997: 527).

6. This description of Bhaktapur's festival is supplemented by several unpublished accounts by Sudarshan Raj Tiwari and by Niels Gutschow and his students, Tessa Fischer, Yvonne Ungerer, and Nadine Plachta.

7. Gutschow sees the festival in Bhaktapur primarily as a rain festival, with the ancestral associations prevalent in Kathmandu relatively unknown. For example, Indrayāṇī's tears are the rain that falls during the festival, and the *mupatra* with his two assistants are the *daityas* who attempt to prevent the falling of the rain (unpublished manuscript). Pauḍyāl echoes this sentiment for the festival generally (1998: 77).

8. He is also called *gumlā lākhe* for his appearance during the Buddhist Newar month of Gumlā that immediately precedes the Indra festival (Toffin 2010: 110).

9. Difficult to render into English, the closest translation of "Śrī Lākhe Ājuḥ" might be "the glorious grandfather Lakhe," a title that directly connects him to Bhairav.

10. Kashinath Tamot (personal communication, September 12, 2018) suggested that all of the different festival dances (Lakhe, Sawa Bhaku, Devi Pyakha, Mahakali Nach from Bhaktapur) were locally performed during the pre-Indrajātrā *yeṃ yāḥ*. The Shah revival entailed a consolidation (via royal invitation, and the power and prestige that it brings to the king and the dance troupe), whereby all of these dances are now performed in Kathmandu proper and especially at Hanuman Dhoka, thus bringing together these groups from all over the city and valley into a single central festival.

11. On Asoj 1, Pulukisi and the three masked figures of Sawa Bhaku—Bhairav, Kumari, and Chandi (or Bhairav, Sawa, and Bhaku)—travel to Lakhenani, where Lakhe, having invited both troupes, takes turns dancing with each, and Lakhe and Pulukisi pay homage to Sawa Bhaku. Here also

several women displayed gestures of trance and possession as they performed puja directly to Sawa Bhaku.

12. One man asserted that since the Taleju temple is immediately behind the main palace area, the mustachioed image represents the goddess Taleju, a gender-bending ambiguity that recurs in other festivals, including the puja to Indra described earlier, where he is depicted as both male and female.

13. Anderson suggests that the rite might reenact the ancient beheading of an ancestral king; display a low-level hatred of Indra, the invading king; or express resentment toward Indra's mother, Dagi, who abandoned the souls of the deceased.

14. In a related narrative from Garhwal, Bhīma places Babrīk's severed head atop a pole from which he can view the remainder of the battle (Sax 2002: 99).

15. Other versions of Yalambar's arrival in Kathmandu, related in the same volume, relate how his head fell from the branches of the tree and dropped into the river amid his continued attempts to get a better view of the battle. Since Yalambar arrived in Kathmandu via the Akash Marg, his severed head began to be referred to as Akash Bhairav, his body residing in Benares (Bajracharya 2003: 19–20).

16. Bajracharya summarizes this transformation even more directly: "According to a tantric viewpoint in which the gods and goddesses are played by [possess] humans, the elders say that the famous Kirāti Rājā Yalambar Yāluṅga through his power was transformed into the powerful and revered deity, Śrī Ākāsh Bhairav of Waṃgha Tol" (2003: 19).

17. Bajracharya asserts the local importance of the festival's central Indra Chowk neighborhood using a similar linguistic argument, tracing the Newar term for Waṃgha to the *hvaṃga* (confluence; Skt. *saṅgam*) of the three rivers that used to flow through this northern neighborhood (2003: 22).

18. Shakya uses such terms as "grotesque," "wrathful," and "infuriated" to describe the physical appearance of Bhairav's mask (2008, p. 125).

19. Maharjan also describes the rites of Bhairav's return to his temple: "The day following the end of the Indrajātrā, Bhairav is lifted back into his temple among tantric and traditional puja. In order that no common people may see these pujas, no outside people are allowed inside at the time of the puja. Once Bhairav is returned to his seat [*āsan*], *jaḥsibu pūjā* is performed with all of the *khalak*—a *sagun pūjā* [*kalaḥ pūjā*], with a buffalo and ram offered as *bali*" (2003: 41). Locke describes a similar establishment of an image of the head of Bhairav in the Jyāpu community at Ituṃ Bāhāl during the Indrajātrā (1985: 290).

20. The Tamil situation resembles that in Kathmandu: "Aravāṉ's ability to see the entire war reflects the practice in the Draupadī cult of setting up a

clay image of his head on a post to watch the ritual proceedings that represent the war, from its beginning to its end" (Hiltebeitel 1988: 325).

21. Newars "want to free Nepal from the unjust rule of "one nation, one culture, one religion and one language' to let flourish, cultures, religions, languages and literatures of diverse nationalities of Nepal so that a truly a multinational, multicultural, multilingual, and multi-religious federal democratic republic of Nepal could to established where all of them can live in peace and harmony with mutual respect" (Shreshta 2010/2011: 4).

22. See Sax (2009: 32–37) and Toffin (2008: 367).

23. Presumably because of this common theme of (self-)sacrifice as boon, many Newars also connect Yalambar to the epic Ekalavya, a low-caste Nishada warrior and student of Drona whose sharp-shooting thumb was requested and subsequently offered as the latter's *gurudakṣiṇā* (Bajracharya 2003: 19; Manandhar 2003: 35). Members of the Nishad caste in Uttar Pradesh remember Ekalavya for his heroic victimization at the hands of brahmins (Narayan 2009: 107–12, 122–30).

24. Ben-Herut (2012) provides a story with a similar historical antagonistic provenance: the retrieval of a self-sacrificed head leads to a twelfth-century sectarian victory of Hindu Vīraśaivas over their Jain counterparts.

25. Hiltebeitel coins the term "free-floating Mahābhārata folklore" in reference to Aravāṉ, whose images, "placed on corners and edges of the temple roof or the top of the compound wall," allow him to guard specifically Draupadi temples "from those of his own kind" (1991: 298).

26. In this act of self-sacrifice, Yalambar-Bhairav serves as a counterpart to the sacrificial *satī*, the woman who mounts the funeral pyre at the death of her husband-warrior, who displays and acquires the *sat*, or truth, of their productive, protective, and sacrificial lives.

27. In the oldest version of the Tamil story (ninth century), Aravāṉ, the multiform of Yalambar, offers himself as a sacrifice to the goddess Kālī (Hiltebeitel 2011: 276), the more standard telling representing a "(probably) fourteenth century version" (2011: 276–77). Vajracharya includes a nineteenth-century painting of this story in his book on Newar art history (2016: 158).

Notes to Chapter 7

1. Mary Slusser's photo in *Nepal Mandala* (1982: vol. 2, plate 442) shows him sitting directly on the ground.

2. Birkenholtz, referring to the Newar text of the *Svasthānī Vrat Kathā*, notes similar ways that Puranic narratives, transformed when incorporated into the local text, "[take] advantage of the fluidity and mobility of narrative elements in both local and translocal sources" (2018: 143).

3. Toffin and Pradhan refer to a specifically "Buddhist version of the myth" (1992: 85; 1986: 395).

4. In his short story, "During the Festival," Samrat Upadhyay uses the festival's underlying narrative of the relationship between Indra and his mother to allow Ganesh, the story's main character, to question his wife's fidelity. As he walks through he city, "Everywhere around him, Ganesh saw people's faces filled with joy and excitement. He knew he should have enjoyed that excitement; instead, he felt as if a giant bird had descended from the sky and spread a shadow over the city" (2001: 88).

5. G. S. Nepali provides a different version of the story in which Indra was arrested for stealing flowers of the Ashok tree and was buried alive at Maru (1965: 359).

6. In Bhaktapur, the stolen object is a *khaisi*, a fruit used in local death rituals and similar to both the *bhagavatya* that is installed on the top of Kathmandu's Indra pole and the *taḥsi* citrus fruit that presides over the *mha pūjā* ritual of the new year's day of Svanti (Nep. Tihar) in October/November (Niels Gutschow, unpublished manuscript) (Vajracharya 2018: 9). Sax describes the similarly playful cucumber thefts that occur during the Small Pilgrimage of Nandādevī in Garhwal, transactions that seem to reflect the fecundity that the goddess brings (1991: 43).

7. The demonic nature of Dagi and Lakhe entails their antipathy to Baumata, whose lights they traditionally attempt to extinguish.

8. Later, Pradhan glosses *baumata* with the Sanskrit *bahumata* (a Sanskrit-Newar hybrid meaning "many lights") (1986: 398). Vajracharya also asserts this (1980: 63).

9. According to Triratna Manandhar (personal communication, August 17, 2005), some years back, the organizers of Baumata refused to fulfill their duties if they were to be abused in the traditional manner, so people now no longer abuse them, and the procession takes place without any disturbances.

10. Triratna Manandhar, personal communication, August 17, 2005.

11. This is the same procession that the *Gorkhāpatra* newspaper asserted was accompanied by soldiers from the Nepali military.

12. In his locally printed pamphlet, Pradip Suvedi provides the only "sinless" end to this story I have encountered: "All of the dead who were walking the road to heaven went with the liberated Indra to Indra Daha at Dahachowk, and then they went to heaven. The dead, being quite disordered, wandered about, jumped into the lake, and thus obtained their liberation" (1998: 8).

13. In one version of this story, Draupadī's postwar chastity was first questioned by Bhīma after one petal of the parijat flower that she kept in her hair began to wilt (Hiltebeitel 1988: 439, n7).

14. Hiltebeitel also identifies the fire pit as the postbattle cremation grounds where the warriors died and their widows weep for them (1999: 476).

15. In his children's book, *Indrajātrā*, Chura Mani Bandhu (2012) applies a middle-class moral to the traditional story to show how "even a king will be punished for his misdeed" and that the people must "maintain justice and respect elders" (personal communication, March 17, 2019).

16. Baburatna Maharjan, a local Maharjan *guthi* leader in Indra Chowk, provided a slightly different rationale for Indra's janai. In the old days, everybody in Kathmandu was wealthy and wore much gold, and on *janāī pūrṇimā*, people are given a yellow or golden janai as a sign of the city's past wealth. In the same way that everyone must wear a janai to reach heaven, Indra wears his for the same purpose. Also on the third day of Svanti (Nep. Tihār), the Newar new year's festival permeated with death imagery, a janai is tied on the tail of a cow, a manifestation of Vaitāraṇī.

17. Campbell reports that among the Rajputs of the Kangra Valley, the festival of *rakṣā bandon* "is said to repeat the paradigmatic act when the dog tied a *raksa* on Indra before he entered battle to give him protection" (1976: 40).

18. He cites other passages from the Brāhmaṇas that transform the ritualist into a winged bird and quotes Frits Staal, who witnessed this ritual act in a 1955 *vājapeya* sacrifice in Pune. See also Gerety (2016).

19. The translations of Ganguli and van Buitenen clearly have Vasu moving: Ganguli translates this passage as: "And when king Vasu took his seat in that crystal car, with the gift of Indra, and coursed through the sky, he was approached by Gandharvas and Apsaras (the celestial singers and dancers)." Van Buitenen writes that Vasu "will ride there above" (1973: 131).

20. Regarding the iconography of Ashokan pillars, Vajracharya (1999) argues that the word *vimāna* refers to stable tower-like structures rather than to a moving chariot.

21. Similarly, Dyczkowski asserts that "Tantrism serves as a vehicle of Sanskritization at the very core of Newar culture, radically rooted as it is in religion that is to a very large degree ritualistic. In this and other ways, notably its art, Tantrism is a ubiquitous part of Newar culture" (2001: 21).

22. Examples of such possessed masked deities in Kathmandu—typically of dancers depicting forms of Bhairav and goddesses—include the Devi Pyakha dance troupe during Indrajātrā, the Nāy Ajimā during the Pachali Bhairav Jātrā (van den Hoek describes the human manifestation of the goddess as being "carried" [2004: 74]), and the Mother Goddesses during the spring Pahāṃ Cāhre and autumn Dasain festivals.

23. A more complete version of this story can be found in Levy and Rajopadhyaya (1990: 503–5).

24. In a similar story, Gayaḥbājyā catches the goddess Caṇḍeśvarī—who had transformed herself into a snake—in his sleeve for seven days; frustrated by her inability to escape, she promised him that "if he freed her, she would stay anywhere he desired" (Sharma 1999: 245–46).

25. In their study of fourteenth-century Tibetan saint Longchenpa, Germano and Gyatso identify the *ḍākinī* in the presence of whom the saint reincarnates as a *tulku,* as "one who goes in space"; the ambivalent *ḍākinī* signifies "a female spirit who can either be a transcendent buddha or a vengeful demoness" (2000: 243). Also present in the text they translate, and equally ambivalent, are Dharma protectresses, whose binding and subjugation by Padmasambhava were meant "to prevent them from hindering Buddhist activities and to bind them into the ongoing service and defense of Buddhism" (2000: 246).

26. The English-language Yomari cartoon series is one of the few sources—primary or secondary—that asserts the tantric nature of the Jyāpu farmer. Here, the farmer with the name and form of a *yomari* (a jam-filled Newar sweet) arrests Indra and declares, "This is no ordinary rope. I use this rope to capture powerful demons." The bound god responds by asserting the identity of the *yomari*-farmer with: "Ah! You must be the famous tantrik" ("Yenya").

27. Lowdin briefly describes the festival "in Sunakothi [where] a *guthi* sets up six Khun dyo (lit., thief Gods), said to be the sons of Indra, on poles" (1998: 89, n34). Bernier describes how the "appearance during Indrajātrā of Indra images . . . defines the sacred geography of the city through their locations and the ritual processions that move past them" (1979: 23).

28. In her study of the Keralan *yakṣī,* Corinne Dempsey (2005) includes several stories with narrative elements common to the tantric stories related to the Indra festival: a ravishing semi-divine female who performs human sacrifice, the possibility of thwarting her power through ritual contest or even domesticating her power through confinement by iron nails, her accidental liberation by an unsuspecting female, and her installation as a powerful local goddess.

29. An alternative interpretation of this image is that Indra's extended and open hands display not his arrest by the Jyāpus but his innocence of the crime of which he is accused.

30. Following Regmi (1966: 1005–6) and anticipating Andrade, Zwilling, and Sweet (2017: 125–26, n487), Vajracharya hypothesizes that this unique iconography of Indra—in the form of a "cross"—was made known to Jesuit missionaries by Newar artisans working in western Tibet in the 1600s (2016: 129; 138; 201, n6; and 1976: 174–75, n1). I argue rather that these icons were unknown to them and that these "crosses" were actually Tibetan Buddhist double *dorje* that would have been displayed during the Newar festival month of Gumlā (Lewis 1993: 334).

31. Vajracharya reiterates this argument elsewhere, referring to the deity as "the Newar ancestral figure" (2020: 87) and connecting Indra specifically to Bhairav-Aju, "the divine grandfather" (2016: 139).

32. Vajracharya also asserts that these aniconic forms of Indra date back to the festival's origins, said to be in the eighth century.

33. Contemporary *Mahābhārata* performances in Gingee provide another example of a vertically oriented hero-deity, that of Indra's epic son, in the famous scene of "Arjuna's penance": "As Arjuna climbs the 'tapas tree,' at each step he pauses for songs and prayers to Śiva. Once he reaches the top, he sits cross-legged—a true pillar saint—on a small platform. There he holds his hands in prayer above his head" (Hiltebeitel 1988: 285).

Notes to the Conclusion

1. More recently, the issue of Newar autonomy vis-à-vis the Nepali government arose in light of a proposed (and eventually failed) state reform of the Newar *guthi* structure (Toffin 2019).

2. Anne Mocko's (2016) excellent book describes this process in great detail.

3. Maharjan and Barata (2017) have written about the Indra festival in the context of UNESCO and heritage in Nepal after the earthquakes.

4. Thus the celebration of the Indra festival among diasporic Newar populations in California, Maryland, Sydney, and Sikkim warrant significant research.

5. Mottin identifies street theater, especially the Jyāpu Nāch (Farmer's Dance), as a significant component of the Indra festival during the Rana period (2018: 10).

6. ekantipur.com, September 8, 2006 (article no longer available).

7. See https://www.facebook.com/newafilmfestival/about_details.

8. "King Attends Indra Jatra Festival amidst Tight Security," ekantipur.com, September 6, 2006, cited in Baltutis (2016: 215).

9. Lecomte-Tilouine describes the Maoist ban on religion—particularly on animal sacrifice—during the People's War in the region of Deurali, some 250 km west of Kathmandu (2009: 123–24).

10. Kashinath Tamot, personal communication, September 12, 2018.

Works Cited

Acharya, Baburam. 1978. "King Prithvi Narayan Shah." *Regmi Research Series* 10 (6): 86–93.

———. 1975a. "Social Changes during the Early Shah Period." *Regmi Research Series* 7 (8): 141–49.

———. 1975b. "Social Changes during the Early Shah Period." *Regmi Research Series* 7 (9): 163–72.

———. 1973. "Annexation of the Malla Kingdoms." *Regmi Research Series* 5 (3): 54–65.

Ahmed, Jamil Ahmed. 2003. "Decoding Myths in the Nepalese Festival of Indra Jatra." *New Theatre Quarterly* 19 (2): 118–38.

Ali, Daud. 2004. *Courtly Culture and Political Life in Early Medieval India*. Cambridge: University of Cambridge Press.

———. 1998. "Technologies of the Self: Courtly Artifice and Monastic Discipline in Early India." *Journal of the Economic and Social History of the Orient* 41 (2): 159–84.

Allen, Michael R. 1984. *The Cult of Kumari: Virgin Worship in Nepal*. Kathmandu: Institute of Nepal and Asian Studies.

Allen, N. J. 1986. "The Coming of Macchendranath to Nepal: Comments from a Comparative Point of View." In *Oxford University Papers on India*, vol. 1, pt. 1, ed. N. J. Allen et al., 75–102. Delhi: Oxford University Press.

Anderson, Mary M. 1971. *The Festivals of Nepal*. London: George Allen & Unwin.

Andrade, António de, Leonard Zwilling, and Michael Sweet. 2017. *"More than the Promised Land": Letters and Relations from Tibet by the Jesuit Missionary António de Andrade (1580–1634)*. Chestnut Hill, MA: Institute of Jesuit Sources, Boston College, 2017.

Aryāl, Rāmjīprasāda. 1990 (VS 2047). *Nepālako Itihāsa ra Arjyāla-Parivāra*. Kathmandu: Bindū Aryāla.

Austin, Christopher R. 2015. "Lifting the Meanings of Govardhana Mountain: A Review Essay." *Journal of Vaishnava Studies* 23 (2): 5–25.

———. 2013. "The Fructification of the Tale of a Tree: The Pārijātaharaṇa in the Harivaṁśa and its Appendices." *Journal of the American Oriental Society* 133 (2): 249–68.

Bajracharya, Manik, and Axel Michaels. 2012. "On the Historiography of Nepal: The 'Wright' Chronicle Reconsidered." *European Bulletin of Himalayan Research* 40: 83–98.

Bajracharya, Manik, Axel Michaels, and Niels Gutschow. 2015. *History of Kings of Nepal: A Buddhist Chronicle.* Kathmandu: Himal Books.

Bajracharya, Nirmal. 2003 (VS 2060/NS 1195). "Nadī Kinārāmā Avisthit Śrī Ākāś Bhairavnāth" (Sri Akash Bhairavnath Established on the Riverbank). In *Śrī Ākāś Bhairavnāth Mandir Jīrṇoddhāra* (*The Renovation of the Śrī Ākāsh Bhairavnāth Temple*), 19–23. Kathmandu: Śrī Ākāś Bhairavnāth Mandir Jīrṇoddhāra Samiti.

Baltutis, Michael. 2018a. "Innovating the Ancient, Instantiating the Urban: The South Asian Indra Festival." In *Strategic Interventions: Ritual Innovation in South Asian Religion,* ed. Amy Allocco and Brian Pennington. Albany: State University of New York Press.

———. 2018b. "Entering the South Asian City: *Praveśa* in Literature and Practice." In *Modern Hinduism in Text and Context,* ed. Lavanya Vemsani, 23–40. London: Bloomsbury.

———. 2016. "Sacrificing (to) Bhairav: The Death, Resurrection, and Apotheosis of a Local Himalayan King." *Journal of Hindu Studies* 9 (2): 205–25.

———. 2014. "Speaking Obscenely and Carrying a Big Stick: The Limits of Textuality in Kathmandu's Indrajatra Festival." *Journal of Ritual Studies* 28 (1): 1–13.

———. 2013. "The Indrajatra Festival of Kathmandu, Nepal." In *Contemporary Hinduism,* ed. P. Pratap Kumar, 83–96. Durham: Acumen.

———. 2011. "Reinventing Orthopraxy and Practicing Worldly Dharma: Vasu and Aśoka in Book Fourteen of the *Mahābhārata.*" *International Journal of Hindu Studies* 15 (1): 55–100.

———. 2009. "Renovating Bhairav: Fierce Gods, Divine Agency, and Local Power in Kathmandu." *International Journal of Hindu Studies* 13 (1): 25–49.

Bandhu, Chura Mani. 2012. *Indrajātrā.* Kathmandu: Ekta Books.

Basu, Subho. 2010. "Nepal: From Hindu Monarchy to Secular Democracy." In *Religion and Politics in South Asia,* ed. Ali Riaz, 98–118. New York: Routledge.

Bell, Catherine. 1992. *Ritual Theory, Ritual Practice.* Oxford: Oxford University Press.

Ben-Herut, Gil. 2012. "Literary Genres and Textual Representations of Early Vīraśaiva History: Revisiting Ekānta Rāmayya's Self-Beheading." *International Journal of Hindu Studies* 16 (2): 129–87.

Bernier, Ronald M. 1979. *The Nepalese Pagoda: Origins and Style.* New Delhi: S. Chand.

Berti, Daniela. 2004. "Of Metal and Cloths: The Location of Distinctive Features in Divine Iconography (Indian Himalayas)." In *Images in Asian Religions: Text and Contexts*, ed. Phyllis Granoff and Koichi Shinohara, 85–114. Vancouver: University of British Columbia Press.

Bharata Muni, Abhinavagupta, and R. S. Nagar. 1981. *Natyasastra of Bharatamuni with the commentary Abhinavabharati: vol. 1, chapters 1–7.* Delhi: Parimal Publications.

Bharata Muni and Adya Rangacharya. 1999. *The Nāṭyaśāstra English Translation with Critical Notes.* New Delhi: Munshiram Manoharlal.

Bhojarāja and Sudarśana Śarmā. 2007. *Samarāṅgana sūtradhāra of Bhojadeva (Paramāra ruler of Dhārā): An Ancient Treatise on Architecture.* Delhi: Parimal Publications.

Birkenholtz, Jessica Vantine. 2018. *Reciting the Goddess: Narratives of Place and the Making of Hinduism in Nepal.* New York: Oxford University Press.

Bledsoe, Bronwen. 2000. "An Advertised Secret: The Goddess Taleju and the King of Kathmandu." In *Tantra in Practice*, ed. David Gordon White, 195–205. Princeton, NJ: Princeton University Press.

Bloch, Maurice. 1986. *From Blessing to Violence: History and Ideology in the Circumcision Ritual of the Merina of Madagascar.* Cambridge: Cambridge University Press.

Bolling, George Melville, and Julius von Negelein (trans.). 1909. *Pariśiṣṭas of the Atharvaveda.* Leipzig: Otto Harrassowitz.

Bourdieu, Pierre. 1990. *The Logic of Practice.* Stanford, CA: Stanford University Press.

Brighenti, Francesco. 2012. "Hindu Devotional Ordeals and Their Shamanic Parallels." *Electronic Journal of Vedic Studies* 19 (4): 103–75.

Brinkhaus, Horst. 1991. "The Descent of the Nepalese Malla Dynasty as Reflected by Local Chroniclers." *Journal of the American Oriental Society* 111 (1): 118–22.

Brockington, John. 2001. "Indra in the Epics." In *Vidyārṇavavandanam: Essays in Honour of Asko Parpola*, ed. Klaus Karttunen and Asko Parpola, 67–82. Helsinki: Finnish Oriental Society.

Brodbeck, Simon. 2019. *Krishna's Lineage: The Harivamsha of Vyāsa's Mahābhārata.* New York: Oxford University Press.

Bryant, Edwin. 2003. *Krishna: The Beautiful Legend of God: Śrīmad Bhāgavata Purāṇa Book X: With Chapters 1–6 and 29–31 from Book XI.* London: Penguin.

Bühnemann, Gudrun. 1988. *Pūjā: A Study in Smārta Ritual.* Vienna: Institut für Indologie der Universität Wien.

Burghart, Richard. 1984. "The Formation of the Concept of Nation-State in Nepal." *Journal of Asian Studies* 44 (1): 101–25.

Campbell, J. Gabriel. 1976. *Saints and Householders: A Study of Hindu Ritual and Myth among the Kangra Rajputs*. Kathmandu: Ratna Pustak Bhandar.

Chalier-Visuvalingam, Elizabeth. 1989. "Bhairava's Royal Brahmanicide: The Problem of the Mahabrahmana." In *Criminal Gods and Demon Devotees*, ed. Alf Hiltebeitel, 157–229. Albany: SUNY Press.

Chaulagain, Nawaraj. 2019. *Hindu Kingship Rituals: Power Relation and Historical Evolution*. Piscataway, NJ: Gorgias Press.

Collins, Brian. 2014. *The Head Beneath the Altar: Hindu Mythology and the Critique of Sacrifice*. East Lansing: Michigan State University Press.

Courtright, Paul B. 1985. *Ganeśa: Lord of Obstacles, Lord of Beginnings*. New York: Oxford University Press.

Dangol, Śarad Kumār. 2003 (VS 2060/NS 1195). *Śrī Ākāś Bhairavnāth ko Choṭo Parichaya* (A Short Essay on Śrī Ākāsh Bhairav). In *Śrī Ākāś Bhairavnāth Mandir Jīrṇoddhāra* (*The Renovation of the Śrī Ākāsh Bhairavnāth Temple*), 37–39. Kathmandu: Śrī Ākāś Bhairavnāth Mandir Jīrṇoddhāra Samiti.

da Rovato, Father Giuseppe. 1970 [1801]. *Account of the Kingdom of Nepal*. New Delhi: India Offset Press.

Darśan, Kumār Prasād. 2003 (VS 2060/NS 1195). *Śrī Ākāś Bhairav ra Indrajātrā ek Pakṣa* (A Report on Śrī Ākāsh Bhairavnāth and Indrajātrā). In *Śrī Ākāś Bhairavnāth Mandir Jīrṇoddhāra* (*The Renovation of the Śrī Ākāsh Bhairavnāth Temple*), 25–26. Kathmandu: Śrī Ākāś Bhairavnāth Mandir Jīrṇoddhāra Samiti.

Davis, Richard H. 2009. *A Priest's Guide for the Great Festival Aghorasiva's Mahotsavavidhi*. New York: Oxford.

Dempsey, Corinne. 2005. "Nailing Heads and Splitting Hairs: Conflict, Conversion, and the Bloodthirsty Yakṣi in South India." *Journal of the American Academy of Religion* 73 (1): 111–32.

Dikshitar, V. R. Ramachandra (trans.). 1939. *The Śilappadikāram*. London: Oxford University Press.

Doniger, Wendy. 2016. *Redeeming the Kāmasūtra*. New York: Oxford.

———. 1984. *Dreams, Illusion, and Other Realities*. Chicago: University of Chicago Press.

Dyczkowski, Mark S. G. 2001. *The Cult of the Goddess Kubjika: A Preliminary Comparative Textual and Anthropological Survey of a Secret Newar Goddess*. Stuttgart: Franz Steiner.

Ekantipur. 2016. "2 Hurt during Indra Jatra Lingo Hoisting." *Ekantipur*.com, September 18.

Emmrich, Christoph. 2014. "Performing Endangerment: Damage, Loss and Maintenance in the Historiography of Newar Religious Artefacts." In *In the Shadow of the Golden Age: Art and Identity in Asia from Gandhara to the Modern Age*, ed. Julia A. B. Hegewald, 257–84. Berlin: EB-Verlag Dr. Brandt.

———. 2007. "'All the King's Horses and All the King's Men': The 2004 Red Matsyendranátha Incident in Lalitpur." In *When Rituals Go Wrong: Mistakes, Failure, and the Dynamics of Ritual*, ed. Ute Hüske, 137–53. Leiden: Brill.

Erndl, Kathleen M. 1989. "Rapist or Bodyguard, Demon or Devotee? Images of Bhairo in the Mythology and Cult of Vaiṣṇo Devī." In *Criminal Gods and Demon Devotees*, ed. Alf Hiltebeitel, 239–50. Albany: SUNY Press.

———. 1993. *Victory to the Mother: The Hindu Goddess of Northwest India in Myth, Ritual, and Symbol*. New York: Oxford University Press.

Feldhaus, Anne. 2003. *Connected Places: Region, Pilgrimage, and Geographical Imagination in India*. New York: Palgrave Macmillan.

Fisher, William. 1993. "Nationalism and the Janjāti." *Himal* 6 (2): 11–14.

Fitzgerald, James L. 2004. *The Mahābhārata: Book 11. The Book of the Women, Book 12. The Book of Peace, Part One*, vol. 7. Chicago: University of Chicago Press.

Gaenzle, Martin, in collaboration with Nutan Dhar Sharma. 2002. "Nepali Kings and Kāśī: On the Changing Significance of a Sacred Centre." *Studies in Nepali History and Society* 7 (1): 1–33.

Ganguli, Kisari M., and Chandra Roy. 1970. *The Mahabharata of Krishna-Dwaipayana Vyasa. 1 Adi Parva*. New Delhi: Munshiram Manoharlal.

Gautam, Dhanuṣcandra. 1965 (VS 2022). "The *Hāsyakadamba*: The Oldest Play in Nepali Language" (*Hāsyakadamba*: Nepālī Bhāṣā ko Jeṭho Nāṭak). *Rūp-Rekh* 6 (7 [55]): 31–43.

Geen, Jonathan. 2015. "Echoes of Govardhana in Jain Literature: The Lifting of *Koṭiśilā* and Consecration as *Ardhacakrin*." *Journal of Vaishnava Studies* 23 (2): 111–30.

Gellner, David N. 2005. "The Emergence of Conversion in a Hindu-Buddhist Polytropy: The Kathmandu Valley, Nepal, c. 1600–1995." *Society for Comparative Study of Society and History* 47 (4): 755–80.

———. 2001. *The Anthropology of Buddhism and Hinduism: Weberian Themes*. Oxford: Oxford University Press.

———. "Introduction." 1999. In *Contested Hierarchies: A Collaborative Ethnography of Caste Among the Newars of the Kathmandu Valley, Nepal*, ed. David N. Gellner and Declan Quigley, 1–37. New York: Oxford University Press.

———. 1992. *Monk, Householder, and Tantric Priest: Newar Buddhism and Its Hierarchy of Ritual*. Cambridge: Cambridge University Press.

Gellner, David N., and Rajendra P. Pradhan. 1999. "Urban Peasants: The Majarjans (Jyāpu) of Kathmandu and Lalitpur." In *Contested Hierarchies: A Collaborative Ethnography of Caste among the Newars of the Kathmandu Valley, Nepal*, ed. David N. Gellner and Declan Quigley, 158–85. New York: Oxford University Press.

Gerety, Finnian. 2016. "Tree-Hugger: The Sāmavedic Rite of *Audumbarī*." In *Roots of Wisdom, Branches of Devotion: Plant Life in South Asian Traditions*, edited by Fabrizio M. Ferrari and Thomas Dahnhardt, 165–90. Bristol: Equinox.

Germano, David, and Janet Gyatso. 2000. "Longchenpa and the Possession of the Ḍākinīs." In *Tantra in Practice*, ed. David Gordon White, 241–65. Princeton, NJ: Princeton University Press.

Geslani, Marko. 2019. "A Comparative Survey of the Indradhvaja Ceremony (Gārgīyajyotiṣa 45)." *History of Science in South Asia* 7: 82–95.

———. 2018. *Rites of the God-King: Śānti and Ritual Change in Early Hinduism*. New York: Oxford University Press.

Geslani, Marko, Bill Mak, Michio Yano, and Kenneth Zysk. 2017. "Garga and Early Astral Science in India." *History of Science in South Asia* 5 (1): 151–91.

Ghimire, Yubaraj. 2016. "Nepal May Be a Secular State, but Rituals and Traditions Still Play Big Role in Politics." *Indian Express*, October 8. https://indianexpress.com/article/opinion/web-edits/nepal-may-be-a-secular-state-but-rituals-and-traditions-still-play-big-role-in-politics/.

Girard, René. 1977 [1972]. *Violence and the Sacred*, trans. Patrick Gregory. Baltimore, MD: Johns Hopkins University Press.

Giri, Girish. 2019. "The Indrajatra Was Made by the Clever Insertion of a Deity. Interview with Gautamvajra Vajracharya." *Setopati*, March 9. https://setopati.com/social/175612.

Gnoli, Raniero. 1956. *Nepalese Inscriptions in Gupta Characters: Part I*. Rome: Is. MEO.

Gold, Ann Grodzins. 1988. *Fruitful Journeys: The Ways of Rajasthani Pilgrims*. Prospect Heights: Waveland Press.

Gonda, Jan. 1967. "The Indra Festival According to the Atharvavedins." *Journal of American Oriental Society* 87: 413–29.

———. 1947. Skt. *Utsava*, "Festival." In *India Antiqua*, 146–55. Leiden: Brill.

Gorkhāpatra. 1932 (VS 1989). Bhadra 21, 32 (21).

———. 1931 (VS 1988). Āśvin 5, 31 (24).

———. 1927 (VS 1984). Bhadra 21, 27 (22).

———. 1926 (VS 1983). Āśvin 12, 26 (24).

Granoff, Phyllis and Koichi Shinohara. *Images in Asian Religions: Text and Contexts*. Vancouver: UBC Press, 2004.

Grieve, Gregory Price. 2006. *Retheorizing Religion in Nepal*. Hampshire: Palgrave Macmillan.

Grimes, Ronald L. 1988. "Ritual Criticism and Infelicitous Performances." *Semeia* 41: 103–22.

———. 1982. *Stadtraum und Ritual der newarischen Städte im Kathmandu-Tal: Eine architektuaranthropologische Untersuchung*. Stuttgart: Kohlhammer.

Gutschow, Niels, and Bernhard Kolver. 1975. *Bhaktapur: Ordered Space Concepts and Functions in a Town of Nepal*. Wiesbaden: Kommissionverlag Franz Steiner.

Halperin, Ehud. 2020. *The Many Faces of a Himalayan Goddess: Haḍimbā, Her Devotees, and Religion in Rapid Change*. Oxford: Oxford University Press.

———. 2019. "Is the Goddess Haḍimbā Tantric? Negotiating Power in a Western Himalayan Sacrificial Arena." *International Journal of Hindu Studies* 23 (2): 195–212.

Hamilton, Francis (Buchanan). 1971 [1819]. *An Account of the Kingdom of Nepal*. New Delhi: Manjusri Publishing House.

Hangen, Susan. 2007. *Creating a "New Nepal": The Ethnic Dimension*. Washington, DC: East-West Center.

Hardy, Adam. 2009. "Drāviḍa Temples in the *Samarāṅgaṇasūtradhāra*." *South Asian Studies* 25 (1): 41–62.

Harlan, Lindsey. 2003. *The Goddesses' Henchmen: Gender in Indian Hero Worship*. New York: Oxford.

Hasrat, Bikrama Jit. 1970. *History of Nepal: As Told by Its Own and Contemporary Chroniclers*. Hoshiarpur: V.V. Research Inst. Book Agency.

Hausner, Sondra. 2007. "Pashupatinath at the End of the Hindu State." *Studies in Nepali History and Society* 12 (1): 119–40.

Hawley, John Stratton. 2015. "Ten Govardhan Poems from the Early Sūrsāgar." *Journal of Vaishnava Studies* 23 (2): 87–99.

———. 1991. "A Feast for Mount Govardhan." In *Devotion Divine: Bhakti Traditions from the Regions of India*, ed. Diana L. Eck and Francoise Mallison, 155–79. Paris: Ecole Francaise d'Extreme-Orient.

Heesterman, Jan. 1993. *Broken World of Sacrifice*. Chicago: University of Chicago Press.

———. 1985. *The Inner Conflict of Tradition*. Chicago: University of Chicago Press.

———. 1957. *Ancient Indian Royal Consecration: the Rājasūya Described According to the Yajus texts and Annotated*. The Hague: Mouton.

Hegarty, James. 2012. *Religion, Narrative and Public Imagination in South Asia: Past and Place in the Sanskrit Mahābhārata*. New York: Routledge.

Heitzman, James. 2009. *The City in South Asia*. London: Routledge.

Hemacandra. 1962. *Triśaṣṭisalākapuruṣacaritra, or The Lives of Sixty-Three Illustrious Persons* (vols. 1 and 5), trans. Helen M. Johnson. Baroda: Oriental Institute.

Hess, Linda. 2007. "An Open-Air Ramayana: Ramlila, the Audience Experience." In *The Life of Hinduism*, ed. John Stratton Hawley and Vasudha Narayanan, 115–39. Berkeley: University of California Press.

Hiltebeitel, Alf. 2018. *Freud's Mahābhārata*. New York: Oxford University Press.

———. 2012. "Buddhism and the Mahābhārata. Boundary Dynamics in Textual Practice." In *Boundaries, Dynamics and Construction of Traditions in South Asia,* ed. Federico Squarcini, 107–31. Cambridge: Cambridge University Press.

———. 2011. *When the Goddess Was a Woman: Mahābārata Ethnographies, Essays by Alf Hiltebeitel,* vol. 2. Leiden: Brill.

———. 2001. *Rethinking the Mahābhārata: A Reader's Guide to the Education of the Dharma King.* Chicago: University of Chicago Press.

———. 1999. *Rethinking India's Oral and Classical Epics: Draupadi among Rajputs, Muslims, and Dalits.* Chicago: University of Chicago Press.

———. 1995. "Dying before the Mahabharata War: Martial and Transsexual Body-Building for Aravan." *Journal of Asian Studies* 54 (2): 447–73.

———. 1991. *The Cult of Draupadi: On Hindu Ritual and the Goddess.* Chicago: University of Chicago Press.

———. 1988. *The Cult of Draupadi. Mythologies: From Gingee to Kuruksetra.* Chicago: University of Chicago Press.

Hiltebeitel, Alf, Vishwa Adluri, and Joydeep Bagchee. 2011. *When the Goddess Was a Woman: Mahābhārata Ethnographies.* Leiden: Brill.

Höfer, Andreas. 2004 [1979]. *The Caste Hierarchy and the State in Nepal: A Study of the Muluki Ain of 1854.* Innsbruck: Universitatsverlag Wagner.

Holle, Annick, Gerard Toffin, and Krishna Prasad Rimal. 1993. "The 32 Maharjan Tols of Kathmandu City." In *The Anthropology of Nepal: From Tradition to Modernity,* ed. Gérard Toffin, 21–61. Kathmandu: French Cultural Centre.

Humphrey, Caroline, and James Laidlaw. 1994. *The Archetypal Actions of Ritual: A Theory of Ritual Illustrated by the Jain Rite of Worship.* New York: Oxford University Press.

Huntington, Susan L. 2015. "Shifting the Paradigm: The Aniconic Theory and Its Terminology." *South Asian Studies* 31 (2): 163–86.

Hutt, Michael. 1991. *Himalayan Voices: An Introduction to Modern Nepali Literature.* Berkeley: University of California Press.

Inden, Ronald. 2006. "Embodying God: From Imperial Progresses to National Progress in India." In *Text and Practice: Essays on South Asian History,* 245–78. Delhi: Oxford University Press.

———. 1998 [1978]. "Ritual, Authority and Cyclic Time in the Indian Kinship." In *Kingship and Authority in South Asia,* ed. J. F. Richards, 41–91. Delhi: Oxford University Press.

Inden, Ronald, Jonathan S. Walters, and Daud Ali. 2000. *Querying the Medieval: Texts and the History of Practices in South Asia.* New York: Oxford University Press.

Irwin, John. 1975. "Asokan' Pillars: A Re-Assessment of the Evidence—III: Capitals." *Burlington Magazine* 117 (871): 631–43.

Jain, Jyotindra. 1984. *Painted Myths of Creation: Art and Ritual of an Indian Tribe.* New Delhi: Lalit Kala Akademi.

Jamison, Stephanie W., and Brereton Joel P. 2014. *The Rigveda: The Earliest Religious Poetry of India.* New York: Oxford University Press.

Jñavāli, Sūrya Bikram. 1983. "Pārivārik Vaṁśāvali-Arjyāl Thar ko" (The Arjyāl Family and Lineage). *Rolamba: Journal of Joshi Research Institute* 3 (3): 9–11.

Juju, Baldev. 2003 (VS 2060/NS 1195). "Vaṁghaḥ ṭol ko Ājudyaḥ Bāre ek Carca" (An Introduction to Ajudyaḥ of Indra Chowk). In *Śrī Ākāś Bhairavnāth Mandir Jīrṇoddhāra (The Renovation of the Śrī Ākāsh Bhairavnāth Temple)*, 15. Kathmandu: Śrī Ākāś Bhairavnāth Mandir Jīrṇoddhāra Samiti.

Juju, Baldev, and Surendraman Shrestha. 1999 (NS 1120). *Nepāḥyā Tāntrika Dyaḥ va Tāntrik Pūjā*. Kathmandu: Koseli Chāpākhānā.

Kane, Pandurang Vaman. 1930–1962. *History of Dharmaśāstra*. 7 vols. Poona: Bhandarkar Oriental Research Institute.

Kaul, Shonaleeka. 2011. *Imagining the Urban Sanskrit and the City in Early India*. London: Seagull Books.

King, Richard. 1999. *Orientalism and Religion: Postcolonial Theory India and "the Mystic East."* London: Routledge.

Kirkpatrick, Colonel (William). 1969 [1811]. *An Account of the Kingdom of Nepaul*. New Delhi: Manjusri Publishing House.

Koirala, Kulchandra. 2003 (VS 2060). "Nepālmā Indrajātrā Parv" (The Indrajātrā Festival in Nepāl). *Prajñā* 98 (33): 90–105.

———. 1985 (VS 2042). *Indrajātrā (Indramaha): Samskṛti-sambandhi Anusandhānātmaka*. Kathmandu: Guthi Samsthan.

Kölver, Bernhard. 1985. "Stages in the Evolution of a World Picture." *Numen* 32 (2): 131–68.

Koolhaas, Rem. 2000. *Mutations*. Barcelona: ACTAR.

Kuiper, F. B. J. 2004. "The Worship of the Jarjara on the Stage." *Indo-Iranian Journal* 16 (4): 241–68.

———. 1977. *Varuṇa and Vidūṣaka: On the Origin of the Sanskrit Drama*. Amsterdam: North-Holland.

———. 1975. "The Basic Concept of Vedic Religion." *History of Religions* 15 (2): 107–20.

Landon, Perceval. 1976 [1928]. *Nepal*. Kathmandu: Ratna Pustak Bhandar.

Lecomte-Tilouine, Marie. 2009. "Political Change and Cultural Revolution in a Maoist Model Village, Mid-western Nepal." In *The Maoist Insurgency in Nepal: Revolution in the Twentyfirst Century*, ed. Mahendra Lawoti and Anup K. Pahari, 115–32. London: Routledge.

———. 2011. "The Transgressive Nature of Hindu Kingship in Nepal." In *Hindu Kingship, Ethnic Revival, and Maoist Rebellion in Nepal*, 193–218. New Delhi: Oxford University Press.

Levy, Robert I., and Kedar Raj Rajopadhyaya. 1990. *Mesocosm: Hinduism and the Organization of a Traditional Newar City in Nepal*. Berkeley: University of California Press.

Lewis, Todd T. 1993. "Contributions to the Study of Popular Buddhism: The Newar Buddhist Festival of Gumla Dharma." *Journal of the International Association of Buddhist Studies* 16 (2): 309–54.

Lewis, Todd T., and Subarna Man Tuladhar. 2010. *Sugata Saurabha: An Epic Poem from Nepal on the Life of the Buddha by Chittadhar Hridaya*. New York: Oxford University Press.

Lewis, Todd T., S. M. Tuladhar, and L. R. Tuladhar. 2000. *Popular Buddhist Texts from Nepal: Narratives and Rituals of Newar Buddhism*. Albany: SUNY Press.

Lidke, Jeff. 1996. *Vishvarupa Mandir, A Study of Changu Narayan, Nepal's Most Ancient Temple*. New Delhi: Nirala Publications.

Lidova, Natalia R. 2004. "Indramahotsava in Late Vedic and Early Epic Traditions." *Journal of the Asiatic Society of Mumbai* 77–78: 85–108.

Lincoln, Bruce. 2014. *Discourse and the Construction of Society: Comparative Studies of Myth, Ritual, and Classification*. New York: Oxford University Press.

Locke, John K. 1985. *Buddhist Monasteries of Nepal: A Survey of the Bāhās and Bahīs of the Kathmandu Valley*. Kathmandu: Sahayogi Press.

Locke, John K. 1980. *Karunamaya: The Cult of Avalokitesvara-Matsyendranath in the Valley of Nepal*. Kathmandu: Sahayogi Prakashan for Research Centre for Nepal and Asian Studies, Tribhuvan University.

Lowdin, Per. 1998. *Food, Ritual, and Society: A Study of Social Structure and Food Symbolism among the Newars*. Kathmandu: Mandala Book Point.

Lutgendorf, Philip. 1991. *The Life of a Text: Performing the Rāmcaritmānas of Tulsidas*. Berkeley: University of California Press.

Maclean, Kama. 2008. *Pilgrimage and Power: The Kumbh Mela in Allahabad, 1765–1954*. New York: Oxford.

Maharjan, Monalisa, and Filipe T. Barata. 2017. "Living with Heritage: Including Tangible and Intangible Heritage in the Changing Time and Space." *Journal of the Institute of Engineering* 13 (1): 178–89.

Maharjan, Śrī Nārāyaṇ. 2003 (VS 2060/NS 1195). "Mūl Thakāliko Choṭo Parichay" (A Short Essay from the Chief Officer). In *Śrī Ākāś Bhairavnāth Mandir Jīrṇoddhāra* (*The Renovation of the Śrī Ākāsh Bhairavnāth Temple*), 39–43. Kathmandu: Śrī Ākāś Bhairavnāth Mandir Jīrṇoddhāra Samiti.

Malagodi, Mara. 2013. *Constitutional Nationalism and Legal Exclusion: Equality, Identity Politics, and Democracy in Nepal (1990–2007)*. New Delhi: Oxford University Press.

Malla, Kamal P. 1985. *Nepālavaṁśāvalī: A Complete Version of the Kaisher Vaṁśāvalī*. *CNAS* 12 (2): 75–101.

———. 1992. "The Nepāla-Mahātmya: A IX-Century Text or a Pious Fraud?" *Contributions to Nepalese Studies* 19 (1): 145–58.

Manandhar, San. 2003 (VS 2060/NS 1195). "Sri Akash Bhairav." In *Śrī Ākāś Bhairavnāth Mandir Jīrṇoddhāra* (*The Renovation of the Śrī Ākāsh Bhairavnāth Temple*), 35–36. Kathmandu: Śrī Ākāś Bhairavnāth Mandir Jīrṇoddhāra Samiti.

McGovern, Nathan. 2019. *The Snake and the Mongoose: The Emergence of Identity in Early Indian Religion*. New York: Oxford University Press.

Meyer, J. J. 1937. *Trilogie Altindischer Machte und Fest der Vegetation: Ein Beitrag zur vergleichenden Religions- und Kulturgeschichte, Fest- und Volkskunde*. Zurich: Max Niehans.

Michaels, Axel. 2008. *Siva in Trouble: Festivals and Rituals at the Pasupatinatha Temple of Deopatan*. New York: Oxford University Press.

Mines, Diane P. 2005. *Fierce Gods: Inequality, Ritual, and the Politics of Dignity in a South Indian Village*. Bloomington: Indiana University Press.

Mitramiśra and Viṣṇuprasāda Bhaṇḍārī. 1916. *Vīramitrodaya: Rājanīti Prakāśa*. Benares: Chowkhamba Sanskrit Series Office.

Mocko, Anne T. 2016. *Demoting Vishnu: Ritual, Politics, and the Unraveling of Nepal's Hindu Monarchy*. New York: Oxford Univeristy Press.

Mottin, Monica. 2018. *Rehearsing for Life: Theatre for Social Change in Nepal*. Cambridge: Cambridge University Press.

Nammalvar and Attipat Krishnaswami Ramanujan. 2005. *Hymns for the Drowning: Poems for Visnu*. New Delhi: Penguin.

Nepali, G. S. 1965. *The Newars: An Ethno-Sociological Study of a Himalayan Community*. Bombay: United Asia Publications.

Nicoletti, Martino, and Fabrizio Gaggini. 2004. *Riddum, the Voice of the Ancestors*. Kathmandu: Vajra Publications.

Oldfield, H. Ambrose. 1974 [1880]. *Sketches from Nepal: Historical and Descriptive with an Essay on Nepalese Buddhism & Illustrations of Religious Monuments & Architecture*. Delhi: Cosmo Publications.

Olivelle, Patrick. 2015. "Explorations in the Early History of the Dharmaśāstra." In *Between the Empires: Society in India 300 BCE to 400 CE*, ed. Patrick Olivelle, 169–90. Oxford: Oxford University Press.

———. 2010. *Aśoka: In History and Historical Memory*. Delhi: Motilal Banarsidass.

———. 2009. *The Law Code of Manu*. Oxford: Oxford University Press.

Olivelle, Patrick, Janice Leoshko, and Himanshu Prabha Ray, eds. 2012. *Reimagining Aśoka: Memory and History*. New Delhi: Oxford University Press.

Ortner, Sherry. 1989. *High Religion: A Cultural and Political History of Sherpa Buddhism*. Princeton, NJ: Princeton University Press.

Palihawadana, Mahinda, 2017 [1981/1982]. "The Indra Cult as Ideology: A Clue to Power Struggle in an Ancient Society" (including a discussion of the semantics of Ṛgvedic ari and its sociopolitical background). Ed. Peter-Arnold Mumm in collaboration with Tina West. *Electronic Journal of Vedic Studies* 24 (2): 19–166.

Panch, "Jyāpu." 2003 (VS 2060/NS 1195). "Śrī Ākāsh Bhairab (Vaṅghaḥ Āju) jiṁ nyanātheṁ, jiṁ syūtheṁ" (Śrī Ākāsh Bhairab [Vaṅghaḥ Āju] as I Have Heard and Understood). In *Śrī Ākāś Bhairavnāth Mandir Jīrṇoddhāra*

(*The Renovation of the Śrī Ākāsh Bhairavnāth Temple*), 9–13. Kathmandu: Śrī Ākāś Bhairavnāth Mandir Jīrṇoddhāra Samiti.

Pant, Dinesh Raj. 1995 (VS 2052). "Indradhvaja Sambandhi Sāit Lekhieko, V.S. 1900 ko Kāgat" (A Document Written in VS 1900 on the *Sāit* of the Indra Festival Tradition). *Abhilekh* 13: 36–40.

———. 1985 (VS 2041). *Gorkhāko Itihās* (*The History of the Gorkhās*). Kathmandu: Sujanā Printers.

Parish, Steven M. 1996. *Hierarchy and Its Discontents: Culture and the Politics of Consciousness in Caste Society*. Philadelphia: University of Pennsylvania Press.

———. 1994. *Moral Knowing in a Hindu Sacred City: An Exploration of Mind, Emotion, and Self*. New York: Columbia University Press.Parry, Jonathan P. 1994. *Death in Banaras*. Cambridge: Cambridge University Press.

Paudel, Bholanath, Dhanavajra Vajracarya, and Gyan Mani Nepal. 2002. "A Historical Gloss on the *Kauṭalīya Arthaśāstra* No. 2." *Ādarśa: Supplement to Pūrṇimā, the Journal of the Saṃśodhana-maṇḍala* 2: 1–18.

Paudyal, Vina. 1998. "Hindū Sāṁskritik Paramparāmā Devrāj Indra (Indra, the King of the Gods, in the Hindu Cultural Tradition)." *Contributions to Nepalese Studies* 25 (1): 71–83.

Pennington, Brian K., and Amy Allocco. "Introduction." In *Strategic Interventions: Ritual Innovation in South Asian Religion*, ed. Amy Allocco and Brian Pennington, 1–14. Albany: State University of New York Press.

Petech, Luciano. 1958. *Medieval History of Nepal (c. 750–1480)*. Rome: Istituto italiano per il Medio ed Estremo Oriente.

Pickett, Mark. 2014. *Caste and Kinship in a Modern Hindu Society: The Newar City of Lalitpur, Nepal*. Bangkok: Orchid Press.

———. 2005. "Ritual Movement in the City of Lalitpur." *Contributions to Nepalese Studies* 32 (2): 243–65.

Pollock, Sheldon. 2009. *The Language of the Gods in the World of Men: Sanskrit, Culture, and Power in Premodern India*. Berkeley: University of California Press.

Pradhan, Rajendra. 1986. "Domestic and Cosmic Rituals Among the Hindu Newars of Kathmandu, Nepal." PhD diss., University of Delhi.

Prasad, Leela. 2007. *Poetics of Conduct: Oral Narrative and Moral Being in a South Indian Town*. New York: Columbia University Press.

Pushpendra, Kumar. 1976. *Devī Purānam: First Critical Devanāgari Edition*. New Delhi: Shri Lal Bahadur Shastri.

Ramanujan, A. K. 1970. "Toward an Anthology of City Images." In *Urban India: Society Space and Image*, ed. Richard G. Fox, 224–44. Durham, NC: Duke University.

Rana, Sagar S. J. B. 2017. *Singha Durbar: Rise and Fall of the Rana Regime of Nepal*. New Delhi: Rupa 2017.

Regmi, D. R. 1975. *Modern Nepal: Rise and Growth in The Eighteenth Century*, 2 vols. Calcutta: Firma K. L. Mukhopadhyay.
———. 1966. *Medieval Nepal*. Calcutta: Firma K. L. Mukhopadhyay.
Regmi, M. C. 2002. *Nepal: An Historical Miscellany*. Delhi: Adroit.
Regmi, Śeṣarāja Śarmā. 1992 (VS 2049). *Śrī 5 Pṛthvīnārāyaṇa Śāhakālika Saṃskṛta Sāhitya*. Kathmandu: Nepāla Rājakīya Prajñā Pratiṣṭhāna.
Riccardi, Theodore, Jr. 1986. "The Nepālarājaparamparā: A Short Chronicle of the Kings of Nepal." *Journal of the American Oriental Society* 106 (2): 247–51.
———. 1977. "The Royal Edicts of Ram Shah of Gorkha." *Kailash* 5 (1): 29–65.
Rodriguez, Hillary Peter. 2003. *Ritual Worship of the Great Goddess: The Liturgy of the Durgā Pūjā with Interpretations*. Albany: SUNY Press.
Rolland, Pierre. 1972. *Le Mahavrata: Contribution a l'etude d'un rituel solennel vedique*. Gottingen: Vandenhoeck & Ruprecht.
Sahlins, Marshall. 1985. *Islands of History*. Chicago: University of Chicago Press.
Sastri, Hara Prasad. 1915. *A Catalogue of Palm Leaf & Selected Paper MSS Belonging to the Durbar Library, Nepal*. Calcutta: Baptist Mission Press.
———. 1905. *A Catalogue of Palm Leaf & Selected Paper MSS Belonging to the Durbar Library, Nepal*. Calcutta: Baptist Mission Press.
Satapatha-Brahmana: According to the Text of the Madhyandina School. 1966. Trans. Julius Eggeling. 1966. Delhi: Motilal Banarsidass.
Sax, William S. 2009. *God of Justice: Ritual Healing and Social Justice in the Central Himalayas*. New York: Oxford.
———. 2002. *Dancing the Self: Personhood and Performance in the Pāṇḍav Līlā of Garhwal*. Oxford: Oxford University Press.
———. 1991. *Mountain Goddess: Gender and Politics in a Himalayan Pilgrimage*. New York: Oxford University Press.
Schnell, Scott. 1999. *The Rousing Drum: Ritual Practice in a Japanese Community*. Honolulu: University of Hawaii Press.
Shaha, Rishikesh. 2001 [1992]. *Ancient and Medieval Nepal*. New Delhi: Manohar.
Shaha, Rishikesh. 1990. *Modern Nepal: A Political History, 1769–1955*. New Delhi: Manohar.
Shakya, Milan Ratna. 2008. *The Cult of Bhairava in Nepal*. New Delhi: Rupa.
Shakya, Rashmila, and Scott Berry. 2005. *From Goddess to Mortal: The True Life Story of a Former Royal Kumari*. Kathmandu: Vajra Books.
Sharma, Nutandhar. 1999. "The Legends of Gayaḥbājya of Patan in the Kathmandu Valley." *Contributions to Nepalese Studies* 2 (2): 239–56.
Shulman, David. 1985. *The King and the Clown in South Indian Myth and Poetry*. Princeton, NJ: Princeton University Press.
Shrestha, Bal Gopal. 2014. "The Death of Divine Kingship in Nepal: Nepal's Move from Autocratic Monarchy to a Fragile Republican State." In *Contesting the State: the Dynamics of Resistance and Control*, ed. Angela Hobart and Bruce Kapferer, 195–223. Wantage, UK: Sean Kingston Publishing.

———. 2010/2011. "Maintenance of Language and Literature: The Case of the Newārs in Nepal." *Newāḥ Vijñāna: Journal of Newār Studies* 7: 4–13.

———. 2006. "The Svanti Festival: Victory over Death and the Renewal of the Ritual Cycle in Nepal." *Contributions to Nepalese Studies* 33 (2): 203–21.

Singh, Nag Sharan. 1985. *Śrīviṣṇudarmottarapurāṇam*. Delhi: Nag.

Slouber, Michael. 2016. "The Herbal Arsenal and Fetid Food: The Power of Plants in Early Tantric Exorcism Rituals." In *Roots of Wisdom, Branches of Devotion: Plant Life in South Asian Traditions*, ed. Fabrizio M. Ferrari and Thomas Dahnhardt, 145–64. Bristol: Equinox Publishing.

Slusser, Mary Shepherd. 1982. *Nepal Mandala*. 2 vols. Princeton, NJ: Princeton University Press.

Smith, Frederick M. 2006. *The Self Possessed: Deity and Spirit Possession in South Asian Literature and Civilization*. New York: Columbia University Press.

———. 1994. "Purāṇaveda." In *Authority, Anxiety, and Canon*, ed. Laurie L. Patton, 97–139. Albany: SUNY Press.

Snellinger, Amanda. 2013. "Shaping a Livable Present and Future: A Review of Youth Studies in Nepal." *European Bulletin of Himalayan Research* 42: 75–103.

Srinivasan, Doris Meth. 2005. "Saṃkarṣaṇa/Balarāma and The Mountain: A New Attribute." *Proceedings of South Asian Archaeological Conference*. London.

Suvedi, Pradip. 1998 (VS 2055). *Dahachowk, "Indra Daha": Samkṣipta Parichaya (Paurāṇik, Aitihāsik, Purātātvik ra Paryaṭakīya Dṛṣṭikoṇa sahit) (Dahachowk, "The Lake of Indra": A Summary Article (With Mythological, Historical, Archaeological and Travellers' Perspectives)*]. Kathmandu: Karna Padma Chapakhana.

Thapar, Romila. 2013. *Aśoka and the Decline of the Mauryas*, 3rd ed. New Delhi: Oxford University Press.

———. 2012. "Aśoka: a Retrospective." In *Reimagining Aśoka: Memory and History*ed. Patrick Olivelle, Lanice Leoshko, and Himanshu Prabha Ray, 17–37. New Delhi: Oxford University Press.

Tiwari, Sudarshan Raj. 2002. *The Brick and the Bull: An Account of Handigaun, the Ancient Capital of Nepal*. Lalitpur: Himal Books.

Toffin, Gérard. 2019. "Why Newars Are Raging." *Republica*, June 26.

———. 2015. "Review of A.W. van den Hoek, *Cāturmāsa: Celebrations of Death in Kathmandu, Nepal*." *Studies in Nepali History & Society* 20 (2): 431–35.

———. 2013. *From Monarchy to Republic: Essays on Changing Nepal*. Kathmandu: Vajra Books.

———. 2010. *La fête-spectacle: Théâtre et rite au Népal*. Paris: Éditions de la Maison des sciences de l'homme.

———. 2007. *Newar Society: City, Village and Periphery*. Kathmandu: Social Science Baha.

———. 2006. "Construction et Transformations d'un Ritual Urbain Nepalais." In *Rites Hindous, Transferts et Transformations,* ed. Gerard Colas and Gilles Tarabout, 49–78. Paris: Purushartha.

———. 1999. "The Citrakārs: Caste of Painters and Mask-Makers." In *Contested Hierarchies: A Collaborative Ethnography of Caste among the Newars of the Kathmandu Valley, Nepal,* ed. David N. Gellner and Declan Quigley, 240–63. New York: Oxford University Press.

———. 1994. "The Farmers in the City: The Social and Territorial Organization of the Maharjan of Kathmandu." *Anthropos* 89: 433–59.

———. 1992. "The Indra Jatra of Kathmandu as a Royal Festival: Past and Present." *Contributions to Nepalese Studies* 19 (1): 74–92.

———. 1984. *Société et religion chez les Néwar du Népal.* Paris: Editions du Centre national de la Recherche Scientifique.

———. 1978. "L'Indra Jatra a Pyangaon: Essai sur une fete newar de la vallee de Kathmandou." *L'Ethnographie* 1: 109–37.

Tree, Isabella. 2015. *The Living Goddess: A Journey Into the Heart of Kathmandu.* London: Eland Books.

Tripathi, G. C. 1977. "Das Indradhvaja-fest in Orissa: Die Uberreste der Indra-Verehrung in Ostindien." *Zeitschrift der Deutschen Morgenlandischen Gesellschaft,* suppl. 3 (2): 1001–14.

Upadhyay, Samrat. 2001. *Arresting God in Kathmandu.* New Delhi: Rupa.

Vajrācārya, Dhanavajra. 1980 (VS 2037). *Śāhakālakā Abhilekha.* Kāṭhamāḍauṃ: Nepāla ra Eśiyālī Anusandhāna Kendra, Tribhuvana Viśvavidyālaya.

———. 1969 (VS 2026). "Śaktivallabh and Kirkpatrick" (Śaktivallabh ra Karkpyāṭrik). *Madhuparka* 2 (2): 93–102.

Vajrācārya, Dhanavajra, and Kamal P. Malla. 1985. *The Gopālarājavaṃśāvalī.* Wiesbaden: Franz Steiner.

Vajracharya, Gautam V. 2020. "Three Licchavi Period Sculptures under One Roof: The Solomon Family Collection of Nepalese Art (Part One)." *Orientations* 51 (2): 86–94.

———. 2018. *Nepal Saṃvat and Vikrama Saṃvat: Discerning Original Significance.* Kathmandu: Himal Books.

———. 2016. *Nepalese Seasons: Rain and Ritual.* New York: Rubin Museum of Art.

———. 2003. "Painted History: The Tuladana Ceremony in a Mediaeval Nepalese Palace." *Orientations* 34 (10): 46–51.

———. 1999. "Symbolism of Ashokan Pillars: A Reappraisal in the Light of Textual and Visual Evidence." *Marg* 51 (2): 53–78.

———. 1976 (VS 2033). *Hanumānḍhokā Rājdarbār.* Kathmandu: Institute of Nepal and Asian Studies.

———. 1974. "Yaṇgal, Yambu." *Contributions to Nepalese Studies* 1 (2): 90–98.

Vajracharya, Punyaratna. 1980 (VS 2036). *Hamro Cāḍh-Parv.* Kathmandu: Ratna Pustak Bhandar.

van Buitenen, J. A. B. 1973. *The Mahābhārata. Book 1. The Book of the Beginning*, vol. 1. Chicago: University of Chicago Press.

———. 1966. "On the Archaism of the Bhāgavatā Purāṇa." In *Krishna: Myths, Rites, and Attitudes*, ed. Milton Singer, 23–40. Chicago: University of Chicago Press.

van den Bosch, L. P. 1978. *Atharvaveda-parisista: Chapters 21–29, Introduction, translation and notes*. Groningen: VRG.

van den Hoek, A. W. 2004. *Cāturmāsa: Celebrations of Death in Kathmandu, Nepal*. Leiden: CNWS Publications.

———. 1996. "The Festival of Indra in Kathmandu: An Archaic Survival or an 18th Century Construction?" Paper presented at the 14th European Conference on Modern South Asian Studies, Copenhagen, Denmark, August 21–24.

Varaha Mihira and M. Ramakrishna Bhat. 1981. *Brhat Samhita*. New Delhi: Motilal Banarsidass.

Vaudeville, Charlotte. 1989. "Multiple Approaches to a Living Hindu Myth: The Lord of the Govardhan Hill." In *Hinduism Reconsidered*, ed. Gunther D. Sontheimer and Hermann Kulke, 202–27. New Delhi: Manohar.

Vergati, Anne. 2002 [1995]. *Gods, Men and Territory: Society and Culture in Kathmandu Valley*. New Delhi: Manohar.

Viśvanārāyaṇa Śāstrī. 1991. *The Kālikāpurāṇa*. Delhi: Nag.

West, Mark. 2005. "Interview with Sunil Pokharel: Questioning Caste: Performance, Parody, and the Political Economy of a Hindu State." *Baylor Journal of Theatre and Performance* 2 (2): 47–63.

Whelpton, John. 1991. *Kings, Soldiers, and Priests: Nepalese Politics and the Rise of Jang Bahadur Rana, 1830–1857*. New Delhi: Manohar.

White, David Gordon. N.d. *Vernacular Ritual Technologies in the South Asian Cult of Bhairava*. Unpublished manuscript.

———. 2010. "At the *Maṇḍala*'s Dark Fringes: Possession and Protection in Tantric Bhairava Cults." In *Notes from a Mandala: Essays in the History of Indian Religions in Honor of Wendy Doniger*, ed. Laurie L. Patton and David L. Haberman, 200–223. Lanham: University of Delaware.

———. 2009. "Bhairava." In *Brill's Encyclopedia of Hinduism*, vol. 1, ed. Knut A. Jacobsen, Helene Basu, Angelika Malinar, and Vasudha Narayanan, 485–90. Leiden: Brill.

———. 2000. "Tantra in Practice: Mapping a Tradition." In *Tantra in Practice*, ed. David Gordon White, 3–38. Princeton, NJ: Princeton University Press.

Witzel, Michael. 1990. "On Indian Historical Writing: The Role of the Vaṃ śāvalīs." *Journal of the Japanese Association for South Asian Studies* 2: 1–57.

———. 1997. "Macrocosm, Mesocosm, and Microcosm: The Persistent Nature of 'Hindu' Beliefs and Symbolic Forms." *International Journal of Hindu Studies* 1 (3): 501–39.

Wollein, Andrea. 2019. "Bhaktapur Revisited: Dīpaṅkara Buddha's Life in a Hindu City." *European Bulletin of Himalayan Research* 53: 108–40.

Wright, Daniel. 2000 [1877]. *History of Nepal, with an Introductory Sketch of the Country and People of Nepal.* Delhi: Adarsh Enterprises.

"'Yenya': A Week-Long Celebration." *Yomari Cartoon Series,* August 29, 2020. https://www.facebook.com/photo?fbid=331854844827869&set=a.328733175140036.

Zotter, Astrid. 2013. "History in Nepalese Chronicles: Report on a Workshop in Nepal (9–22 March 2013)." *European Bulletin of Himalayan Research* 42: 138–43.

Index

www.ingramcontent.com/pod-product-compliance
Lightning Source LLC
Chambersburg PA
CBHW030344270326
41926CB00009B/953